PATRON ACCESS

ACCESS

ISSUES FOR ONLINE CATALOGS

by Walt Crawford

G.K. HALL &CO.

70 LINCOLN STREET, BOSTON, MASS.

Professional Librarian

Patron Access: Issues for Online Catalogs

Library of Congress Cataloging-in-Publication Data

Crawford, Walt.
  Patron access.

  Bibliography: p.
  Includes index.
  1. Catalogs, On-line. 2. Library catalogs and
readers. 3. On-line bibliographic searching.
4. Libraries—Automation. I. Title.
Z699.3.C694 1987   025.3'13   86-20861
ISBN 0-8161-1850-7
ISBN 0-8161-1852-3 (pbk.)

Printed in the United States of America

10   9   8   7   6   5   4   3   2   1

Table of Contents

List of Figures   iv
Acknowledgments   vii
Preface   viii

 1. The Online Catalog: A View of a Library   1
 2. The Database Engine: Computer, Files and Indexes   15
 3. Presentation: Context in an Online Catalog   39
 4. System Clarity   61
 5. Terminals: Input and Display   77
 6. Printers, Workstations and Dial-In Use   106
 7. Commands and Menus   117
 8. Feedback and Help   137
 9. Retrieval and Browsing   157
10. Searching   173
11. Display Issues   192
12. Specific Displays: Single and Multiple Items   214

Glossary   235
Annotated Bibliography   241
Index   251
About the Author   259

List of Figures

Figure 3.1   Hypothetical Opening Screen   45
Figure 3.2   Poor Redirection Signpost   50
Figure 3.3   Better Redirection Signpost   51
Figure 3.4   Possible Signposts for Result Position   52
Figure 3.5   Possible Signpost for Access Point   53
Figure 3.6   Possible Signpost for Multiple-Item Display   55

Figure 4.1   Unambiguous Terminology   69
Figure 4.2   Poor Response to Situational Command
               Problem   73
Figure 4.3   Better Response to Situational Command
               Problem   73

Figure 5.1   Possible Response for Unused Keystroke   81
Figure 5.2   Soft Labels on Last Two Lines of Display   85
Figure 5.3   Multiple-Item Display with Capitalized Titles . .   99
Figure 5.4   Single-Item Display with Capitalized Title   100

Figure 7.1   Hybrid System, Pure Menu Screen   118
Figure 7.2   Hybrid System, Completion Screen   118
Figure 7.3   Command System with Options   119
Figure 7.4   Overcrowded Options Screen   123
Figure 7.5   Ordered Options, First Screen   123
Figure 7.6   Ordered Options, Screen Following Figure 7.5 .   124
Figure 7.7   Layered Options, First Screen   124
Figure 7.8   Layered Options, Result of "Find T" on Figure
               7.7   124
Figure 7.9   Ordered Options with Numbered Alternative . .   125
Figure 7.10   Response Screen from Figure 7.9   125
Figure 7.11   Menu Screen with Explicit Command
               Alternative   126
Figure 7.12   Possible Synonyms for Verbs and Index Names
                 130

Figure 7.13   Possible Command Editing Screen.   132
Figure 7.14   Error Correction Results   133
Figure 7.15   Very Simple Error Correction.   133
Figure 7.16   Fairly Simple Error Correction   133
Figure 7.17   Moderately Complex Error Correction   134
Figure 7.18   Complex Error Correction.   134
Figure 7.19   Ambiguous Command Error   135

Figure 8.1   Simple Status Line   138
Figure 8.2   Possible Command Feedback from Menu
               Choice.   140
Figure 8.3   Boolean Explanation, First Example   144
Figure 8.4   Boolean Explanation, Second Example   145
Figure 8.5   Boolean Explanation, Third Example   145
Figure 8.6   Boolean Explanation, Fourth Example   146
Figure 8.7   Boolean Explanation, Fifth Example.   146
Figure 8.8   Boolean Explanation, Modified Version of Fifth
               Example   146
Figure 8.9   Functional Index Expansion Screen   148
Figure 8.10   Possible Material Format Breakdown   149

Figure 9.1   Bibliographic Display Supporting Related Work
               Search.   161
Figure 9.2   Display with Related Work Search.   161
Figure 9.3   Hierarchical Class Browse, Top Level.   167
Figure 9.4   Hierarchical Class Browse, Second Level.   168

Figure 10.1   Parser Interpretation of Known-Item Search, A   178
Figure 10.2   Parser Interpretation of Known-Item Search, B   178
Figure 10.3   Possible Handling of Ambiguous Boolean
               Search.   183
Figure 10.4   Boolean Expansion for Zero Result   185
Figure 10.5   Spelling Check for Zero Boolean Result   186

Figure 11.1   Labeled Display Without Vertical Spacing   195
Figure 11.2   Labeled Display with Vertical Spacing   195
Figure 11.3   Cardlike Display with Some Vertical Spacing . .   196
Figure 11.4   Descriptive Elements with ISBD
               Punctuation   197
Figure 11.5   Descriptive Elements with Modified
               Punctuation   197
Figure 11.6   Multiple-Item Display with Capitalized Titles . .   198

v

Figure 11.7   Single-Item Display with Capitalized Title   199
Figure 11.8   Partial Entry Using Title Citation.   204
Figure 11.9   Partial Entry Using Labeling.   204
Figure 11.10   Partial Entry with Title Citation, Sound
               Recording.   205
Figure 11.11   Labeled Display, Version 1   206
Figure 11.12   Labeled Display, Version 2   207
Figure 11.13   Labeled Display, Version 3   207
Figure 11.14   Labeled Display, Version 4   208
Figure 11.15   Labeled Display, Version 5   208
Figure 11.16   Multiple-Item Display with Labels.   212

Figure 12.1   Fully Columnar Single-Line Display   215
Figure 12.2   Partially Columnar Single-Line Display   216
Figure 12.3   Subject Search Result in Reverse Chronological
               Order.   219
Figure 12.4   Machine-Readable Data File, Brief Cardlike
               Display   223
Figure 12.5   Machine-Readable Data File, Brief Labeled
               Display   224
Figure 12.6   Sound Recording, Medium Cardlike Display . . .   225
Figure 12.7   Sound Recording, Medium Labeled Display
               with Spacing.   226
Figure 12.8   Visual Material, Medium Labeled Display with
               Spacing.   229
Figure 12.9   Map, Medium Citation Display with Labels,
               Holdings.   230
Figure 12.10   Map, Second Screen.   231

Acknowledgments

The J. Paul Getty Trust provided grant funding for the RLG Patron Access Project. Without that support, this book might not have been written.

David Richards, director of research and development at RLG, asked me to serve as investigator for Phase 1 of the Patron Access Project. Glee Harrah Cady, assistant director for applications development, agreed to the choice. Kathleen Bales, Wayne Davison, Charles Stewart and Lennie Stovel all helped refine the Patron Access Project reports that provide background for this book.

Several people read and commented on early drafts of this manuscript. My editor at Knowledge Industry Publications, Karen Sirabian, made crucial suggestions at the rough draft stage and offered the expert editing I have come to expect at later stages. My wife, Linda Driver, brought two perspectives to bear: her recent experience in helping to select and implement an integrated system at a public library, and her keen eye for the language. She also provided her broad professional library background, her common sense and her uncommon patience. Lennie Stovel, Glee Cady, Sarah How and Kathleen Bales provided useful comments on various drafts.

This book builds on, but does not supplant, the landmark books on online catalogs by Charles Hildreth, Joe Matthews and Emily Fayen (all cited in the Bibliography). Although I don't agree with everything in those sources, I would be remiss not to express my appreciation for their work.

Finally, I should acknowledge the librarians who, over the years, have shown that the most important aspect of patron access is the concerned, professional librarian. Many names at UC Berkeley, Stanford, Palo Alto City Library and Menlo Park Public Library come to mind; Virginia Pratt of UC Berkeley's Library School library deserves special mention.

While many hands have helped polish this manuscript and my thinking, none of the people named here should be held responsible for my opinions and statements. Opinions and suggestions expressed here are mine, and subject to change. Errors are also most likely mine, and corrections are always appreciated.

Preface

In 1984, the J. Paul Getty Trust funded a two-year Research Libraries Group (RLG) project with a number of aims. One portion of the overall project was the Patron Access Project. The goal of that project was stated in one of the final reports from its first phase:

> To develop a design for a workstation-based patron access system to work with an online catalog based on RLIN [Research Libraries Information Network] software. The project rests on several assumptions:
> - Online catalogs, and particularly patron access, are just beginning to undergo a long process of development, evaluation and improvement.
> - Scholars as information users, and research libraries as information providers, may have special needs that are not likely to be fully addressed by commercial online catalog development.
> - By the end of the decade, scholars will have access to powerful microcomputer-based workstations and can reasonably expect to have access to library catalogs through such workstations.
> - RLIN represents an unusually sophisticated database engine and retrieval methodology, proven in large-scale use, but it is not designed for direct use by scholars or other patrons.
> - RLG should focus on the access needs of scholars as part of its overall goal. Even if no online catalog based on RLIN software ever reaches full production in any library, the development effort should yield useful information and lead to improvements in other online catalogs.[1]

I was assigned to carry out the first phase, an investigation into the literature of patron access to develop a documented sense of what was being done and suggested. That phase resulted in an outline of more than 250 specific issues relating to patron access. The outline finally emerged as a three-part document, completed in late 1985.

In the spring of 1985, I attended the Conference on Online Catalog Screen Displays, Lakeway Conference Center, Austin, TX, sponsored by the Council on Library Resources (CLR). The conference brought together a mix of system designers, librarians and others; we were able to sample 20 online catalogs and to discuss display-related issues. This conference resulted indirectly in RLG's Bibliographic Display Project and the book *Bibliographic Displays in the Online Catalog*.[2] It also led me to believe that a thorough examination of issues related to patron access was needed, partly because so many designers are relying on different sets of unstated assumptions.

This book is not based on my own experience designing or implementing online systems, since I don't have any such experience. My background at RLG has been with batch products and accounting, not with building the online RLIN system. My experience as an RLIN user, not builder, certainly influences my thinking. I regard RLIN as a fairly complete search design with a good command syntax; however, I do not regard it as a reasonable model for patron access.

Although this book originated with a survey of literature, it is not a scholarly survey of opinion on online catalogs. It is an examination of issues, things to consider in designing and implementing online catalogs. Except where sources are specifically cited, most opinions and assertions are my own. Two paragraphs from the report of the Patron Access Project should help to clarify my stance during that project and in this book:

> In no case should the assertions be considered final or unarguable. These assertions are generally my own opinion, based on reading, experience and reflection. In some cases, the assertions are stated simply as a starting point for discussion. The project team and reviewers may reasonably come to different conclusions. Some assertions may even be in conflict with other assertions; no particular effort has been made to ensure overall consistency. Perhaps most significantly, little or no consideration has been given to questions of machine efficiency. The development process will certainly involve trade-offs not considered during Phase I.
>
> This document includes a great many possibilities for patron access design, including many different access methods. It isn't clear that a workable patron access interface could incorporate all of the recommended features without becoming so complex as to be unwieldy.[3]

DEFINITIONS AND ASSERTIONS

A few terms have been shortened in this book; such use does not suggest that these terms must be used in any reasonable patron access design. They are as follows:

- *Record* is sometimes used to represent an item or edition that normally would be described by a single MARC record. It does not imply that a system must or should store all elements of a record in one location or structure. A record may be assembled by drawing together headings from authority files and circulation information from a separate database. A record may also be a single item within a database.
- *Index* is used to represent an organized means of access. Its use implies that patrons can access information through a particular path but does not imply that the path itself uses a particular technique.
- *OPAC (Online Patron Access Catalog), patron access system, online catalog, catalog* and *system* all serve as synonyms for patron access systems, present and future.

Most sample screens are deliberately fictional, but all bibliographic examples are real, taken from RLIN or from other works in the field. Sample screens are not intended to be examples of the best possible patron access system. The full set of examples is not even consistent internally. All examples were printed on RLG's Xerox 9700 printer using RLG's documentation character set and were reduced for this book. Vertical ellipses, four dots on each side of the screen, are used to represent missing portions of a screen.

Highlight boxes such as the one below represent thoughts that may or may not be repeated in the text. They are my own opinions and are intended to provoke thought, not to be accepted on faith.

Online catalogs that do not provide holdings and status information are inferior to card catalogs for known-item searches.

ISSUES, NOT ANSWERS

Good patron access systems exist, and more are being developed. Online catalogs, though still in their infancy, have the potential to provide more and better access to all forms of bibliographic material, including materials never represented in card catalogs.

This book's subtitle expresses its primary intent and focus: *Issues for Online Catalogs.* After some years of discussion, early research and early examples of online catalogs, the time seems right to discuss a broad spectrum of issues related to patron access. Some issues appear to be obvious and to have obvious answers. Some issues may appear extraneous to patron access. Many issues are controversial, and some may be impossible to resolve.

My intent in this work is to stimulate further thought and development, not to devise the perfect patron access system. Assertions should encourage challenges; if those challenges produce demonstrably better patron access, my goals will be achieved.

Patron access catalogs will improve. By 1991, many of the discussions in this book should appear quaint because the issues I discuss will already be resolved. That's as it should be. I am building on the work of others, with the expectation that others will add more and better work to mine.

NOTES

1. Crawford, Walt. *Patron Access Project, Phase I; Report to Phase II: Development Issues.* Stanford, CA: The Research Libraries Group, Inc.; 1985. (RLG Document Code 85-52.) p. 3.

2. Crawford, Walt. *Bibliographic Displays in the Online Catalog.* White Plains, NY: Knowledge Industry Publications, Inc.; 1986.

3. Crawford, *Patron Access Project,* p. 5.

1

The Online Catalog: A View of a Library

A library catalog links library patrons with library collections. A good library catalog brings readers together with materials they need and with materials they can use but were not aware of.

Library card catalogs show the results of decades of thought and action, and provide fast access to each item in a collection via a few access points. Shelf lists provide inventory control for a library; authority work ensures consistent use of names, series and subjects; catalogs establish the state of the collection while providing access to its members. Much of catalog maintenance and most authority work serves to maintain a clean catalog. The catalog may be an end product for some librarians, but it is no more than a means for most patrons. With few exceptions, patrons want materials, not bibliographic records.

Cards represent constancy. While card sets may be replaced, a given card should be unchanged as long as it is in the catalog. Any user wishing to see the card approaches it through a single sequence, and every user sees the same information. A card catalog represents database, access methods and presentation all in one package; all aspects are identical for all users in all situations.

When bibliographic records are converted to machine-readable form, the constancy of catalog cards is no longer necessary or desirable. Online catalogs offer many virtues that are not available with card catalogs, however, and present challenges for catalog designers.

Library professionals come to online catalogs burdened by the history of card catalogs and with grand expectations of online miracles.

We sometimes feel that the computer will solve everything, and all we need do is a bit of fine tuning. Library professionals assume that the terms *library catalog* and *online catalog* are essentially self-explanatory. This book makes no such assumption. While providing no final answers, this book examines some of the issues involved in patron access.

DEFINING THE ONLINE CATALOG

An online catalog can be defined as any computer-based set of bibliographic data that can be accessed by library users working directly at a terminal. That broad definition underlies most literature written on the subject during the early 1980s and was the implicit definition used for the 1981–1982 study funded by the Council on Library Resources (CLR).[1]

The CLR study created an unfortunate tautology. Since it was a study of patron use of online catalogs, the systems studied must be considered online catalogs. By more recent standards, however, CLR's definition of an online catalog is too broad. Putting a terminal in a public place doesn't create a good patron access interface, and connecting that terminal to a circulation system doesn't create an online catalog. The CLR study included circulation systems with limited bibliographic access, pilot systems with small databases, and both OCLC and RLIN, neither of which was ever intended to provide patron access. A narrower definition of online catalogs is needed to guide future thinking, but it is difficult to arrive at a suitable one.

Online catalogs should serve patrons at least as well as card catalogs do. The best online catalogs will provide each patron with access that suits his or her needs.

This book defines online catalogs as *primary* links between patrons and items—not toys off to one side of the card catalog, or pilot projects including only new items, but systems that offer the only alternative (or at least the primary alternative) to browsing the shelves. This type of catalog is not very prevalent today; few libraries have systems designed to replace card catalogs completely, and even fewer have actually abandoned card catalogs. Although another generation of catalog design is needed before online patron access can be satisfactory, the working definition of online catalogs used in this book places us at the beginning of the era of online catalogs.

Online Catalog as a View

A card catalog has physical existence and can be an end in itself. Patron access—the public online catalog—has no such physical existence.

An online catalog is not a thing, but a perspective; it is a particular view of underlying functions and data.

A database (or set of databases) and a computer (or set of computers) may deal with many different views, such as the view from acquisitions, the view from serials checkin, the view from the circulation desk, the view from accounting, the view from cataloging and the view from interlibrary lending. Some form of computerized or manual system must serve each of these views. Each differs in requirements but has some overlap with other views.

Patron Access and Integrated Systems

Librarians are looking for better patron access at the same time that they are being asked to consider integrated systems. Kenneth Dowlin of Pike's Peak Library System defines an integrated system as "one that appears to the user as if all desired functions are in one database and are available from the same device."[2]

Dowlin makes a point that is central to this book. A system should be defined by its functionality, not by its internal techniques. There are good reasons to combine multiple library functions into a single database and to use a single set of software to access that database, but the success or failure of an online catalog does not depend on the existence or absence of an integrated system.

Patrons don't care whether a system is integrated or linked. As long as patrons can get the information they want when they want it, they don't care where it comes from.

Functions, Not Techniques

Designers of patron access systems should focus on results rather than on underlying mechanisms—functions, not techniques. Focusing on results permits library professionals to maintain a library perspective without bogging down in the details of database design and coding techniques. Librarians need to be concerned with MARC compatibility, machine capacity, response time and availability of access points, but they do not need to be concerned with "B-trees" or "hashed indexes." Librarians need assurance that techniques will work now and in the future, but they should not have to concern themselves with the details of the techniques.

THE ONLINE CATALOG AND THE CARD CATALOG

An online catalog should not be a computerized card catalog. This isn't because online catalogs are inherently superior to card catalogs, but because each type of catalog has different problems and advantages.

Card catalogs are relatively new in the history of libraries and represent a substantial improvement over previous links between user and collection. Doing as well as the card catalog, in all respects, is no mean feat because card catalogs have many attributes that can't be equaled by any known online system.

Advantages of the Card Catalog

Card catalogs support many users simultaneously, provide immediate feedback and rarely become wholly unavailable because of mechanical breakdown.

A good card catalog provides immediate feedback, much faster than most online catalogs. Patrons need not type to use card catalogs. A typical card catalog supports many searchers working simultaneously, far more than the number likely to be supported by an online catalog for the same size library.

Card catalogs provide fast browsing with immediate access to additional information as desired. A patron can scan through catalog cards rapidly, glancing at headings, and at any point in that scan can look at more of any given card. That combination of fast browsing and extensive added information, immediately available with no added steps, is something no currently known online catalog can provide.

Contemporary automated systems provide very good reliability, but no automated system will ever provide the assurance of a card catalog. As Emily Fayen notes, "The card catalog is always 'up,' and if there is light enough to see, people can use it."[3]

Online Improvements

Most online catalogs will fall short of a card catalog in some ways. They can balance those deficiencies by improving on the card catalog in other ways. Word searching, Boolean logic, internal-phrase searching and immediate access to help are just some of the potential improvements over card catalogs.

Perhaps the greatest single improvement that online catalogs can offer is status information. The patron can see not only what items may be useful and whether the library has an item, but whether an item is (or is likely to be) on the shelf.

Many early online catalogs appear successful partly because they are an additional means of access. Card catalogs continue to serve those searching for known items and those whose needs can't be met by unsophisticated online systems. When the card catalog freezes or dies, that won't be possible. Known-item searches pose a special problem. Card catalogs work very well for such searches, and it may be difficult to design online catalogs that will provide the same information as quickly or as conveniently. A good online catalog will provide status information, and that may make up for some loss of speed and convenience.

Real improvements over card catalogs don't come easily and can be undermined by incomplete databases or slow response. That may be one reason why the death of cards has been greatly exaggerated. In 1980, RLG introduced a new catalog card production system with the confident expectation that, by the end of its five-to-seven-year life span, card production would be so diminished that the program could be patched to continue as long as needed. That expectation was too optimistic; RLG produced more catalog cards in 1985 than in any previous year.

Some claims made for current online catalogs are extreme—for example, that an online catalog provides faster access than a card catalog for almost all searches. Other claims rest on unwarranted assumptions as to what an online catalog does or should provide. When online catalogs are oversold, to libraries or to patrons, the libraries suffer; a poor online catalog can be a step backward for patron access. Online catalogs have the capability to provide better access than the card catalog, but improvements will take time.

Costs and Benefits

This book contains many possibilities for patron access, probably more than should be offered in any single system. Every library must consider direct and indirect costs of features and decide whether the benefit from a feature justifies its cost. Such cost/benefit analysis is beyond the scope of this book. Cost factors change as we learn more about online catalogs and as computers become faster and cheaper; benefits differ from one library to another.

There are no perfect patron access systems, just as there are no perfect card catalogs. A library must settle for something less than perfection.

Even if computers were free and had infinite power, no single catalog would meet all patron access needs for all patrons in all libraries equally well. One cost associated with new features is the time it takes to have them explained and made available; new features require more complex screen design and command methodology. This cost can't be negated by cheaper and faster computers, and it is a cost not always factored in to decision making.

The most powerful catalog won't serve patrons who can't use it. Simple catalogs may not serve patrons who need more power. A good online catalog must blend power with clarity. If patrons need a full week's training to find a known title, the patron access system is a failure, no matter how efficiently it performs searches. If patrons need no training but must go through six screens and seven steps to arrive at the call number of a known item, the patron access system may be a failure compared to a card catalog, even if each of the six screens is lucid.

PRESENTATION, PROCESS AND PROTECTION

Every use of an online system involves one or more aspects of user interaction. These can be classified as Presentation, Process and Protection.

- Presentation is how the system interacts with the user: the devices used by the user, what the user can tell the system and what the system can tell the user.
- Process indicates system activities that the user can initiate. A process is something that changes the state of the database or the state of the library. All perspectives involve searching, and searching does not change the state of the database; thus, searching is not a process. Charging a book, placing a hold and maintaining a catalog record are all processes.
- Protection signifies ways in which users are shielded from the other users, the system is shielded from the user and the user is shielded from the system.

This three-part analysis, the three-P model, is an artificial construct. Its virtue is simplicity. Some views of a system require little attention to presentation and much attention to process; some involve little or no protection.

The three-P model focuses on the system as perceived by a particular category of user. It separates issues relating directly to that perception from issues that form part of the underlying support for library automation. That underlying support is the *database engine*—a computer or computers, database or databases, and program or programs. Whether the database engine is one computer system or a network of systems, it must provide the necessary storage, indexing and retrieval power to support various views of the system.

Patron access may be the richest view in terms of presentation and protection; it is certainly the leanest in process. Most patron access issues relate directly to presentation. The remainder of this chapter considers issues of process and protection. Chapter 2 deals with the database engine. Chapters 3 through 12 discuss presentation issues.

PROCESS

What can a patron do to cause a change in the underlying system? What should take place within patron access other than searching? The sections that follow discuss activities that are possible within patron access—activities that are also processes because they alter the system.

Messages to the Library

Patrons should be able to send signed or anonymous messages to "the system" while using a patron access system.

Patrons frustrated by using an online catalog must be able to relieve that frustration by expressing opinions or making suggestions. Direct anonymous messages can provide valuable feedback, alerting libraries to problems with a catalog or to desirable new features. Patrons should have the option of signing messages, but also must know that messages can be anonymous.

For patrons to send messages, the system must offer instructions and an editing function. *Send a message* may not make sense as a prompted option, but should be present in help screens and appear on a printed summary of system functions. Editing capabilities need not be fancy. A library can place a one-screen limit on a single message, but a single-line limit is too short.

A message function will be more useful if a patron can leave a display, key a message relating to that screen and send the message along with a copy of the screen. Such a function may be difficult to explain (although people familiar with microcomputers, and especially with programs such as SideKick, will find it natural), but it allows patrons to alert the library to real or perceived problems. A patron's comment, "this result doesn't make sense," will be more useful if the result is attached.

Message functions can result in prank messages and obscenities. The staff assigned to read and distribute messages has to be aware of that but should also try to distinguish juvenile obscenity from the language of extremely frustrated patrons.

A message function helps patrons and the library much more if patrons know that the messages are being read and acted upon. Libraries should post the most interesting and useful messages on a bulletin board, with responses as appropriate. Seeing such an up-to-date bulletin board tells patrons that the library cares about them and takes their problems seriously.

Holds and Recalls

Patrons should be able to place holds on items and should be able to request that items be recalled.

Holds and recalls, and other processes discussed below, require that patrons identify themselves. That need for identification will increase problems of protection, as it is equally important that one patron's identification not be used intentionally or accidentally by the next patron.

A library might require that a patron key in an identification number as part of each request for an action, retaining that identification only for the single request. A library may also provide a bar code reader—a light pen or other mechanism—and allow the patron to scan a library card. Requiring the patron to place a machine-readable library card in a reader serves the same purpose, but leaves open the possibility that the patron will forget to retrieve the card.

Some systems prompt for a hold whenever a circulated item is displayed. Libraries may not want to encourage holds to that extent, but should make them fairly straightforward because the system has to enforce whatever restrictions are placed on holds and recalls.

Library policies on recalls vary. Public libraries may not provide for recall under any conditions; academic libraries typically allow recall past a certain initial due date and may allow earlier recall for certain special reasons. The patron access system should enforce those conditions as part of recalls. Some libraries may wish to review any recalls that are placed, rather than allowing automatic notice generation based on patron request.

Orders

Patrons should be able to suggest that items be ordered but, in most libraries, should not be able to initiate orders without library review.

Many public libraries already invite patrons to suggest orders; academic libraries frequently restrict that privilege to faculty members. Some ingenuity may be needed to design a good way for patrons to suggest an order while using an online catalog. One possible solution is a suggestion form with areas for author, title, edition, publisher, etc. Another and perhaps more realistic possibility is to use free-text suggestions. That may not require a separate process, if patrons know that order suggestions can be made by sending a message.

Some libraries charge patrons for the privilege of suggesting an order, just as some libraries charge for holds. In either case, the online system may pose a problem unless such fees are handled in the same way that overdues are handled and added directly to a patron's record.

Interlibrary Borrowing

Patrons should be able to initiate Interlibrary Lending (ILL) requests, either directly or with library verification. If a system supports nonlocal searching, patrons should be able to use the results of that searching directly in formulating an ILL request.

Nonlocal searching (see Chapter 10) should lead directly to an ILL request as one possible action. That allows the system to combine exact bibliographic information and the name of a library known to hold the item, substantially reducing the overhead of interlibrary borrowing.

Should patrons be able to initiate interlibrary borrowing, or only to request that the library borrow something for them? That will depend on the library and, in most libraries, on the patrons and the items involved. Interlibrary borrowing is, and probably always will be, an expensive function; as a result, most libraries must maintain some control over the flow of interlibrary borrowing requests. Libraries that participate in regional delivery services should offer direct interlibrary borrowing within the region.

Channeling interlibrary borrowing requests through the patron access system serves another useful function—alerting a library to possible collection problems. If the same in-print item costing less than $30 is requested twice in one year, many libraries will order the item. If requests within a classification area begin to pile up, a library may wish to evaluate its holdings in that area and consider the possibility that the needs of its patrons have changed.

PROTECTION

A good patron access system protects the patron from the system, the patron from other patrons and agencies, and the system from the patron.

"For the majority of online catalog users the interface must be both a link . . . . and a barrier (protecting the user from all other aspects of the computer system) as Stewart (1976) has correctly noted."[4]

Protection means limits. While patrons should have unlimited access to bibliographic information and indexes, patrons should not have access to other information within the system. Providing those limits may require two specific restrictions on system access, restrictions that may irritate some staff members:

- Patron access terminals should not be able to reach privileged functions, even if a staff member with appropriate keyword and privileges is using such a terminal. Inevitably, staff members will walk away from terminals without logging off or will enter keywords without noticing an eager computer enthusiast looking over their shoulders. The inconvenience of requiring staff members to go to a terminal behind the desk in order to check on a patron's status, modify an order or use other sensitive information is much less significant than the "inconvenience" of opening complete system access to a computer sociopath.
- Telecommunications ports, specifically those available by telephone, should have the same restrictions as patron access terminals. If a library staff member must have dial-up access to privileged functions, some form of encoding or dial-back modem can be used to prevent unauthorized access.

Confidentiality of Current Borrowing

While patron access systems should show that items are charged out, and may show when they are due, no patron should be able to find out who has items charged out.

Ideally, information on a current borrower should be strictly internal to the system, used only to generate recalls and overdues. In practice, some public service staff may require access to information on current borrowers. In any case, no public terminal should ever provide access to the name or other identification of current borrowers.

One process not listed earlier is a function that allows a patron to see what he or she has currently charged. That omission is deliberate; in order to assure confidentiality of other patron records, public access terminals should deny any access to patron-linked circulation records, a concept discussed further below.

The omission is also controversial, since many patrons want the ability to check their current borrowing records without asking library staff. If a request to view current circulation is accompanied by immediate entry of a patron's identification, and if that identification is eliminated immediately after the request is fulfilled, a system may be able to show a patron his or her current charges without too much compromise of confidentiality. A library must balance this service against the danger to confidentiality that is always present when information appears on a public terminal.

Confidentiality of Previous Borrowing

No records should link a patron to returned items, and no records should link an item to the patrons who have borrowed and returned it.

Past borrowing records represent the strongest, most important protection issue for patron access and for library computer systems in general. When an item is returned, any link between that item and the borrower should be permanently severed, leaving no history to be traced. Even statistical records should be broad enough to ensure confidentiality.

Most current library automation systems function properly in this regard. Some systems provide the option of maintaining a linked history, but libraries should be very wary of choosing that option. Government abuse of circulation records is a known phenomenon, not simply paranoia. Investigative agencies can and do demand access to library circulation records for a variety of reasons. In many cases, a library has no legal right to deny access to such records. In most cases, however, a library has no requirement to *retain* circulation records.

If patrons believe that their reading habits are subject to monitoring at any level, they will not use libraries freely. Libraries have a duty to protect patrons from undue scrutiny, and eliminating historical links between items and borrowers helps to fulfill that duty. Most current circulation and patron access systems reflect this need—links between patron and item disappear when an item is returned. A library may worry about defaced items, but that worry does not justify maintaining a historical record that, based on real evidence, may lead to fishing expeditions by government agencies.

Anonymity of Command Logging

Records of commands entered at a catalog should never identify the patron who is using the system.

Systems should provide some record of commands entered—usually called command logging—because that information is useful for a number of legitimate purposes. Even if patrons can review their own activity during a session, the system should detach patron identification from stored command logs. Specific identification of user search activity is potentially even more dangerous than specific identification of borrowing history for a book or a patron.

Command logs serve two purposes: statistical analysis of system performance and use, and direct analysis of searching behavior and problems. In neither case is the identity of a patron useful, though the system may wish to record when a new user is present.

Abusive Searching

A patron access system should have some protection against abusive searching, but such protection is not easily defined.

Patrons abuse the system when they issue searches that require system resources at a level that prevents other patrons from performing searches rapidly. That makes abusive searching dependent on system load, time of day and other measures that are not easily predictable. An abusive search at noon is simply a difficult search at midnight.

Research and analysis may suggest areas where excessively difficult searches can be spotted and trapped, and either rejected or deferred until the system is less heavily loaded. A better path for investigation may be index and access designs that reduce the possibility of abusive searches. If an access system is well designed, it may not require additional safeguards against difficult searches.

NOTES

1. *Using Online Catalogs.* Joseph R. Matthews; Gary S. Lawrence; Douglas K. Ferguson, eds. New York: Neal-Schuman; 1983. p. 117.

2. Kenneth Dowlin, cited in "INDEX: Education—LITA at Infomart." *LITA Newsletter*. 23: 1986 Winter. p. 2.

3. Fayen, Emily Gallup. *The Online Catalog: Improving Public Access to Library Materials*. White Plains, NY: Knowledge Industry Publications, Inc.; 1983. p. 19.

4. Matthews, Joseph R. *Public Access to Online Catalogs: A Planning Guide for Managers*. Weston, CT: Online; 1982. p. 29.

2

The Database Engine:
Computer, Files and Indexes

A patron access system represents an underlying set of computers, storage media, indexes and information. That underlying system is the database engine.

At a minimum, an online patron access system consists of one or more computers, a database (one or more files), a set of indexes and software to maintain the database and indexes. These elements are also needed for a circulation system, a technical processing system or any other online system, or for a single system that offers several functions.

This book uses the term *database engine* to refer to the combination of computers, files, indexes and software that support patron access. A patron access system may use several computers that serve only that function, or may share a single computer that performs many other functions. Decisions to use one computer or several, to integrate all functions, to provide links between functions or to keep functions separate all affect the quality of the database engine.

Patron access is one perspective on a database engine. Circulation is another perspective or view, as are serials control and acquisitions. The design of a database engine must take into account all the perspectives that will be supported. This chapter discusses some aspects of the database engine such as content and arrangement; computer power and response time; authority and heading files; and indexes.

15

Poor presentation of a good database engine results in a poor patron access system. Even the best presentation of a poor database engine will result in a poor patron access system. If the information isn't there or isn't properly indexed, or if the computer isn't powerful enough, no amount of user-friendly design will produce good results.

CONTENT

The most sophisticated indexes and search techniques won't retrieve records that are not in the database. Similarly, sophisticated access can't make up for inadequate content within records. Overly brief records restrict access to material. If a field isn't in the record, it can't be used to find the record.

No single issue is more important for patron access than complete records in a complete database.

MARC Compatibility

The database should be fully compatible with USMARC. USMARC compatibility is the ability to accept all USMARC records and recreate them, without loss of content designation or content. Lack of USMARC compatibility forecloses a library's options for future development.

Some vendors and writers argue that the USMARC formats include more detail than patrons require, and that online systems can safely discard or combine elements of USMARC records. If full USMARC records are kept current, in some other portion of a system, that attitude may be reasonable. In practice, though, systems that take shortcuts on USMARC compatibility also tend to take shortcuts in using records.

MARC and *USMARC* do not mean Library of Congress cataloging. Both terms are shorthand for a family of machine-readable formats that provide flexible storage for bibliographic information. *USMARC* is the general term for all MARC formats within the United States, specifically those that include all fields defined in the *MARC Formats for Bibliographic Data*. USMARC provides the only general means of exchanging bibliographic information in machine-readable form. Libraries should avoid database engines that can't handle USMARC properly.

If a library maintains its information in USMARC form, it will be able to exchange that information with other libraries or move it to another online system at a later date. Elements of USMARC that are not currently needed may be useful later. A library's investment in machine-readable cataloging, through new cataloging and retrospective conversion, may be larger than the investment in an online catalog. Retaining full USMARC content designation protects that investment.

USMARC indicators and subfield codes provide the information to build better indexes, more flexible access and proper labels during display. Systems that discard those content designators may restrict patron access.

Some current database engines store full USMARC records in one set of files, but build online systems from another set of files that lack some of the USMARC content designation. It's perfectly reasonable (and almost necessary) to transform USMARC records to a different format for online retrieval, but throwing away content designation may cause problems.

If a vendor says that USMARC is not a proper format for online retrieval, the vendor is telling the truth. The formats were never designed for that purpose. If a vendor says that indicators and subfield codes aren't useful for online catalogs, the vendor is mistaken. Indicators specify the display constants that make some notes and linking entries useful. Subfield codes make it possible to index author-title added entries properly, with authors going to name indexes and titles going to title indexes. The added entries should still display in combined form.

A vendor may choose to use different mechanisms to serve the same functions as indicators and subfield codes. If so, the library should insist on a detailed explanation of the mechanisms, and make sure that they will actually serve all useful functions of indicators and subfield codes, now and in the future. Recent experience suggests that online systems that discard content designation usually do not offer equivalent support and usually reflect an incomplete understanding of the USMARC formats.*

*An extended discussion of MARC compatibility appears as Chapter 11 of Crawford, Walt. *MARC for Library Use: Understanding the USMARC Formats*. White Plains, New York: Knowledge Industry Publications Inc.; 1984. That discussion bears reading for librarians dealing with issues of MARC compatibility, as does Chapter 12 of the same book. A good starting point for negotiation is that any database engine should be no lower than Level I as described in *MARC for Library Use*, and that even Level I should be specified in considerable detail.

Nonprint Materials

All forms of material should be included in the database. No modern library system should discriminate against any material that can be described in a bibliographic record. If it is in the library, it should be in the database.

Most modern libraries have more than just books and serials, but many library catalogs include only books and serials. "It's not fair to the whole category of materials we call *audiovisual* or *nonprint* to either not catalog them at all (which is extremely possible) or to treat them in a second-class way vis-a-vis books."[1]

Ten years from now, if all goes well, researchers will read this section and ask why this point needs to be raised at all. Today, however, a single integrated catalog is by no means common in the traditional library. Libraries may have good reasons to shelve special materials separately, but all too often that physical segregation leads to segregated (or nonexistent) cataloging.

Microform sets, invaluable to researchers but inaccessible in most catalogs, have traditionally presented the most severe access problem. Cooperative national projects are improving the situation, but unless those sets are represented in a library's general online catalog, the material remains inaccessible to all but the most dogged researcher.

Books will continue to be the most important source of knowledge in most fields for decades to come. But books don't represent the only valuable sources of information. The subject *Evolution* yielded 2688 books on RLIN in February 1986. It also yielded one serial, eight sound recordings, 117 films, videocassettes, slides and filmstrips, and four archival control records.

Most patrons think of nothing but books when looking for information. When patrons retrieve nonbook items through a good patron access system, they may discover whole new areas of information.

Fully integrated systems can cause difficulties for patrons, particularly in large libraries. Maintaining separation by default has much the same effect as leaving nonprint materials out of the access system—only those patrons who know about nonprint resources will ever find them. Patron access systems should combine all forms of material for searching and display, but patrons should also be able to explicitly limit searches to specific types of material when necessary.

When a patron wants only to listen to a piece of music or to read the score, he or she should be able to request limits on a search. Unless a patron places that limit, however, the search should yield books, pamphlets, paintings and data files alike.

Integrating nonprint materials goes one step further in providing access to works, not just items. A work can cross media, and the system should not discriminate in advance. Discrimination isn't needed by default for the listener; that patron will learn quickly to qualify searches. Nonprint media enhance a library only if patrons have full access to them.

Completeness

Older material deserves the same treatment as new material. If the item deserves to be on the shelf, it deserves to be in the online catalog and fully indexed.

Most writers agree on the need for nonprint materials in the database, but a surprising number feel that older materials can be left out. Paul Fasana says that "it is less clear whether the fully on-line catalog will need to be complete in terms of coverage of a library's collection."[2] Hugh Atkinson suggests "that somewhere between 10 [and] 25 years' worth of material be stored online and that the catalog be weeded or purged yearly; [and that] those items older than 10 to 25 years be transferred to microfiche in accumulating single file."[3] Emily Fayen says, "Considering that the use of most library materials falls off very rapidly with age, in a very few years the online catalog should be meeting the needs of its users—even though it includes only a part of the collection."[4]

One can only assume that some people either don't regard the online catalog as a serious replacement for the card catalog, or that people confuse "most" with "all." Scholars in the humanities and in many sciences would be startled to hear that material more than 25 years old is of no value; it is hard to think of a field in which there are no useful materials more than 25 years old. Millions of dollars have been spent, and tens of millions will be spent in the future to preserve the printed word and make it accessible; to understand a field is to study more than its current state. Many other writers, not cited here, do call for completeness. Users specifically want older materials in online catalogs. Since most users do not look through more than one catalog, older materials that are represented only in card catalogs are largely inaccessible.

Many public libraries must weed older material, but very few libraries of any size discard *all* materials more than 25 years old. Weeding is a proper library activity, but it should be carried out deliberately, not by making books inaccessible through the catalog.

Brief Records

Retrospective conversion and other methods for building a database may result in brief records. Brief records may limit access to materials, but limited access is better than no access at all. Brief records should include control numbers such as ISBN, LCCN, OCLC Record ID or the like, even if those numbers are never displayed online. The control numbers may improve the possibility of replacing brief records with full records in the future.

Enhanced Records

Enhanced records might improve access, but large-scale studies are needed to demonstrate cost-effectiveness and to discover the balance between finding more items and finding too many items.

Enhanced records in this context are records with portions of the table of contents or index added as searchable fields. Patrons will clearly retrieve more items, and retrieve items by a wider variety of terms, if more terms appear for each item. The questions that arise are whether the results will be more useful and whether the improvement will be worth the cost.

Early studies using enhanced records for searching have been limited to items in a narrow discipline or have been so small in scale as to eliminate loss of precision as a factor. Terms that yield good results when limited to one discipline may yield uselessly large results in a complete database. For example, the word *affect* might be a useful search term in a database dealing only with psychology, but would be useless in a general database.

For many years Pauline Atherton Cochrane has argued for enhanced records in order to improve subject access. The possible improvement in recall can't be denied, but precision problems can't be addressed realistically until and unless a large-scale study is done. She has also suggested eliminating subject entries for works more than 10 years old. This reduces the problem of large results, but is a poor solution, for reasons noted above.

Most patrons will use only one catalog, particularly if they find any results. Adding more material to the online catalog is more important than adding more information to existing records.

Budgetary realities suggest that libraries can either include more items in online catalogs or enhance the contents of some items, but probably not both. It has been demonstrated over and over again that most patrons will go no further than the first catalog they encounter. Enhancing existing records might improve access to a few materials, but without retrospective conversion and increased cataloging for all library materials, a great many materials will be wholly inaccessible.

Other methodologies can be used to improve subject access; some of them are discussed later in this chapter or elsewhere in this book. Possibilities include Dewey Decimal and LC classification schedules searchable by phrase or word, subject thesauri for various fields, and other techniques to match patron vocabularies to the language of subject headings and titles.

Titles on Order and in Process

Titles on order and in process should be represented in the database. These titles should be accessible to patrons, and should include clear status information.

Many card catalogs provide at least one access point for titles that are on order. Any patron access system should provide more access to such titles by treating ordered items the same as fully processed items, but with appropriate circulation statuses.

In many libraries, particularly those using shared technical processing systems for acquisitions, records for ordered material may be nearly as complete as records for material on the shelves. In other libraries, these records may be brief, thus limiting access. In either case, acquisition records should be indexed and displayed along with other records.

Holdings Information

Holdings information should appear for all cataloged items and be accessible in clear, readable form.

An online catalog without holdings information may tell the patron less than a card catalog would, though perhaps through more access points. An online catalog with arcane or overly detailed holdings information may fail to tell the patron how to obtain the material.

In order to be clear, holdings information must be brief. For serials, that may require that the database maintain two forms of holdings: summary holdings and detailed holdings. Summary holdings should be designed for fast reading and easy comprehension. Detailed holdings, preferably following national standards, should be available on request. Researchers and those needing a specific item need access to detailed holdings, but not at the expense of clear default displays.

Holdings have to be designed for usefulness. When a library has more than one location, it may present those holdings in the present location first, but there are also advantages to listing all locations together. In a patron access system serving several library systems, holdings for the local library should appear first. Some libraries may prefer to limit default holdings display to items available within the same building as the terminal, displaying other holdings only on request. A good patron access system will let the library choose the extent and order of holdings displays.

Circulation Status Information

Circulation status should appear automatically as part of every single-item display.

As with holdings, circulation status should be clear and terse. The status of an item includes whether holds are present and when the item is due. Circulation status and holdings information must be part of the database engine, available to patrons without visible delay. This does not mean that circulation and holdings must be on the same computer or in the same files as bibliographic information, but it does mean that any linking should be fast and transparent enough that patrons are not aware it is taking place. Patrons need to know whether an item is available, and should generally get that information on the first screen of a single-item display. They do not need to know where the information came from, as long as it is current and correct.

AUTHORITY AND HEADING FILES

Authority and heading files should be browsable, should display as upper and lower case text strings, and should show the number of items containing each heading. References are desirable and should be expressed clearly.

A proper authority file is internally consistent, includes references, and should control a database, serving as the authority for forms of names, series and subjects—hence the name. Authority files may include headings with no items, i.e., names representing authorized headings that are not currently represented in a library's collection. Such headings may or may not be displayed in a patron access system.

A *heading file* is based directly on the bibliographic records and represents those records but does not control them. A heading file does not need to be internally consistent, and rarely includes references.

The distinction between authority and heading files may be fuzzy, particularly since some online authority files do not actually control the bibliographic files. I rarely make a distinction between the two varieties of files in this book because, from a patron's perspective, there is little significant difference. A patron should be able to browse through heading files and authority files, and should see the same information in all cases.

Name Authority Files

Good online catalogs include access to name authority or heading files, which should be compatible with the USMARC authority format and include cross references. Such files should also include scope and verification notes to be as useful as possible for technical processing. Scope and verification notes should not appear on browsing screens, but a library may choose to make them available to patrons through a separate command.

Subject Authority Files

Subject authority files should be available and inclusive. The Library of Congress now makes the Library of Congress Subject Headings (LCSH) available in USMARC authorities form, with updates retaining stable record numbers, which makes LCSH useful as a form of ongoing subject authority or heading file. But libraries use sources in addition to, or in place of, LCSH. "The authority file should accommodate and distinguish multiple sources of headings, i.e., LC, NLM, Sears, and locally established controlled vocabularies."[5]

Well-presented subject authority files provide a view of subject relationships not readily available from subject card catalogs.

Innovative design can make that view even more powerful, but certain forms of innovation require that subjects be established in controlled relationships—broader terms, narrower terms and related terms. LCSH and some other subject systems don't fit neatly into such relationships, and LCSH represents the bulk of subject cataloging currently available to American libraries.

Title Authority or Heading Files

Patrons can make good use of browsable title files, and some titles also serve as authorities. Series and uniform titles may be useful as authorities. Libraries should consider whether series titles should be separated from other titles or included with them, or whether series titles should appear in two heading files. Title headings should include title subfields as well as title fields.

Author-Title Heading Files

A browsable heading file combining authors and titles will not improve patron access. When patrons search by author and title, they expect immediate bibliographic results and should get them. The database engine may have an index combining authors and titles, depending on the way that author-title searches are keyed and supported, but that index does not appear to have much use as a browsable heading file. Browsable author-title headings are not the same as screens displaying multiple author-title search results; such screens are a basic part of any patron access system.

Dewey and LC Schedule Files

Several subject access activists support the notion of searchable classification schedules as an enhancement to subject access. Searching classification schedules by words and terms should provide a broader subject access vocabulary than LCSH provides, though word searches may yield some peculiar results. For example, a patron might search a schedule file by the words *California History*. The search will result in one or more call numbers or call number ranges, showing the number of items held for each such range. The patron could then retrieve the call number ranges or, if one appears to be most interesting, go directly to the shelves.

One substantial problem with such access, however, is a more acute version of a perceived problem with subject headings—there aren't enough of them, and interdisciplinary works aren't handled well. Access by classification results in precisely one access point per item. That needn't be true, as additional "searching classes" could be assigned, but it is certainly true for most material. If an average of 1.9 subject headings don't provide sufficient access, even though nonfiction works frequently have four or more subject terms, how will one access point per item improve the situation?

A project to add "searching classes" seems inefficient; the money can be spent more effectively by adding subject terms directly rather than indirectly. USMARC allows for subject headings using uncontrolled vocabulary. The vocabulary problems of LCSH do not prevent librarians from adding whatever subject headings will serve their patrons.

Although interdisciplinary works and works for emerging disciplines may be some of the most important in a library's collection, they tend to be some of the least accessible. Call number access will not help in such situations. To the extent that subject searchers come to think of class schedule searching as a primary tool, searchable schedules will worsen access to such materials.

The CLR/OCLC/Forest Press project on use of the Dewey Decimal Classification (DDC) online represents the first actual research in this area. That project yielded inconclusive results.

Entry Vocabulary Files

Should a catalog include a searchable thesaurus to help patrons identify synonyms? Some researchers argue that it should, but with few suggestions as to how such a thesaurus can be prepared. Any thesaurus will include large numbers of synonyms that are only similar in meaning. The English language has many approximate synonyms, but few true ones.

A searchable thesaurus, allowing access to terms used in subject headings by way of synonyms used in common language, could enhance subject access.

Building a thesaurus covering not only words but expressions is a formidable task. A patron access system that allows optional access to such a thesaurus, presumably labeling synonyms as related terms, will provide patrons with a range of possibilities for broadening a search. A patron access system that implements synonyms as an inherent part of subject searching will serve patrons badly, by forcing them to deal with items they did not directly request and may not want.

A patron access system can improve access for all patrons by including absolute synonyms such as color and colour, cooperative and co-operative or data base and database. Such equivalent words result from alternatives in spelling, hyphenating and compounding words. When synonyms go beyond such straightforward cases, access through synonyms should be optional.

INDEXES

The database engine must provide sufficient indexing so that patrons have at least as much access to items as they would have in a card catalog. A good database engine will provide more access than a card catalog.

Authority and heading files provide browsable access from approximate entries. Indexes provide specific results from approximate or exact searches. This section discusses various index possibilities, including those already in use and some that may not yet be employed.

An *index*, for this book's purposes, is any method that can provide direct access to one or more bibliographic records or, in some cases, to one or more headings.

The distinction between an index and an authority/heading file is one of presentation; the distinction may not exist within the database engine itself. As part of patron access, an authority/heading file is browsable, with the initial search representing merely an entry point from which the patron can proceed forward or backward. An index is not browsable, but yields a discrete set of results. That distinction can become muddy but is generally useful.

A complex patron access system could plausibly view all indexes as heading files and could index all authority/heading files. In that case, *find subject word ethics* would retrieve all subject headings with the word *ethics* in them, where *scan subject ethics* would drop the patron into the subject authority file at *Ethics*.

Card catalogs provide reasonably fast access through full fields: names, subjects, titles and series. Online database engines can and should provide similar access, but they should also provide new kinds of access.

Word Indexes

Word indexes (frequently called keyword indexes) provide access through each word within fields. They may include words from one type of field, from several related fields or from the entire record. The only decisions that have to be made regarding word indexes are (1) What fields should be indexed by word? and (2) What words should be suppressed from an index—that is, what words should be stopwords?

Almost every database engine uses some stopwords. It is possible, however, to maintain very large word indexes with very small sets of stopwords. RLIN may represent the nation's largest word-indexed library database, and the only words stopped in RLIN word indexes are one- and two-letter words and a few conjunctions, pronouns and prepositions. Such natural stopwords as *states, history, art* and *report* are all indexed in RLIN.

Stopwords should be used sparingly, if at all. They protect the system, not the patron. Good software design may reduce or eliminate the need for stopwords.

The usual reason for stopwords is to protect the database engine from extremely large searches. Do stopwords somehow improve access, or do they simply make certain entries difficult to locate? What if a title contains only stopwords and the system provides only word indexes? The best word indexes do not use extensive lists of stopwords.

Full-Record Word Indexes

A single-word index, offered instead of multiple indexes more narrowly defined, makes precise retrieval much more difficult. A full-record word index places greater stress on the database engine by requiring extensive Boolean logic in order to attain useful results. Such an index may also yield meaningless results.

Some current patron access systems use a single-word index, including all words in the bibliographic records, as the only index other than a name index. Further research into the relative ease of searching such a system might be useful. Can users retrieve known items rapidly using such a system? Does the ease of learning such a system and the ease of obtaining large results make up for problems in narrowing a result to manageable proportions?

Boolean logic helps solve most of the problems that arise when too much source data is included in a single word index, but no amount of Boolean logic will eliminate retrieval through words that have nothing to do with the substance of the item retrieved.

Headings

Every heading file should have a word index. Every recognized access point should be retrievable by word searching.

Subject word searching presents a difficult problem for direct searching because of extremely large result sets. This problem can be eliminated or eased, however, if subject word searches yield a set of subject headings rather than a set of bibliographic records.

Further research may help to determine the best blend of word indexes for given libraries, or for patron access in general. How many and what types of word indexes should be provided? Should a single word index include all access points, or should titles, series, subjects and names each have separate word indexes? Should each bibliographic field be indexed separately, with the database engine providing transparent combinations except when patrons (or staff) want very specific searches? The answers to these questions may depend on the library and its needs.

Contents, Summaries and Special Notes

Word indexes to contents, summaries and some other special note fields will retrieve more items, at some cost to specificity. Contents notes can provide access to works that do not have separate (analytic) cataloging—for example, collections of short stories or plays. Contents and summary notes also enhance topical or subject access, at least in terms of retrieving *more* items through a broader vocabulary. The problem of specificity (precision) may be a substantial one, arguing for a separate contents/summaries word index. Research into the effects of combined access point/contents word indexing is needed to determine whether patrons retrieve more of what they need with this type of indexing, or whether they retrieve too much that is not useful.

General Notes and Publication Statements

General notes (field 500) seem to have little retrieval value, but they can make precise word searches more difficult. A merged word index that includes publication (imprint) statements will add a new form of retrieval but will make some useful terms effectively unsearchable.

General notes, specifically MARC field 500, seem least useful for word indexing of any field in MARC records. Words used in general notes may not have any relation to the topic of a book. Indexing 500 notes is likely to yield essentially useless search results.

The case for access to publisher name is strong, at least for small and specialized presses—but that access can be through separate added entries for the publisher. Patrons might even be served better by an ability to qualify a search by publisher's name. Word indexes that include the publication statement will make *publications, publisher, publishing* and some other terms useless for topical retrieval because of their frequent use in company names (just as a merged index that includes corporate names may make *company* useless as a topical search). Quite a few geographic terms will also become largely useless, unless it is assumed that a patron looking for books about San Francisco is equally interested in seeing all books published in San Francisco. A separate word index for publication statements would eliminate the precision problem, but might not be very useful.

Term Indexes

*Term indexes can improve patron access significantly if they
are supported clearly and efficiently.*

As used here, a *term index* is an index consisting of portions of
fields; specifically, a *term index* contains a series of phrases built from
each field, with the first phrase starting at the first word, second phrase
at the second word and so on, including a final phrase containing the
last word in the field. Portions could be indefinitely long, going up to the
end of the field, or could be terminated at a reasonable length such as 60
characters.

Since term indexes are not currently used, examples may help to
clarify the concept. The film *On the Little Big Horn; or, Custer's Last
Stand* would generate the following terms, always eliminating articles
and conjunctions in search and index alike.

ON LITTLE BIG HORN CUSTERS LAST STAND
LITTLE BIG HORN CUSTERS LAST STAND
BIG HORN CUSTERS LAST STAND
HORN CUSTERS LAST STAND
CUSTERS LAST STAND
LAST STAND
STAND

That's a total of seven index entries, exactly the same as what is
required for a word index (except that a word index would probably
eliminate *on*). The special virtue of the term entries can be seen in the
second and fifth entries. Without the Boolean overhead and false drops
of searching *Little Big Horn or Custer's Last Stand* in word indexes,
the two phrases can be retrieved easily even though they occur within a
title.

The title of this book provides another example. It generates the
following:

PATRON ACCESS ISSUES FOR ONLINE CATALOGS
ACCESS ISSUES FOR ONLINE CATALOGS
ISSUES FOR ONLINE CATALOGS
FOR ONLINE CATALOGS
ONLINE CATALOGS
CATALOGS

The search FIND TTERM ONLINE CATALOG* (where *tterm* is a term index and * is the truncation symbol) will pull together this book; Joseph Matthews' book *Public Access to Online Catalogs*; Emily Fayen's *The Online Catalog: Improving Public Access to Library Materials; Users Look at Online Catalogs*, a summary report on the CLR study on online catalog use; several CLR publications reporting on conferences; and some other useful materials. As with many other powerful tools, this one is imperfect. It would give a result that apparently includes most of the significant words in the field, but it would miss Charles Hildreth's *Online Public Access Catalogs*.

A term index combines the functions of a field or phrase index and a word index, with the substantial added value of providing direct access to internal phrases—and omits the cumbersome and imperfect chore of building a table of "likely internal phrases."

Term indexes solve one serious problem with title searching. People remember a form of the title, but the form they remember may not be the form used in cataloging. As long as the form remembered is some set of contiguous words actually found in the title, a term index will work. A subject term index also overcomes some of the problems with the structure of subject headings.

Term Indexes and Boolean Word Searches

Most implicit (and many explicit) Boolean word searches may actually be term searches in disguise. When a patron keys FIND TWORD ART HISTORY (where *tword* is a title word index), the patron is probably more interested in titles with the phrase *art history* than in all titles with *art* somewhere in a title field and *history* somewhere in a title field.

The difficulty of Boolean searching, implicit or explicit, is well known. Term searching offers a clearer, more powerful, and simpler alternative in most cases. Term searching with implicit word level truncation should perhaps replace all implicit Boolean word searching. The rare patron who really needs to find all titles with American somewhere and Scientific somewhere else can always enter an explicit Boolean term search, e.g., FIND TWORD AMERICAN AND TWORD SCIENTIFIC.

Proximity Searching

Adjacency searching, another name for term searching, may be the only form of proximity searching that most patrons need or can use within an online catalog.

Proximity searching is a specialized form of Boolean *and* searching in which the words must be within a certain proximity, that is, one word must be no more than a set number of words away from the other word. Few patron access systems support proximity searching, but the tool is found on Dialog, BRS and similar online bibliographic searching systems. The amount of explanation required before a patron can formulate a proximity search makes it unfeasible for any patron access system.

Adjacency searching, where two words must be next to each other, represents a special form of proximity searching and duplicates the function of term searching. Term searching does not require special operators or any explanation of special symbols and verbs.

Name Indexes

Most patron access systems should use browsable name heading or authority files in place of name indexes.

Name searching presents several problems. Corporate and conference names don't mix well with personal names, and patrons may not know the proper form of personal names. Command parsing routines should be able to normalize name searches in order to provide access to heading files. FIND NAME GORE, DANIEL and FIND NAME DANIEL GORE should both result in a heading file screen in the region of GORE.

For those systems without heading files, some approximate name index may be needed. Approximate name indexes can be difficult to design. The pn (personal name) index provided in RLIN (and available in several similar systems) discards portions of the search term and yields results that may bear little resemblance to the search. That algorithm was a useful early attempt to improve approximate name searching, but it does not provide the quality of access that patrons should expect. Word searching within a name file may be an even worse solution.

Special Indexes

Special indexes require special sensitivity to search and index normalization and to required length of search term. Except for call number indexes, patrons should not require special indexes.

Special indexes are those that index something other than textual information. Examples include Library of Congress Catalog Number, ISBN, ISSN, record ID, publisher's number and call number.

In practical terms, leaving special indexes out of the options normally displayed will not injure those few patrons who can make use of the indexes. If a system has a clear and consistent command syntax, such patrons will be able to make intelligent guesses as to additional indexes. Just as a visiting librarian may guess that a command such as DISPLAY MARC will bring up a tagged display, a patron can probably guess that FIND ISBN or FIND ISSN will access the appropriate index, if it exists. As with the tagged MARC display, control number indexes should be represented in online descriptions and should be represented in written documentation, but need not be part of the primary information presented to patrons.

Most special indexes are phrase indexes, but many require special handling. The special handling is needed for internal access and for occasional patron access. Some special index problems follow:

- LCCN searches should be acceptable with or without the alphabetic prefix, with or without the trailing revision codes, with or without leading zeros after the year and with or without a hyphen. *76005123, 76-5123* and *765123* should all retrieve *The child from five to ten*.
- ISBN and ISSN searches should be accepted with or without hyphens. Both searches should be checked for valid check digits, particularly if the search does not yield a result. Truncated ISBN searches do make sense; it isn't clear that truncated ISSN searches ever make sense.

Other special indexes may require similar considerations. Only one special index, call numbers, has specific value for patrons, either as a browsing file or as a direct index. Unlike most other indexes, it must be possible to truncate call number searches to as little as one or two characters. Patrons interested in naval or military science or gypsies will need two-character LC call number truncation, even if it would be nearly useless for many other classifications in large libraries.

Should ISBN searches be provided as a method of searching for works from a specific publisher? The method has some virtues, but a publisher subfield index would provide much better results. The following three problems with ISBNs make them less than ideal for publisher access:

1. Patrons must understand ISBN hyphenation to make good use of an ISBN index. Since ISBN hyphenation varies, this is not

an automatic process. While the catalog should accept searches with or without hyphens, the second hyphen specifies the end of a publisher prefix.

2. Early works have no ISBNs. More recent works may have ISBN prefixes that represent an imprint, a publishing house or some other concept. An ISBN prefix does not always represent a publisher.

3. Newer publishers and growing publishers will have more than one ISBN prefix, making the results of truncated ISBN searches deceptive.

The publisher of this book represents a good example of the third problem, which may be the most important problem. A search on *0-86729** will yield recent books from Knowledge Industry Publications, but will not yield its earlier books, some of them still valuable. On the other hand, a patron familiar with *Microcomputers and Libraries: A Guide to Technology, Products and Applications* would enter *0-914236**, and might assume that KIPI has published nothing since 1982, when that prefix ran out of numbers.

Those problems do not make ISBN indexes useless, but they do suggest that a library wishing to provide access by imprint should support a publisher index based on text subfields.

Derived-Key Indexes

Derived-key indexes have no place in contemporary public access systems. Hidden derived-key indexes, without proper filtering, represent a substantial disservice to patrons.

A *derived-key index* is one that uses leading letters from one or more words of one or more fields to form a search key. In the best known derived-key system, this book can be searched by two methods. One takes the first three letters of the first title word, the first two each of the second and third and the first from the fourth, yielding *pat,ac,is,f.* The second takes the first four letters of the author's last name and the first four letters of the first title word, yielding *craw, patr.* Another derived-key system has TLS/PATRACCESS and ATS/CRAWPATRO as equivalent searches, using a four letter–five letter combination in both cases.

Some existing systems use *hidden derived-key indexes*, where patrons key authors and titles and the system derives the key internally.

If the system proceeds to filter the results, making sure that each one actually fulfills the search as keyed, hidden derived-key indexes can function fairly well. In any other case, hidden derived-key indexes are likely to yield unexpected and unwanted results, since most of the patron's search is ignored.

Derived-key indexes require little machine overhead, but they reduce searching precision, lead to an odd and unnatural searching style and generally seem unsuited for patron access.

SUPPORTING THE PATRON ACCESS SYSTEM

Good patron access requires much more computing capacity than has generally been acknowledged.

Good patron access requires a complete database consisting of high-quality records. It requires extensive indexes, well-designed access, a good command system and intelligent feedback. But none of that will be of much use if the system lacks sufficient capacity to serve patrons rapidly.

Early estimates of computing requirements were very optimistic. Librarians were told that minicomputers would support up to 256 terminals, with a relatively small minicomputer supporting up to 64 terminals. Neither estimate proved to be reasonable, as libraries discovered when they actually started providing patron access.

Pioneering online systems that add the dozens or hundreds of terminals required for full online access find that computers must be substantially upgraded to provide good performance. More research and real experience may help to provide reasonable estimates for CPU requirements.

Computing power gets cheaper every year. Libraries should plan to increase computing power as they add terminals and improve the database. Computing power, disk storage (capacity and speed) and terminal capabilities will continue to improve, providing more leverage for the library dollar.

Searching Large Catalogs

Large catalogs are more difficult to search than small ones.

This statement has always been true for card catalogs. Finding a particular work related to Shakespeare takes seconds in a 50,000-item library, but may be a formidable task in a 4,000,000-item library. The problem may be more extreme for online catalogs. Result sets are larger, truncated searches can yield absurdly large results and multiple item displays may go on for many screens. Patron problems in searching large catalogs can be eased by adding search limiting and encouraging precise searches. That shifts searching difficulty from the patron to the computer. Boolean searches, one key way of reducing result sets, require much more computer power than simple searches. Boolean searches may cause difficulties for patrons as well as for computers.

Machine requirements for a large library can't be predicted by using straight-line projections based on small library or pilot catalog use. If a computer processing 1 million instructions per second (MIPS) provides good response for a library with 100,000 titles and 10 terminals, that doesn't mean that a computer able to do 10 MIPS will be as fast for a million-title library and 100 terminals. The larger system might be faster, or might be so slow as to be useless.

The factors are complicated and hard to predict. With good database design, computing power needed to support a larger database may not rise as rapidly as the size of the database. However, the power (computing power, communications speed and disk access speed) needed to support more terminals may rise much more rapidly than the number of terminals involved. Librarians must also be aware that "the better the searching tool we create, the more it will be used, and thus the more processing power will be required by the system."[6]

A speaker on online catalogs recently suggested that future catalogs may recognize design limits, with no more than 500,000 items in a catalog. That limit rules out online catalogs for large academic libraries, large public libraries and many library systems. In fact, good design and sufficient computing power can support a patron access system with millions of titles and hundreds of terminals.

Queuing and Response

Heavy use of a slightly underpowered patron access system will result in unacceptable response. Response can go from very good to very bad with a small increase in usage.

Every system has a "knee," a point at which gradually worsening response gets much worse very quickly. That knee may be predictable. If system designers can determine how long a system needs to fulfill a request, and a library can predict the rate at which requests will arrive, queuing theory can be used to predict the point at which requests begin to pile up and interfere with each other. That point is the knee of the curve, the point at which response suddenly goes bad.

Patron access loads may be somewhat complex, requiring a combination of theory and testing. Since requests may vary from a simple title phrase search to a Boolean search involving five logical operators and three indexes, a designer can only determine the length of time needed to fulfill a request if the mix of requests can be predicted.

The surest way to determine what load a system can handle effectively is to exceed that load.

The knee of the curve can come at a point that is regarded as very satisfactory. A system may go from one-second average response to two-minute average response when five more terminals are added. For most online systems, the only way to be sure where the response curve will suddenly go bad is to reach that point. At least one vendor of online catalogs is now using exactly that method.

If a vendor or library can create a legitimate load testing system, a catalog can be tested to determine maximum acceptable capacity. Such testing requires a full-scale database and some means of providing realistic simulation of patron search patterns. A good load test should be designed by people with no direct knowledge of the system's internal design because it is too easy to slant a test to take advantage of a system's strong points, even without intending to do so.

Response Time

Fast response is a fundamental attribute of a successful, user-friendly patron access system.

The Council on Library Resources study on online catalogs found that a full 43% of public library online catalog users were unhappy with response time. Other libraries didn't fare much better; the overall rate of unhappiness was 30%.[7]

Patrons do not expect half-second responses to all searches, but will be delighted to get instant feedback on heading searches, which should be possible in a well-designed system. Reasonably fast response may make the difference between a well-liked system and one that patrons avoid; any delay of more than a few seconds may cause patrons to wonder if the system is working and will discourage them from pursuing search strategies.

A patron access system should keep the patron informed as to whether a search or any other transaction will take more than two or three seconds. If a search takes more than five seconds, the patron should have some way to interrupt it.

Good messages, and good times to display them, require some creativity. Some systems display changing numbers as searches are analyzed. If those numbers can be combined with some sort of INTERRUPT key, so that a patron can abandon an extremely large search in progress, such feedback may assure the user that something is happening and can also help to avoid unnecessary large searches.

Patrons must feel that they control the catalog. Fast response to searches encourages patrons to enter more searches. A signal that a search may take a long time gives the patron a chance to reconsider. Systems that offer no such chance and that take minutes to offer results place a barrier between patrons and the collection.

NOTES

1. Berman, Sanford. "Cataloging for Public Libraries." *Nature and Future of the Catalog.* Maurice J. Freedman; S. Michael Malinconico, eds. Phoenix, AZ: Oryx Press; 1979. p. 225.

2. Fasana, Paul J. "1981 and Beyond: Visions and Decisions." *Journal of Library Automation.* 13(2): 1980 June. p. 101.

3. Atkinson, Hugh C. "The Electronic Catalog." *Nature and Future of the Catalog.* Maurice J. Freedman; S. Michael Malinconico, eds. Phoenix, AZ: Oryx Press; 1979. p. 102.

4. Fayen, Emily Gallup. *The Online Catalog: Improving Public Access to Library Materials.* White Plains, NY: Knowledge Industry Publications, Inc.; 1983. p. 20.

5. Corey, James F. "Search Retrieval Options." *Online Catalog Design Issues: A Series of Discussions.* Brian Aveney, ed. Washington, DC: Council on Library Resources; 1984 July. p. 23.

6. *Online Catalog: The Inside Story.* William E. Post; Peter G. Watson, eds. Chico, CA: Ryan Research International; 1983. p. 120.

7. *Using Online Catalogs.* Joseph R. Matthews; Gary S. Lawrence; Douglas K. Ferguson, eds. New York: Neal-Schuman; 1983. p. 117.

3

Presentation:
Context in an Online Catalog

A library is a system, an interacting and interdependent set of items that form a unified whole. Any system establishes a context within which each component part works. If the component parts make sense within that context, the system is well designed. If the parts are at odds with each other, the system has contextual problems.

A catalog must make sense within the context of a library. In the same way, elements of a catalog should fit together within the context of the catalog.

Like many other elements of a library, a catalog is a working system. In order to use a catalog effectively, patrons must understand how that system functions in the context of the library.

Some libraries use dictionary card catalogs, with cards in a single alphabetic sequence including subjects, authors and titles. Other libraries use divided catalogs, usually combining authors and titles in one sequence, with subject headings in a separate sequence. When patrons accustomed to dictionary catalogs go to a library with a divided catalog, they may at first assume that the library doesn't have what they want. If the library has rows and rows of cabinets, and the only labels are alphabetic ranges on individual drawers, the user may not recognize that the new card catalog is a different kind of system from the old one, and that it requires different actions.

Confusion arises because the user has a mental model of a card catalog and, quite naturally, applies that model to this new case, not realizing that the case doesn't fit the model. Libraries can avoid that problem and other contextual problems by placing signposts on and around catalogs, to help guide users toward proper models.

39

Online catalogs are more complex systems than card catalogs and represent a broader range of models. Patron actions are also more varied when they use online catalogs. These actions must make sense within a context and must be part of a consistent overall presentation.

This chapter and the next raise some issues that specifically affect overall presentation and context. All the elements mentioned in this book work together to form an online system, and all must be considered within that context. This chapter also introduces the draft *American National Standard Common Command Language for Online Interactive Information Retrieval, dp Z39.58*, proposed in 1986 by Standards Committee G of the National Information Standards Organization [Z39] (NISO). That proposed standard, henceforth called the *Standard Command Language*, is mentioned often in the rest of the book. While it is only a draft as of mid-1986 and may be adopted in a different form or may not be adopted at all, the proposed Standard Command Language provides a basis for discussing commonality among online catalogs.

SESSION BOUNDARIES

An online catalog begins to establish its context by the way that patrons begin and end a session. Clear and effective starting and stopping establish a clear and effective presentation.

For most patrons, catalogs are tools to use to find material. Patrons expect to start using the tool and stop using it as soon as they find the information they need. The boundaries of a searching session are determined by resolving the following issues:

- What appears on the screen as a patron approaches a terminal?
- What must a patron do in order to begin searching?
- What are the steps required to begin and end a session? Are they clear, quick and consistent?
- How does a patron end a search session? What happens if a patron fails to end a session?

An online patron access system should use explicit starting and stopping points to establish separate sessions for each patron.

Card catalogs present an analogy that may be faulty. A patron approaches the card catalog, finds an appropriate drawer, uses that drawer and leaves the catalog. Each use of a card catalog is a "session." By analogy, online patron access consists of searching sessions for each patron, and should have a known beginning and end.

But a patron using a card catalog does not go through an introductory ritual. Few libraries require that patrons inform a staff member that they are about to use a card catalog. The card catalog is present, and is always ready to handle searches. Most patrons don't look at informative material before plunging in to find an appropriate drawer. A patron begins a session at a card catalog by opening a drawer; polite patrons end a session by returning drawers to their proper locations or closing open drawers. That explicit ending is desirable, but neither required nor universal; some patrons end a search by simply walking away from the catalog.

Explicit session boundaries assure patrons that their work will not be affected by the work of the previous user and provide all catalog users with a consistent starting point.

Although most existing patron access systems use explicit session boundaries, some do not require them. In almost any system, if one patron fails to finish a searching session, another patron can start searching at the point the first patron left off, without starting a new session. If the online catalog is as anonymous and independent as the card catalog, this does no harm because the lack of boundaries reassures patrons that their activity is not being recorded in any way that could harm them. In fact a case can be made against requiring explicit sessions. Even though lack of boundaries may be reassuring to some, patrons should at least have the option of explicitly starting a session.

Starting Point

The starting point for patron access should be obvious, self-instructing and welcoming.

Patrons should always be able to start a session explicitly, in order to clear away residue from the previous user and establish the ground rules for the session. The ideal starting point will depend on the library, but some points should be considered.

The first step to designing good starting points is avoiding bad starting points. A blank screen may be appropriate, if the terminal has a bright, obvious instruction for starting. A public terminal should never show an operating system prompt such as A> or a blank screen with a message such as *Logon:, Function:* or *Command:*.

START Function Key

Patron access systems should use a function key labeled START, or the text string "START," to begin a new session. Libraries must decide whether START should clear stored search results without asking for confirmation.

A good patron access system must provide a way to start a new session that is visible from any point within a session, including a blank screen. For dedicated public terminals, one obvious solution is a prominent function key labeled START.

Good design suggests that the function key START should be accompanied by a label elsewhere on the terminal saying something such as *Press START to start using the catalog.* Less desirable, but suitable as an option for dial-up or workstation use, is a label referring to a function key. *Press F2 to start using the catalog* will make good sense to a scholar using an IBM PC or equivalent, but a dedicated terminal should call the function key what it is: START.

A START function key should always take a patron to an opening screen from any other point in the system. That doesn't necessarily mean that START should always act immediately. If the patron access system allows results to be stored and manipulated, and if a stored result set is present, a library may wish to allow for the possibility that START was pressed accidentally. In that case, some suitable message can appear, along with a request for confirmation (either a Y for Yes or, possibly, another press of the START key). At public terminals, that safeguard may not be reasonable; most libraries will prefer to treat START as an absolute and immediate command.

START is not the only possible verb. LOGON is possible but is computer jargon. BEGIN is equally clear, but the proposed Standard Command Language uses START, abbreviated STA, and it does not seem to have any drawbacks.

First Screen

The first screen of a new session should identify the library, be clear and inviting for new users and allow experienced users to start searching immediately.

The first screen for a session does more to establish the system context than any other screen. A first screen should be sparse, clear and not wasteful.

- If at all possible, no more than 15% of available text spaces should be used, or a total of 294 characters (on a standard screen of 24 lines with 80 columns each). Thirty percent, or 588 characters, should be an absolute maximum for the opening screen; a screen with 588 characters is surprisingly full.
- The screen should indicate the type of catalog, what the patron's options are, how to get help and what to do next. A small set of options (usually five to nine) ensures that the patron will not become overwhelmed by too many choices.
- An experienced patron should be able to enter any valid command from the first screen, and a new user should be able to begin searching or get help directly from the first screen. If an online catalog has more than one welcoming screen, it requires more steps to complete a known-item search than does a card catalog. If the first screen offers several information sources including the online catalog, the extra step may be justified.

Many starting screens either identify the vendor of the catalog, or say *Welcome to the online catalog, press any key to continue*. Neither seems to serve patrons well. The first serves as free advertising for the vendor and wastes the patron's time. The second wastes the patron's time paging past opening screens to get some work done. The second example also demonstrates a common mistake: *Press any key* is not a good suggestion. An experienced user will be ready to enter a search; a novice user, particularly one who is ill at ease with computers, needs to know *exactly* what to do, not be invited to press any key.

If a library's system requires a second screen before work can be done, the first screen should offer a specific instruction, such as *Press + to continue* or *Press C to continue*. The system may actually treat all keys identically, but at least the uneasy novice has a clear instruction to follow.

No single opening screen suits all libraries in all circumstances. The criteria mentioned above allow for a wide range of designs. The opening screen sets the context for the catalog and is the only screen a library can expect every user to see. These two facts suggest several other questions to be considered by catalog designers:

- Does the opening screen provide a consistent model, followed in the rest of the design?
- Should the opening screen include an area for special messages from the library to its patrons, such as holiday schedules, special events, milestones or requests for assistance? If so, should that area be fixed or variable in length?
- Should the opening screen suggest that librarians are available to provide assistance, or should that offer be made only in help screens? Is the statement true? That is, will there always be librarians within a few feet of each public terminal who will be able to respond to any question? Should the patron access system point out librarians as the first place to go for help, or should it offer an internal help function as the first level of support?
- Since a complete patron access system will have more command possibilities than can fit on a sparse first screen, what possibilities should be on the first screen and how should extended possibilities be presented?

Figure 3.1 shows one example of an opening screen for a mythical patron access system serving college students. The screen contains 553 characters and spaces between words, not including two lines of dashes. This represents a screen density of 28%, which is approaching the recommended maximum for any advisory screen and is considerably more than the 15% that some regard as ideal. While Figure 3.1 may not be an ideal opening screen, it meets the basic criteria stated here.

Restarting

Patrons will walk away from terminals without explicitly stopping their session. A good design will automatically restart the session in some manner; a restart might result in a blank screen to preserve the terminal.

When a patron looks for a terminal to use, he or she may be reluctant to use one if it displays a bibliographic record or otherwise

Figure 3.1: Hypothetical Opening Screen

```
┌─────────────────────────────────────────────────────────────────────────┐
│CCCCCAT: Cougar Canyon Community College Catalog                 OPENING   │
│New Session: No search in progress                                         │
│---------------------------------------------------------------------------│
│                                                                           │
│March 15, 1988                   Messages From The Library                 │
│                                                                           │
│The Carmody Library will close at 5:00 p.m. Friday.  The Francher Natural   │
│Science Library will remain open until midnight as usual.                  │
│                                                                           │
│Remember: March 23 is Visitor's Day.                                       │
│                                                                           │
│                                                                           │
│                                                                           │
│                                                                           │
│You may begin a search or press H or the HELP key for more information.    │
│                                                                           │
│---------------------------------------------------------------------------│
│Possible NEXT ACTIONs: ? for Help              T for Title search          │
│                       N for Name search       W for Word search           │
│                       S for Subject search    M for More search choices   │
│          NEXT ACTION? _                                                    │
│                                                                           │
└─────────────────────────────────────────────────────────────────────────┘
```

shows that somebody else is using it. An opening screen welcomes the new patron; a session in progress deters the new patron. A blank screen may not be as welcoming as an opening screen, but at least should not deter. Most libraries will need some means of clearing public terminals not in current use. Designers should not assume that patrons will explicitly end a searching session and should make provisions for those who do not.

Patron access systems should automatically end a session if no keys are pressed in a set period of time, possibly 10 or 15 minutes.

One sensible provision is a timed restart. If no keys have been pressed on a terminal for a given period of time, the session is assumed to be over. The system can go blank, go to the opening screen or perform some combination of the two. A system may go to the opening screen for a similar period of time, then blank the opening screen if no activity takes place.

Timed restarts serve the library and the patrons, but must be considered carefully. Following are some of the questions surrounding timed restarts:

- Should a warning be given before the restart occurs? If so, should the warning include a beep or other audible signal?
- What should the time limit be? Five minutes? Or 10, 15 or 30 minutes?
- Should the time limit be consistent for all public terminals or should some high-demand terminals have shorter time limits?
- Should workstations and other nonpublic terminals have the same time limits? Different time limits? No time limits?
- Should dial-up users have similar time limits? If so, should the line be disconnected when the limit is exceeded?
- Should the restart blank the screen or go to the opening screen? Should different time limits have different effects—for instance, blanking the screen after 10 minutes, then going to the opening screen only after another 10 minutes have passed?
- Should terminals alternate between blank screens and opening screens on a timed basis, so that patrons have a better chance of seeing a welcoming message?

A timed restart with blanking helps to prevent the possible hardware problem of phosphor burn-in. On most terminals, if the same characters stay on the screen for an extended period of time, their shadow burns indelibly into the screen phosphor, making the screen more difficult to read. Modern CRTs may be less prone to burn-in than older devices, but blanking still serves as a protective measure. In fact, many contemporary terminals include timed blanking within the terminal itself.

Explicit Stop

If patrons can explicitly start sessions, they should also be able to explicitly stop them using a STOP function key or the command "Stop."

Any system that uses explicit sessions should have a STOP key to match the START key. Even if a system does not use explicit sessions, STOP should be available. The same patrons who always return card drawers to the catalog and always close the drawers will use the STOP to assure themselves and others that they have finished a searching session properly.

Polite patrons will always use STOP, since it should return the terminal to a welcome screen, leaving it ready for the next patron. Nervous patrons will use STOP to be sure that their session is properly completed. Some patrons will not use STOP, just as some patrons leave catalog drawers in a state of disarray.

STOP should work immediately and without confirmation, terminating a session and clearing any results. If possible, a STOP function key should take effect while a search or display is in progress, terminating the other action.

Questions for an explicit stopping point are similar to those for timed restarts: (1) What happens to the screen when the STOP button is pressed?; and (2) Do patrons who have saved search results have to confirm the STOP? Assuming that STOP is not easy to press accidentally, the answer to the latter question seems straightforward: STOP should take effect immediately, going to an opening screen with no additional questions. STOP also makes a good "panic button" if the function key is always active, even during searches, displays and print commands.

At least six different terms can be used to end a session: END, EXIT, LOGOFF, QUIT, STOP and TERMINATE. EXIT, LOGOFF and TERMINATE are all somewhat jargony. END is commonly used in microcomputers to mean "go to the end of the line" or "go to the end of the document." Anyone familiar with microcomputers will be startled to find END leaving a session. Some people may expect STOP to suspend a search or display rather than to leave a session, but that is not a common usage. QUIT might be preferable, except for two factors: STOP is directly parallel to START and the proposed Standard Command Language recommends STOP. The first factor is probably sufficient to make STOP the best choice to end a session.

SIGNPOSTS

Signposts should always show patrons where they are, how they got there and where they can go.

Signposts are those portions of a display that show where the system is and how the patron got there. Signposts serve to maintain context and to assure patrons that they control the access system. They should be brief, clear and unambiguous.

Most Recent Action

Every screen should show a user's most recent action. When a screen is the result of a search, the screen should also show that search. The most recent action should be capitalized and should appear as a command, not as menu numbers or function keys.

Every well-designed patron access system shows users how they got where they are. Some considerations for showing the most recent action include the following:

- Normalization. The patron's action should stand out, and for that reason should probably appear in all capital letters rather than exactly as keyed.
- Function keys. In order to show the most recent action, any function key must have a textual equivalent, which should be displayed. For example, if key F4 starts a title search, the next screen could show *You keyed F4: FIND TITLE* or *You keyed FIND TITLE*, but should not show *You keyed F4*. A signpost such as *You keyed F4* is appropriate only if F4 has no meaning and the remaining message is something like *No function has been assigned to F4*.
- Menu choices. Any menu choice must also have a textual equivalent, and the signpost should work as for function keys (above).
- Searches. When a search retrieves more than one item, the most recent action includes the search itself and the actual command that retrieved the current screen. The search may be more significant than the command that produced this particular display.
- Boolean searches. For systems that support search qualification, the most recent action could be either the last term entered, e.g., *and name asimov*, or the entire search statement, e.g., *find word robots and name asimov*.

Several existing systems do not consistently provide signposts for most recent action. One commentator defends the absence of such signposts: "The search argument does not remain on the screen if there is a match; this causes no real problems, although there are occasionally displays that disconcert the user who has inadvertently entered a search for the wrong record."[1] A system that displays an unexpected record, with no indication of why the record is there, gives the patron no way to see what has gone wrong.

Next Action

A patron access system should always give the patron some choices for the next command. Options displayed should be appropriate for the current context. A highlighted or prompted "most likely action" should not preclude other commands.

Most illustrations in this book divide the screen into three sections. The top shows where the system is and how the patron got there; the middle shows results, headings or other information; and the bottom part of the screen shows where the patron can go next. This bottom section requires careful design and analysis.

Should a system display a most likely next action, either as a prompted command line or by highlighting one of a set of options? This form of suggestion can save keying and help guide a patron through a series of actions, but can also cause inconsistency, since the system will frequently be in a state where no one action is most likely.

A complex system will usually have more options than can reasonably be displayed on part of a screen. Some systems solve that problem by limiting the patron to those actions that appear, which does not seem justified. As long as the same key sequence does not mean different things at different times, the patron's ability to use known commands should not be restricted.

Figure 3.1 includes a fairly minimal next-action signpost, one that would change depending on the state of the session. By including an option that calls up more possible actions, the need for completeness can be satisfied without using too much of the screen or providing too many choices.

Several current online catalogs provide no next-action signposts or provide them only at some points within searching. The most typical gap is at the point of item display. Quite a few systems omit any prompting once an item is displayed. Such systems do not mislead the patron with an incomplete signpost but they also leave the user with no idea of where to go.

Chapters 7 and 8 discuss some of these issues in more detail.

Redirection

When a patron searches one form of heading and the system identifies an equivalent form actually used in the catalog, the system must inform the patron of the situation. If the patron searches for "Samuel Clemens," the catalog should not give results for "Mark Twain" without making the redirection clear.

Redirection can take place only when a system has authority control with references or some equivalent mechanism. A system capable of redirection can either indicate that an authorized form exists and offer to redirect the search to the authorized form; or do the redirection automatically, retrieving the authorized form.

Signposts must be used in either case, and the nature of the signpost depends on the option chosen. If redirection is prompted, the signpost must explain what is being offered in a clear, nontechnical manner and should provide some indication of the outcome of redirection. Figure 3.2 shows a poor signpost for prompted redirection and Figure 3.3 shows a better alternative.

Figure 3.2: Poor Redirection Signpost

```
You keyed: N CLEMENS, SAMUEL                              AUTHORITY
Your search retrieved 1 authority record.
---------------------------------------------------------------------

#    Name                                    Items

1    Twain, Mark                              415
     x Clemens, Samuel                          0
:                                                               :
:                                                               :
---------------------------------------------------------------------
Possible NEXT ACTIONs: # to retrieve items       T for Title search
                       ? for Help                W for Word search
                       N for Name search         M for More search choices
                       S for Subject search      Q to Quit searching
           NEXT ACTION? 1_
```

If redirection is automatic, the signpost must indicate what has happened. Careful wording should make it clear to the patron why a search for CLEMENS, SAMUEL retrieves items for TWAIN, MARK. The signpost should not say *Your search: NAME TWAIN, MARK.* The patron didn't key that search and will lose control of the context and the process. At worst, the patron may assume that the system is malfunctioning or that the search was incorrectly entered. The signpost should show what was keyed, what was retrieved and why the two differ.

Figure 3.3: Better Redirection Signpost

```
You keyed: N CLEMENS, SAMUEL                                      REDIRECT
Your search retrieves 0 items.
--------------------------------------------------------------------------

The name CLEMENS, SAMUEL is not used in this catalog.
The name TWAIN, MARK is used instead.

N TWAIN, MARK will retrieve 415 items.

:                                                                        :
:                                                                        :
---------------------------------------------------------------------
Possible NEXT ACTIONs: ? for Help              T for Title search
                       N for Name search       W for Word search
                       S for Subject search    M for More search choices
                       [RETURN] to perform the search shown below
               NEXT ACTION? N TWAIN, MARK_
```

Request and Response

---

*A patron access system should give patrons what they request.
Unless the result of a patron's request is a browsable display,
the system should never give patrons more than what was
requested.*

The fundamental roles of signposts are to show the patron why
the current screen appears and how that screen functions within the
context of the overall design. Besides showing how the patron got here
and where the patron can go, the contents of the current screen should
make sense in terms of what the patron asked for.

Some systems always retrieve a response for every search, taking
the next item alphabetically if there is no proper response. Other
systems will fill a multiple-item display with items, even though the
search retrieves fewer items than will fill a screen. A search for *kesner,
richard* from an authority display may yield four books, but the multi-
item screen has room for seven items. Some systems will display the
four Kesner books and fill the screen with three books by Kespali.

In addition to showing items the patron didn't ask for, this type of
system makes the screen denser than necessary. The worst case is one
in which a search retrieves a single item. Such a search should yield a
single-item display rather than a screen full of many items.

A screen containing four Kesner titles and three Kespali titles
makes perfectly good sense if it is part of a browsable author/title file.

But when a patron has already chosen *kesner, richard* after browsing a name index, the patron should retrieve only items for that author.

Results: Extent and Relative Position

A search result screen should show the size of the result and the location of the patron within that result. Signposts should also show how to move back and forth within the result, if appropriate.

Some online catalogs do not display the relative position or overall result size once the patron displays a single item. This makes it more difficult for a patron to go on to other items. Signposts to give the needed information should be straightforward. Figure 3.4 shows one simple possibility.

Patrons should know how large a result is, but they do not necessarily need an exact number. Some online catalogs pause when a search yields a certain number of items, display a message such as *Your search retrieves at least 100 items. Continue?*, and wait for confirmation before completing the search. Some systems can handle large searches efficiently but do not count large result sets as efficiently. A message such as *Your search retrieves more than 100 items*, presented as a result, may be sensible in such cases. The patron can still display all the items, but is more likely to refine the search.

Figure 3.4: Possible Signposts for Result Position

```
Your search: N TWAIN, MARK                                    MEDIUM
Your search retrieves 415 items.
You keyed: DIS 1-3, 5, 7-10
Item 2 of 415        Screen 1 of 2
-------------------------------------------------------------------

        TITLE: Sketches of the sixties
    PUBLISHED: San Francisco : John Howell, 1927

        NAMES: Harte, Bret, 1836-1902.
               Twain, Mark, 1835-1910.
:                                                                   :
:                                                                   :
-------------------------------------------------------CONTINUED--
Possible NEXT ACTIONs: + for Next Screen      F for Full Display
                       I+ for Next Item       ? for Help
                       I- for Previous Item   M for More options
        NEXT ACTION? _
```

Result Clarity—Single Record

Designers should consider a signpost that shows the field that causes an item to be retrieved, particularly when that field does not appear on the first screen of the bibliographic display.

The argument against such a signpost is that displays should be clear and consistent. Adding a field that could come from anywhere in the item tends to destroy that consistency. The argument in favor is that the patron must always be in control. Items that don't show the term used as a search tend to weaken the sense of control. The patron may wonder why an item was retrieved.

Figure 3.5 shows one example of such a signpost. Four different aspects of this issue require careful thought:

1. How should a field, used for retrieval but not normally displayed on a given screen, be displayed and properly identified?
2. How should a field that appears on the first screen, but is not the first element displayed, be identified so that the patron clearly understands why the item was retrieved?

Figure 3.5: Possible Signpost for Access Point

```
You keyed: N FOX, ROBIN                                          MEDIUM
Your search retrieves 8 items.
Item 1 of 8          Screen 1 of 2
[Retrieved by ADDITIONAL AUTHOR: Fox, Robin, 1934-, joint author]
-----------------------------------------------------------------------

    AUTHOR: Tiger, Lionel, 1937-
     TITLE: The imperial animal / [by] Lionel Tiger & Robin Fox.

   EDITION: [1st ed.]
 PUBLISHED: New York: Holt, Rinehart and Winston; 1971
DESCRIPTION: xi, 308 p. 24 cm.

  SUBJECTS: Civilization, Modern--20th century.
            Psychobiology.

LOCATION              CALL NUMBER          STATUS
Horvath               HM107 .T5            On Shelf

-----------------------------------------------------------CONTINUED--
Possible NEXT ACTIONs: + for Next Screen      F for Full Display
                       I+ for Next Item       H for Help
                       I- for Previous Item   M for More options
            NEXT ACTION? _
```

3. If access points are ever identified by special signposts, should they always be identified by special signposts in order to maintain a consistent display?
4. Can these goals be met when an explicit or implicit Boolean search involves terms from two or more fields?

If the last line in the upper portion of a screen is *TITLE: Little Women* and the first line of the bibliographic display window is the same thing, the signpost is redundant and may seem silly. On the other hand, the signpost provides consistency.

The fourth question above may not have any good answer. One reasonable but possibly false assertion is that patrons who are sophisticated enough to use Boolean logic will recognize that items may appear for reasons that are not immediately obvious.

Result Clarity—Multiple Items

Signposts to show the access point for each item in a multiple-item display are desirable but may not be workable.

When a screen full of items appears, how does the patron know why each item is included? Is it possible to show the access point that retrieved each item while retaining an open and intelligible multiple-item display?

Possibly not. Multiple-item displays should be uncluttered. Single-line displays should concentrate information so that patrons can browse rapidly and displays with brief bibliographic information for several items should be open and easy to read. Patrons may need to page through several dozen or several hundred items to find the specific items needed. More space taken for each item means more screens and more time for the patron. Adding an extra line to show retrieval points increases display density and reduces the number of items per screen.

Other factors argue in favor of clarifying the source of items. Assuming that multiple-item displays appear alphabetically by main entry or title, a patron may be wholly confused by the first screen when the search term was late in the alphabet. The patron may feel that the system has gone haywire, particularly if the access points are somewhat obscure. Figure 3.6 demonstrates the problem and one possible solution. That solution shows the difficulty with such signposts—Figure 3.6 is not an attracive display.

Figure 3.6: Possible Signpost for Multiple-Item Display

```
You keyed: N TWAIN, MARK                                          MULTIPLE
Your search retrieves 415 items.
Items 1-4 of 415
------------------------------------------------------------------------
1.  AUTHOR: Buranelli, Vincent.
    TITLE: Tom Sawyer
    [ADDITIONAL ENTRY: Twain, Mark, 1835-1910. Tom Sawyer.]

2.  AUTHOR: Harte, Bret, 1836-1902.
    TITLE: Sketches of the sixties
    [ADDITIONAL AUTHOR: Twain, Mark, 1835-1910.]

3.  AUTHOR: Hoffman, Heinrich, 1809-1894.
    TITLE: Slovenly Peter (Struwwelpeter)
    [ADDITIONAL AUTHOR: Twain, Mark, 1835-1910.]

4.  AUTHOR: Miller, Roger, 1936-
    TITLE: Big river
    [ADDITIONAL ENTRY: Twain, Mark, 1835-1910. Adventures of Huckleberry Finn.]
--------------------------------------------------------------CONTINUED--
Possible NEXT ACTIONs: + for Next Screen          ? for Help
                       D1-D415 to display an item  M for More options

        NEXT ACTION? _
```

MODEL AND METAPHOR

Patrons will form their own ideas or models of how an online catalog works. If those models match the catalog, patrons will use the catalog effectively. If those models are incorrect, patrons will be frustrated by the catalog.

People cope with new situations in two ways—by relating new situations to old ones (establishing a metaphor) and by building internal models for the new situations. Appropriate models and metaphors speed the learning process; inappropriate models and metaphors slow learning and inhibit use. Online access represents a new and fairly complex activity for most library patrons. Designers should be alert to the potentials and dangers of models and metaphors. Designers should also give some consideration to patrons who use more than one library and more than one patron access system.

Establishing a Model

An online catalog should be based on a clear and consistent model. An open-ended model is better than a closed and limiting one, but any model is better than none at all.

Some online catalogs appear to lack a single model. This may happen for one of two reasons. In some cases, the system may start out with a clear model but, as new functions are added and old ones are revised, the system becomes inconsistent because revisions do not follow the original model. In another case, each function within a system may be designed independently because methods that are most effective for one function may not be effective for another function. When these functions are combined, the system may not have any single model.

The second problem can be avoided by proper design and by coordinating functions as they are developed. The first problem, inconsistent revisions and added functions, is more difficult to avoid. Some online systems show two distinct models: the old model for functions that were part of the original design and a new model for functions added later. If the two models conflict, patrons may never become wholly comfortable with the system.

When different parts of an online catalog behave differently, patrons can't transfer knowledge of one part for use with other parts. Inconsistent systems are a deterrent to fast learning.

People build models as part of the learning process. Few academic libraries and even fewer public libraries can hope to reach many patrons through formal catalog instruction. Most patrons will develop a model of the online catalog by using it. If the catalog has a consistent and clear design, patrons will succeed.

The points to consider are the same for those developing online catalogs and for those evaluating them:

- It should be easy to develop a working model of the online catalog by using it.
- A model developed by using one function should not conflict with other functions. Learning one function well should make other functions familiar.
- A library professional, acting as a patron with no previous knowledge of the catalog's design, should be able to develop a model that matches the stated design.

Metaphor: Communicating a Familiar Context

Appropriate metaphors help to make new systems familiar. Inappropriate metaphors make learning more difficult.

The fastest way to establish a mental model for a new thing is to assume a familiar metaphor. Calling an automobile a horseless carriage established such a metaphor and eased people's transition to automobiles. One sure way to slow learning and damage patron effectiveness is to suggest an inappropriate metaphor.

People try out metaphors as an easy way to build a model. When a metaphor works, a model is available; the new system's operation can be predicted from previous experience. If predictions work and do not restrict use of the new system, the metaphor serves the patron well. For example, a patron's ability to treat a computer keyboard as "like a typewriter," and the fact that letters typed on the keyboard will indeed appear on the screen, helps make communication between patron and system possible.

Mixed metaphors make a catalog difficult to use. If a patron access system sometimes looks like a card catalog, sometimes like Dialog and sometimes like a session of Twenty Questions, the patron may be amused but will never be comfortable with the catalog.

The card catalog is not a good model or metaphor for an online catalog. Care should be taken to block the card catalog metaphor.

Designers must be sensitive to the question of metaphor. The natural metaphor for a patron access system, especially if it is called an online catalog, is the card catalog. One task for designers may be to block this metaphor in such a way that patrons do not, under any circumstances, think of a patron access system as an "online card catalog."

It is easy to underestimate the strength of the card catalog metaphor. At the 1985 Lakeway Conference, one nonlibrarian (invited to comment on various catalog displays) consistently used the phrase online card catalog. This person had considerable difficulty with all the systems, possibly because none worked like card catalogs.

Good OPACs will differ from card catalogs in many important ways. If patrons come to the online catalog with the card catalog as a model, they may fail to use the more powerful features of the online catalog and become frustrated by online search techniques. Librarians who suggest that the online catalog is just a replacement for the card catalog, or an "electronic card catalog," reduce patron effectiveness and make the online catalog less useful.

STANDARD COMMAND LANGUAGE: A COMMON MODEL?

Command language plays a major role in establishing the model for a catalog. The National Information Standards Organization [Z39] appointed Standards Committee G in 1984 to develop a common command language for online interactive information retrieval. A draft proposal was issued for initial review and comment in March 1986. That draft, with some revision, appears likely to gain approval as an American National Standard.

American National Standards are voluntary, and no government agency will require that online catalogs conform to a Standard Command Language. No matter how effective the standard, some developers will choose to ignore it for legitimate reasons. Others may ignore it out of ignorance. Naturally, any online catalog developed prior to 1987 (or whenever the standard reaches final approval) cannot be expected to follow the standard.

Pros and Cons

The proposed American National Standard Common Command Language can provide a common basic model among different patron access systems. Such a model will ease the task of those patrons who use more than one library and may simplify design questions for new online catalogs.

"The requirement to learn and remember how to use several online catalogs is an enormous and unnecessary burden."[2] A suitable standard language would establish part of a commonly understood model, allowing patrons to retain expertise from one system to another.

Commonality benefits only those patrons who use multiple catalogs, probably a small fraction of any library's patrons. If a standard language limits the capabilities of an online system or forces inefficient methods, most patrons will suffer from use of the standard. Possibly for that reason, attendees at a 1982 CLR conference on subject searching said that "it is too early to look for, or seek, standardization of features . . . among the many online public access catalogs available."[3]

Nevertheless, it can be argued that a standard command language will help designers by establishing a basic vocabulary for online information retrieval. With a common vocabulary as a basis, designers can concentrate on other issues in an online catalog.

The Proposed Language

The proposd Standard Command Language (Z39.58) provides a defined set of common verbs, a general command structure and some criteria for punctuation and command normalization. The standard is open-ended and does not restrict future development.

The Standard Command Language proposal defines scope, conformance and implementation. A section on general features and rules of syntax is followed by descriptions of 27 primary commands, a table summarizing those commands and a table summarizing command operators, symbols and punctuation. An appendix offers a list of recommended field labels, but the list is not part of the standard.

The proposal says that a system should recognize the commands defined in the standard. If the system does not implement the function or implements it in a nonstandard way, the system should inform the user. New functions may be added, but commands for those functions should follow the same syntax as standard commands. The draft does not deal with implementation techniques.

The proposed standard syntax is flexible and will be familiar to users of RLIN, MELVYL, TOMUS and some other existing systems, though it is not identical to the syntax of those systems.*

The general syntax consists of a command word followed by a command specification. The specification may include search terms, numbers identifying lines on a screen, index or field labels, qualifiers and truncation symbols, along with some other expressions. Command words are always single words, can always be abbreviated to three letters and can frequently be abbreviated to a single letter.

All of the following search statements conform to the standard:

FIND ecosystems
FIND conversion tables
FIN AU elliot AND TI wasteland
F TI radiation NOT TI solar
FIN SU (catalog or catalogue) and library
FIN AB nuclear & stockpile? & PD > 1982
F TI,SU behavio#r

The 27 primary command words are all common words and include some useful distinctions. EXPLAIN provides online tutorials,

---

*The committee did not include representatives from the organizations that created those systems.

while HELP provides context-sensitive information and SHOW provides variable information such as files selected, time of day and sets of stored results. Other primary command words will be mentioned elsewhere in the book, as appropriate.

While the proposed standard Command Language is imperfect, it provides an excellent basis for development. If a standard along the same lines is adopted, designers should consider the advantages of conforming to it. The draft does not restrict the creativity of designers and does not limit future possibilities for patron access. It does establish a well-defined common vocabulary for those functions provided by many systems.

NOTES

1. Furlong, Elizabeth J. "Index Access to On-Line Records: An Operational View." *Journal of Library Automation.* 11(3): 1978 September. p. 238.

2. Matthews, Joseph R. *Public Access to Online Catalogs: A Planning Guide for Managers.* Weston, CT: Online; 1982. p. 107.

3. *Subject Access.* Washington, DC: Council on Library Resources; 1982 December. p. 68.

4

System Clarity

A computerized system is effective if it is transparent to the knowledgeable user and lucid to the new user. A good patron access system should ease the way for less knowledgeable patrons, make learning easy and reward that learning with faster, more effective use.

LEARNING THE SYSTEM

Each library patron comes to the online catalog with a unique combination of need, general background and specific experience. "A system is a user friendly one if it provides the right number of appropriate features and functions for the user to perform the current task."[1] Although most online catalogs have to provide more features and functions than any specific user needs for any specific task, the system is clear if it leads patrons to the appropriate features as quickly and effectively as possible.

How Patrons Learn

Good instructional materials should accompany any online system.

Libraries may offer patrons many methods for learning to use online catalogs: brief classes, pamphlets, personal instruction, posters, command summary cards, even videocassettes and other instructional media. Although such tools are outside the scope of this book, any or all of them can be effective, depending on a library's resources and the nature of its user population.

Some written explanation should accompany any new patron access system. Posters should alert users to the presence of public terminals. Pamphlets should explain the purpose of the system and the relation of the online catalog to the card catalog (this becomes particularly important when the card catalog is frozen or removed). Tutorial pamphlets can be effective, as can brief pamphlets that serve as quick references to the commands and indexes of the catalog. Patrons who use other computer systems will welcome command summary cards.

Following are some guidelines for written (explanatory) materials, though books on library instructional materials will cover these in more detail:

- Accuracy. The access system must work in the way it is described. Examples used in written materials should be on the system. Users may well wish to repeat examples to confirm their reading. No library can ensure that a given search will yield the same result as that in a brochure, but it can determine that the search is correctly stated and likely to return some result.
- Completeness. A command summary card should list all commands normally available for users and a quick reference leaflet should include all indexes and options and illustrate all available display screens. The primary use for a command summary card is to extend the next action space available on a screen. If a command summary card is incomplete and the function needed by the patron does not appear, the card is useless.
- Illustrations. Leaflets and pamphlets should use at least one or two screen displays that are legitimate and accurate.
- Conciseness. If a patron access system requires a 50-page handbook to list each command, index and option and provide an example of each, the system is too complex. It should be possible to provide a quick summary on both sides of a card, possibly folded once or twice, and to provide a complete (if terse) command reference in a pamphlet of no more than 12 to 16 small pages (preferably fewer).
- Clarity. Written materials should be as clear as the access system itself. Since quick-reference pamphlets and cards must be easy to find and use, an alphabetical arrangement may be suit-

able. A tutorial pamphlet, on the other hand, serves a different purpose than a reference pamphlet and may require a different arrangement.

Most users won't use external instruction, help screens or online tutorials. Patrons will learn the best online access systems (those that are clear, consistent and responsive) simply by using them.

Command summary cards and brief pamphlets are most useful for, and most used by, those who want to get the most out of a catalog. Would-be experts will read the material, act on it and keep the material for use as needed. For most users, however, the system is the only instructor.

The Learning Curve

The assumption behind good patron access design is that a patron will start out slowly and learn rapidly, making the learning curve smooth and easy.

Most library users are, by definition, more literate than average Americans and, therefore, should be able to learn to use patron access systems skillfully. On the other hand, "most people will not use the OPAC as part of everyday routine, and hence their knowledge and skills will not be constantly reinforced."[2]

The second time a patron uses an online catalog within a month, the patron will work more cleverly and efficiently than on the first try. By the third or fourth use, many patrons will want the system to stay out of the way and simply respond to commands. Online catalogs have to accommodate a fast learning curve for patrons. At the same time, even experienced patrons need help occasionally and should be able to get it without difficulty.

Consistent systems can respond to the learning curve more effectively than systems with different modes. Patrons should be able to work at their own level without being aware of what that level is or how it is changing.

Types of Users and Needs

A patron access system should serve all potential library users at their current level of background and need. To do otherwise abridges their right to use the library and damages intellectual freedom and the library itself.

Most libraries serve all types of users, from the person who wants some light fiction to the person preparing a local history or a genealogical study. Public libraries may serve researchers and research libraries may serve casual readers. Elementary school libraries, corporate libraries and some other libraries may serve very specific communities with very specific skills. Except for a few types of special libraries, however, it is difficult to categorize libraries by type of user in any way that has meaning for catalog design.

When Matthews, Lawrence and Ferguson summarized findings of the CLR-sponsored online catalog study, they noted that "problems experienced by users are similar regardless of type of libraries . . . the similarities between all types of libraries, including ARL and public libraries, are much greater than the few differences that exist."[3]

Point Six of the Library Bill of Rights states that "a person's right to use a library should not be denied or abridged because of origin, age, background, or views."[4] Serving patrons at all levels of need serves intellectual freedom; it also makes good sense.

Command and Menu Modes

Patron access systems should not require separate command and menu modes of operation. A single mode should be able to serve novices and experts alike.

Advocates of menu-driven systems assume that menus help beginners to get started with online catalogs. Command-driven systems allow knowledgeable users to get more work done in a shorter time. Some systems offer both command and menu modes and require that users choose one or the other.

Separate modes may be justified by arguing that only a constrained menu-driven system can provide enough protection for the occasional user, while a command-driven system with little or no prompting will provide the power that only the experienced user can appreciate. Charles Hildreth takes issue with that argument: "Perhaps the fundamental error is the mistaken assumption that expertise or naivete are global attributes of a given user or user class. A user may be proficient with some parts of the system but incapable of using other features. The level of motivation . . . may not always remain commensurate with the level of training or experience."[5]

Systems with separate menu and command modes require patrons to make distinct transitions from one mode to the other. Distinct transitions transform a learning curve into a barrier, making movements in either direction more difficult.

A system can combine commands and heavy prompting as needed without requiring separate modes. One example of modeless design with variable menuing that is a classic in the microcomputer field is the "timed menu" technique used in WordStar since 1979, now found in other interactive programs. The technique works by waiting for a set period, usually a second or so, after the user begins to key a command. If the set period elapses and the next element of the command has not been keyed, a menu offering appropriate next steps appears automatically. If there are three elements in the command, another menu will appear if the user does not key the third element within a preset time, and so on. Experienced users may never see a menu in WordStar; new users see them constantly.

Chapter 7 discusses further menu and command issues.

Search Encouragement

Library patrons tend to stop searching too soon, often assuming incorrectly that the library doesn't have what they want. Designers should look for ways to make online catalogs encourage patrons to persist.

"Most people do not persevere in catalog searches. More than 50 percent will look up only one entry and then stop, regardless of whether or not they have found what they are looking for. Most subject searches are attempted under a single subject heading."[6]

Card catalogs make persistent searching somewhat cumbersome, since moving from one heading to another may mean locating another catalog drawer many feet away. Online catalogs should be able to do much better. One basic strategy is to make searching fast. Another is to make it easy to search for related items once an item is displayed, that is, to search for items with the same subject heading, series or other access point. Browse screens and other techniques may help to avoid incomplete results such as a patron finding some items but failing to locate a broader range of suitable items.

Search Review

Patrons can learn to use an online catalog more effectively if they can review their activity during a session. However, patrons are unlikely to use review functions enough to make them worthwhile, even if privacy and other problems can be solved.

Part of efficient learning is seeing what you've done. If a patron access system maintains a command log during a session, patrons can review their current search strategy or compare the effects of different search strategies.

Command logs for patron review pose several problems:

- Unless patrons explicitly start and stop sessions, a review function raises privacy questions.
- Reviews of activity may be more time-consuming than helpful.
- Patrons may not use a review function often enough to make it worthwhile.
- If a review includes system responses, displaying or printing it may be slow and cumbersome. If not, the review will not provide sufficient information.

Review can be valuable, but not if it goes unused. Patrons using public terminals are unlikely to spend longer reviewing their activity than they spent performing searches. Unless a library has more terminals than it will ever need, the library may not wish to encourage lengthy review sessions.

Scholars using workstations and those using the system by dialing up from home computers can maintain their own logs on their own computers. Such logs raise no privacy questions and involve no system overhead because they are maintained on the patron's own equipment, not on the library system.

User Profiles

Patron access systems should not treat individual patrons in different ways or require user profiles in order to serve patrons effectively.

Some writers have suggested that sophisticated patron access systems should store and maintain individual user profiles in order to meet special needs. Such profiles could include the preferred form of display, the order in which items should appear, what forms of material a patron searches, and the patron's level of experience and proficiency.

Although they have the potential to be very useful, user profiles raise serious privacy issues. Most public libraries don't even require catalog users to have library cards, but profiles require absolute identification of each patron. Patrons may be nervous about privacy when using online systems in any case, and requiring that they enter an identification code will surely increase such nervousness, and rightly so. If a session begins by asking for identification, those seeking known items and other short-session users will find the catalog unsatisfactory, as it will be more cumbersome than a card catalog. Requiring identification may also pose problems when a patron fails to end a session because the next user will have the previous user's profile.

Designers should look for ways to achieve the benefits of user profiles without actually using profiles. It should be possible for all sessions to start identically and still provide each patron with the power to use the catalog in a personal manner.

A well-designed patron access system should not require customizing. The better the system, the less use patrons will have for individual profiles.

Workstations and other nonpublic terminals pose different concerns. If a profile is stored on a microcomputer and acts to transform the character of the patron access system, the patron's privacy is protected and other users are not affected by the profile. A workstation-based profile may be heavily customized. Given the availability of keyboard enhancement or "macroprocessing" programs such as Pro-Key and SuperKey, any microcomputer user can customize the patron access system to a great extent without the knowledge of the library. If dial-up users want to use the combination of ALT and N to mean FIND AUTHOR, they can establish that combination temporarily or permanently. Such customization may slow the user down when using a public terminal at the library, but that is not the library's problem.

LANGUAGE

The language used in an online catalog can help or hinder learning and use. Terms, messages and other text should be treated as carefully as any other part of catalog design.

Language seems to be an afterthought in some online catalog designs. Language problems can be obvious or subtle: subtle language problems can make the catalog annoying and language techniques that make it more approachable for new users may irritate frequent users.

Clear and Consistent Usage

An online catalog should use consistent terminology.

An online catalog should always use one term to refer to one thing. If a screen full of text is called a "page" in one part of the catalog, it should not be called a "screen" in another part. If the system uses "screen" to refer to that which is on the screen, it should not use "screen" to refer to the physical device.

Consistent terminology speaks well for any system. Real or apparent inconsistency suggests sloppy design or implementation and can hinder understanding. The two common forms of inconsistency involve using the same name for more than one thing and using two or more names for the same thing. Both should be avoided.[7]

Text used in an online system may come from several sources. The designer may establish a basic set of system messages; programmers may add error messages; any number of people may contribute to online tutorials, help screens and messages added by the library. With so many sources of text, inconsistency can enter any design.

A dictionary should be maintained for an online system, showing what nouns and verbs are used and how they are used. New text should be checked against that dictionary before it is added to the system.

Usage should be consistent from a patron's view, not from a designer's view. A browsing screen, a help screen, a single-record display screen and an online tutorial screen are all quite different from a programmer's perspective, and a designer might reasonably call one a segment, one a page, one a display and one a frame. Those subtle distinctions should be masked from patrons; the same term should be used for all four sets of characters on a video display.

Figure 4.1 shows a possible screen top and bottom. The terms used on the screen may not be ideal, but they are distinct. Compare Figures 3.5 and 3.6 in the previous chapter. In Figure 3.5, *display* is a noun, referring to a particular way of showing bibliographic data. In Figure 3.6, *display* is a verb. Either one is clear enough, but the combination may be confusing.

Figure 4.1: Unambiguous Terminology

```
You keyed: NAME FOX, ROBIN
Your search retrieves 8 items.
Item 1 of 8            Page 1 of 2
:                                                    :
:                                                    :
Possible NEXT ACTIONs: + for Next Page       F for Full Version
                       V+ to View Next item  H for Help
                       V3-V8 to View an item M for More options
           NEXT ACTION:+_
```

The proposed Standard Command Language provides a set of verbs for most functions that an online catalog will provide. If a system uses those verbs, they should be used consistently in help screens, messages and online tutorials.

Appropriate Vocabulary

Online catalogs should avoid jargon and codes; the vocabulary used should be familiar to most users. Terms should never be abbreviated: spell it out or leave it out.

The jargon of librarianship and of automation serves communication within those fields. But since very few library patrons are librarians or automation experts, use of jargon in a patron access system will block understanding.

A surprising number of "user-friendly" designs use *Collation, Main Entry* and other library jargon to label elements. No patron access system would use *245* to label a title; to most patrons *Collation* for the physical description is equally mysterious. Even the most ardent defenders of AACR2 and MARC will agree that such terms need not be used for public labels. They serve no special purpose and fail to communicate.

Professionals use jargon without being aware of it. *Monograph* is a more precise word than *book* (and covers a different range of materials), but patrons look for books, not monographs. Some terms are questionable. For example, *record* as a name for a bibliographic item may or may not be jargon, but it is a poor term in any case because it is the common word for a phonograph disc.

Use of abbreviations is not optional: they have no place in an online catalog. If *Imprint* is jargon, *Im* is much worse. Brevity serves the user, but not at the expense of clarity. Abbreviations require mental effort to expand and may require special training that most patrons do not have. Little can be done about abbreviations within the bibliographic record, but the patron access system should avoid any additional ones.

Wording and Tone

The system should neither judge the user nor condescend to the user. Messages should be clear and neutral, not hostile or congratulatory. System failures should always be masked from the patron.

Current systems fail the patron in different ways. Inappropriate messages fall into three general categories: mysterious messages resulting from system problems, negative messages resulting from poor communication between patron and system and condescending messages that can appear either when the patron is successful or when the patron is having problems.

ERROR 46 IN RUNTIME ENVIRONMENT has no place on a public terminal. Neither does MEMORY OVERFLOW, COMMUNICATIONS PATH INTERRUPT or—possibly worst of all—SYSTEM PANIC. When something happens that prevents the user's command from being executed, the message should be neutral and helpful. If the

problem is due to a general system problem, a message such as TEM-
PORARY COMPUTER PROBLEMS—PLEASE WAIT will let the
patron know why nothing is happening without causing panic.

---

*When problems arise, the system should let patrons know what
the problem appears to be, let them maintain control and
inform them of appropriate steps, if any.*

If the system is running properly, but the user's command causes
problems, another type of message is needed. SEARCH TOO GEN-
ERAL seems judgmental, but is better than UNABLE TO COM-
PLETE SEARCH. TRY AGAIN, which almost invites the user to try
the same problematic search a second time.

INCORRECT COMMAND is a poor, judgmental message. COM-
MAND NOT UNDERSTOOD is better, though not ideal. I'M NOT
SURE I KNOW WHAT YOU MEAN or I DON'T KNOW HOW TO
. . . are anthropomorphic and somewhat condescending, as well as
being too wordy.

Patrons need carefully worded messages to help them recognize
and resolve problems. Most of all, patrons need messages that do not
discourage them from using the system.

---

*The computer is a tool, not a friend. Overly friendly messages
are condescending and inappropriate.*

A message such as YOU'RE DOING GREAT! may be appropri-
ate for a computer learning system or for a game, but not for an online
catalog. Patrons will know they're succeeding when they get results. A
user-friendly system works rapidly and effectively to fill the user's
needs but does not engage in small talk at the expense of efficiency.

Anthropomorphism and Humor

---

*A computer is not a librarian, and it is certainly not a comic.
Online catalogs should never pretend to be human, and should
generally avoid humor.*

When a miskeyed search returns I DON'T UNDERSTAND
rather than SEARCH NOT UNDERSTOOD, the system is being an-

thropomorphic. The computer is a thing, not an "I." Personalization may make the catalog more accessible, but will offend many users; with few exceptions, humor is equally inappropriate.

Syntax: Voice, Order and Clarity

> *Messages and prompts should be direct, terse and clear. Messages that don't make immediate sense will be misunderstood or ignored.*

Consistent command syntax contributes to a clear online catalog. Command options should be presented in brief, unambiguous phrases, in either direct or inverted order. *Key + to see next screen* uses direct order. *To see next screen, key +* uses inverted order. Arguments can be made for either. The argument for direct order is that direct statements are simpler and more readily understood; the argument for inverted order is that patrons want to know how to do something, not what will happen when they key something.

Help screens and online tutorials will use more text than messages and prompts should ever use. Most text within such screens should consist of simple sentences in the active voice. However, passive sentences do make sense within long tutorial screens, where a succession of short active sentences may become choppy and tiresome.

ACCESS: USER CONTROL AND CLARITY

> *Good online catalogs are clear and consistent but do not restrict access or sacrifice power.*

A system can increase clarity by restricting command choices, but that restriction limits overall power. As a general rule, there seems to be no excuse for denying a patron access to any bibliographic display or search. Certain functions seem vital to maintaining user control and power. The remainder of this chapter considers miscellaneous issues of power and clarity.

Access to Commands

Patrons should always be able to issue a meaningful command. If possible, any command should be carried out even if it does not appear as a menu choice or prompt.

A patron should be able to enter a new search at any point. Some commands don't make sense at certain points—DISPLAY 4 doesn't make sense if no search has been issued or if the search results in two items—but a sensible command should always work.

If a command is part of the system's vocabulary but won't work at a certain point, the message should indicate the special problem and not suggest that the command does not exist. Figure 4.2 shows a poor response to a command that cannot be honored; Figure 4.3 shows a better response.

Commands should be unique within a system. Even if menus offer numbered choices, textual equivalents should always work. A system may reasonably offer a set of choices where *1* will start a personal name search and *3* will start a subject search. The system should also permit FIND AUTHOR, FIND SUBJECT, or some equivalent commands. If those commands are not available, patrons must always work their way back to the searching menu before initiating a search.

Numbers have meaning only within context. If numbered menu choices are the only way to initiate actions, the user cannot learn shortcuts to make searching and display more efficient. Numbered

Figure 4.2: Poor Response to Situational Command Problem

```
Your original search: TITLE SHOGUN# retrieves 2 items.
You keyed: V3.
ILLEGAL COMMAND
:                                                                      :
:                                                                      :
```

Figure 4.3: Better Response to Situational Command Problem

```
Your original search: TITLE SHOGUN# retrieves 2 items.
You keyed: V3.
Search retrieved fewer than 3 items; unable to honor view command.
:                                                                      :
:                                                                      :
```

menus without text equivalents keep the system in control; if text commands work, the patron can retain control. "The user should feel like he is driving the machine rather than the other way around."[8]

Many existing online catalogs refuse to recognize choices other than those displayed at any point. More recent systems tend to honor any intelligible command. Systems that limit recognition may require the patron to back out through several steps in order to modify a "successful" search. While a restrictive design can guarantee clear pathways through the system, it does so at the expense of flexibility.

Access to Displays

Patrons should be able to see any bibliographic display, including a display showing MARC tags, indicators and subfields. The only secret displays should be those containing confidential information.

Common sense suggests that very few library users know much about MARC, and that very few will gain much information from the tagged displays used in technical services. That is true, but it may be beside the point. An online catalog that maintains some version of a MARC format will support a display that provides tags, at least for catalog maintenance. Since the system supports the display, and since the information in a tagged display is not confidential, patrons should have access to it.

Patrons should not be able to see confidential information but should have no artificial barriers to information. A tagged display will contain some coded information not provided on any other displays and will include more explicit content designation for some information. A small fraction of a library's patrons doing bibliographic research will understand enough of MARC to be able to use that extra information.

Backup and New Search

Patrons stay in control when they can correct errors and problems easily. Backing out of a bad command and starting a new search at any point can help patrons take charge of the system.

System designers should consider a BACKUP function key, one that will undo the most recent command, whatever that command may be. People make mistakes. Knowing that the last action can always be reversed provides some security and encourages people to take some chances. A good BACKUP key maintains clarity by always undoing the most recent command, regardless of what it was.

What happens when a patron presses BACKUP two or more times? Three possibilities exist:

- The second BACKUP has no effect and returns a message saying something like *BACKUP already performed; no action taken.*
- The second BACKUP backs up the first BACKUP. In other words, BACKUP becomes a toggle between the two most recent situations.
- Further BACKUPs back through further system states (some systems already do this). While it requires that the system maintain a record of its activities, this solution will probably help users more than either alternative.

Any good online catalog will permit a new search at any point. Menu-driven systems with many layers of menus need an explicit new search command more than command-driven systems; otherwise, the patron must go back through several layers to start a new search.

Consistency

Consistent commands, syntax and function keys help patrons learn to use an online catalog. Consistency should not prevent patrons from carrying out commands in any workable order.

Good system design can blend consistency with efficiency. Patrons should never become lost in a maze of inconsistent commands, nor should they ever have to wait because the system is maintaining a consistent path. Consistency is more important than computer efficiency, but patron efficiency is more important than system consistency.

Clear systems place the user in control and act in a predictable manner so that users retain control and improve their use of the system.

NOTES

1. Noerr, Peter L. "Are Micros Friendly?" *7th International Online Meeting*. Oxford: Learned Information; 1984. p. 1.

2. Reynolds, Dennis. *Library Automation: Issues and Applications*. New York: Bowker; 1985. p. 432.

3. *Using Online Catalogs*. Joseph R. Matthews; Gary S. Lawrence; Douglas K. Ferguson, eds. New York: Neal-Schuman; 1983. p. 127.

4. *ALA Handbook of Organization, 1985/1986*. Chicago: American Library Association; 1985. p. 223.

5. Hildreth, Charles R. *Online Public Access Catalogs: The User Interface*. Dublin, OH: OCLC; 1982. p. 54.

6. Atherton, Pauline L. "Catalog Users' Access from the Researcher's Viewpoint." *Closing the Catalog*. Phoenix, AZ: Oryx Press; 1980. p. 107.

7. Examples in this book do not use consistent terminology, partly to avoid suggesting a preferred model for a catalog.

8. Shaw, Ward. "Design Principles for Public Access." Clinic on Library Applications of Data Processing (17th: 1980: University of Illinois at Urbana-Champaign). *Public Access to Library Automation*. Urbana-Champaign: Graduate School of Library and Information Science; 1981. p. 6.

5

Terminals:
Input and Display

Good patron access requires good ways to accept and display information. Inadequate terminals and terminal techniques can undermine the best system.

Any online catalog must accept information from, and display information to, patrons. For most patrons using online catalogs, a terminal serves these purposes. In this chapter I discuss several important aspects of terminals, including input devices, special input techniques, display quality and special display features.

INPUT DEVICES

The primary device patrons use for input should be familiar, easy to use, sturdy, fast and clear. A standard typewriter-like keyboard is the best input device for most public terminals.

Patrons communicate with the system through some form of input device. Several input devices may be useful for patron access; for example, an online system may combine a primary input device with one or more secondary devices that are used for special purposes. The following characteristics are important for input devices:

- Familiarity. The best device is one that most patrons have used in other settings. If it is not familiar, a device must have such an

obvious design and use that a patron can learn to use it within seconds.
- Ease of use. The device should make it equally simple to enter menu choices and complex commands.
- Sturdiness. The device should be difficult to break and impossible to misuse in a way that makes the system fail.
- Speed. The device should not slow the patron down.
- Clarity. Input should not be ambiguous.

Keyboards

Any patron access system designed during the next 5 or 10 years will probably use a standard keyboard as an input device. Some catalogs may assign certain functions to a mouse, touch screen, function keys or other techniques, without providing an equivalent way to use the functions from the keyboard. A terminal that requires patrons to use multiple devices is inherently less clear and direct than one that can channel all input through a single device. An online catalog that requires devices other than standard keyboards will not be able to support remote users with workstations or home computers.

Although some people view keyboards as relics of the nineteenth century and feel that they are less user-friendly than other devices, keyboards do have certain advantages: most adults have used keyboards and most children now become familiar with standard keyboards in early school years; modern keyboards are extremely sturdy and reasonably inexpensive to replace; and keyboard entry is more flexible and less ambiguous than any other input device currently available. Keyboards aren't new, but neither are books. To date, no other technology has appeared that can replace the unique qualities of either.

Quality

Good keyboards are familiar. Most terminals come with good keyboards, but some work better than others.

Terminal keyboards are like microcomputer keyboards and should follow the same guidelines, some of which are outlined below:

- Separation. The keyboard should be detached from the terminal, so that patrons can adjust it. High-demand, short-use terminals don't call for detachable keyboards, and some libraries may have security problems that argue against using them. Most modern terminals include detached keyboards as a matter of course.

- Thickness. Good contemporary keyboards are less than 40mm (1.5 inches) high at home row (the row of keys beginning ASDF) so that patrons can rest their hands on the desk while keying. Some thin keyboards are noisy or tiring for long use. Felt pads under the keyboard's feet, or a foam pad under the keyboard, will generally help.
- Key design. Each keytop should be concave, lower in the center than around the edges. Keytops should be separated by 3mm to 6mm from edge to edge so that thick-fingered typists don't hit the wrong key or two keys at once. The outer edges of each key should be nearly level. Keys should actually move and should provide a distinct physical feedback when keystrokes are accepted. Keys should be 13mm to 16mm from edge to edge and the center of one key should be 19mm from the center of the next key. Keys should have neutral colors and matte finishes and should be clearly labeled.
- Keyboard design. The keyboard should slope, with a "stair step" of horizontal rows, each row 3mm to 5mm lower than the row above. The center of the Q key should be 171mm from the center of the P key. All alphabetic and numeric keys should be the same size and shape.
- Repeating. All keys should repeat if held down for an extended period (typically more than a second). No key should repeat accidentally.
- Rollover. A keyboard should be able to accept at least five or six successive keystrokes no matter how quickly they are entered.
- Feel. A keyboard should be pleasant to use. It should not feel like a toy or like an old manual typewriter. Feel is a subjective criterion and one of the most important measures of a good keyboard.

Libraries should consider one additional criterion—good keyboards should not clatter or be offensively noisy.

Layout

Terminal keyboards should use the traditional typewriter layout, with "QWERTY" beginning the top alphabetic row of keys.

Although QWERTY keyboards (with QWERTYUIOP on the upper alphabetic row, ASDFGHJKL on the home row) are by far the most common, the layout has long been regarded as less than ideal. An alternative design called the *Dvorak keyboard* supposedly permits faster and less tiresome keying, though recent studies suggest that the potential advantage of the layout is minor at best. For those totally unfamiliar with typewriter keyboards, an alphabetic keyboard with ABCDEFGHI on the top row might be easier to use.

Most present users know QWERTY or no layout at all. Good typists will find alphabetic keyboards startling and disruptive. Nontypists typically learn to cope with QWERTY and are not speed users in any case. Even if the Dvorak layout could be proven to be significantly more effective, it would be much less familiar. Since QWERTY is clearly not a handicap to most typists and users, the most familiar solution is the best for public terminals.

Strength

A terminal should be able to accept any keystroke or sequence of keystrokes without beeping, breaking out of the online catalog, causing the system to fail or making the terminal unusable. Any key sequence should yield some response on the screen so that the patron knows the terminal is working properly.

Sturdy keyboards require good manufacturing and robust keyboard handling requires good design. Good design means preparing for the unexpected. No matter what a patron does at the keyboard, it should not be possible to break out of the patron access system and into the computer's operating system or freeze the keyboard. If clumsy keying can make the terminal useless, patrons will properly regard the system as fragile and unreliable and will be less likely to try new techniques.

A system that ignores unexpected keystrokes is better than one that allows the possibility of frozen terminals or an exit to the operating system, but may cause patrons to wonder whether the terminal is working properly. Some systems beep when any unexpected keystroke is received. While this assures the patron that the keystroke was accepted, it is a somewhat hostile action, particularly when no message appears. A better solution is a line within the terminal's feedback area, such as the one illustrated in Figure 5.1.

Figure 5.1: Possible Response for Unused Keystroke

```
Your search: N TWAIN, MARK    retrieves 415 items.          MULTIPLE
You keyed: %  -- which is not used to begin any command.
No action taken.
------------------------------------------------------------------
:                                                                 :
:                                                                 :
```

Function Keys

Special function keys can speed use of a patron access system and can provide command options without taking up screen space. Function keys can also confuse patrons and slow down expert users.

Function keys include all keys other than those on a typewriter keyboard and the cursor arrow keys. On an IBM PC and many terminals, function keys are labeled F1, F2 and so on. Other terminals use labels from PF1 through PF16 or similar notations. Function keys tend to be found to the left of, above or to the right of a standard keyboard layout, and typically have keytops that are a different color from alphabetic keys.

Public terminals for patron access systems may use special keytops labeled with specific phrases. Those keys, such as START, AUTHOR, QUIT and NEW SEARCH, are also function keys.

Chapters 3 and 4 identify START, STOP, BACKUP and NEW SEARCH as valuable function keys. This section considers some other possible uses for function keys.

Standard Function Keys

Standard function keys should either perform in sensible ways or be removed from the keyboard.

Several function keys appear on almost all modern terminals and computer keyboards. These include ESC, CTRL and RETURN or ENTER. Other common special keys include ALT, HOME, END, DEL, INS and BREAK.

A library supporting dial-in users and scholar workstations should assume that most or all of these keys will be present and must determine how to respond to them. These keys can be removed, relabeled or ignored for public terminals, but a good design takes into account every key on the keyboard.

Standard function keys have expected uses, but not necessarily clear ones. Consider the following points:

- The oversized ENTER or RETURN key is almost always used to complete a command and most online systems will also use it that way. The problem with the key is inconsistent labeling. Some keyboards (such as the standard IBM PC) have no word at all, only a curved arrow. Some use ENTER, some use RETURN. Some keyboards have a second key as part of a numeric keypad performing the same function. For any public terminal, the key should have a proper label; ENTER may be more sensible than RETURN, since the key enters the command. RETURN is a holdover from typewriter keyboards.
- Some computer programs use the ESC key to allow the user to undo a command or escape from a situation. In other words, the key functions as a panic key. Online systems can take advantage of this familiar usage by labeling the key ESCAPE and using it to stop a search or undo a command. Some systems disable the key; in that case, it must still be recognized, since nearly every dial-in and workstation user will have access to an ESC key.
- The CTRL and ALT keys rarely work independently, normally serving to modify other keys. For instance, the combination of CTRL and N is a special keystroke, as is ALT and N. Such keystrokes are sometimes called *control-shifted* or *alt-shifted* keys. Patron access systems will typically have no use for such keys, but should be able to recognize and cope with control-shifted and alt-shifted keystrokes. A message such as *CTRL W has no meaning in this system. Command ignored.* should suffice.
- HOME, END, INS, DEL are not as common as the keys above and have no single standard use. Except for the earlier caution that END should not be used to stop a session, these keys can be treated as available for use similarly to any other function keys. Note that some dial-in users will not have these keys, and must be able to use textual equivalents.

Help and Restart

Patrons should always be able to call for help and start over again.

A key labeled HELP should always yield some help that is appropriate to the situation. HELP is a better label than ?, since a question mark already appears on the screen. A question mark keyed by itself should probably have the same function as HELP. However, a question mark may appear as part of text; a HELP key should always work, even if a patron has keyed part of a command.

A key labeled RESTART or START OVER may reassure patrons that they can always start over, even if a search or command sequence has become confused. In most systems, RESTART and START may do exactly the same thing.

Function Keys for Searching

Labeled function keys for possible searches may help new users but should never preclude use of the regular keyboard.

"Special function keys on the terminal could be employed to aid the user in conducting a search . . . labeled AUTHOR, TITLE . . . ISBN, etc. When a [SUBJECT] key is pressed . . . the screen would display the heading 'Subject Search' and provide the command for a subject search and ask the user to enter the search request."[1]

A sophisticated patron access system will have more indexes than function keys, unless the terminal is cluttered with as many as two dozen function keys. That means that some searches are handled differently from others. That does not rule out such use, but does show the need for careful evaluation before assigning function keys. Some smaller systems may have few enough indexes to permit every index to have a function key; in those catalogs, search function keys may be desirable.

Unfortunately, searching function keys have other drawbacks. Keyboards with too many special function keys may be more difficult to use. Good typists and experienced users may prefer to issue all commands directly from the standard keyboard, making the function keys superfluous. Dial-in and workstation users will not have the labeled function keys.

Further research will be useful. Can a subset of indexes have function keys without straining the consistency of the system? Should function keys be used as widely as possible, or kept to a few uses? Charles Hildreth argues that "the user should not have to learn specialized keyboard techniques. The use of special function keys . . . should be kept to a minimum."[2] Microcomputer software experience may be useful. Software targeted at new users tends to use only 2 or 3 of the 10 IBM PC's function keys, while software for experienced users may assign as many as 40 functions to the 10 keys (using SHIFT, CTRL and ALT combinations).

Screen Labels

Function keys that are not labeled on the keys should be labeled on the screen, but screen labels are not as clear as keytop labels.

Soft labels or *screen labels* are labels on the screen that describe the actions of the function keys. Such labels typically appear on the 25th line of a display. On some terminals, labels are two or three lines high and the screen has more than 25 lines. Figure 5.2 shows a possible screen bottom for soft labels. Such labels frequently appear in reverse video or half intensity to set them apart from text. Unless terminals have explicit labels on the keytops, soft labels on the screen should be used. If a library provides a special program for dial-in users, soft labels might be used in the program to help overcome the lack of special keytop labels.

Function keys should have the same function throughout a patron access system. Keys that mean different things at different times will confuse new patrons and irritate experienced patrons.

Some systems use function keys for different purposes at different times, with soft labels that change to suit the situation. Other systems leave the same functions active at all times, even when they may not make sense. There are two problems with function keys that change

Figure 5.2: Soft Labels on Last Two Lines of Display

```
:                                                                    :
:                                                                    :
F1:New Search   F3:Help       F5:Author     F7:Subject    F9:More Indexes
F2:Backup       F4:Quit       F6:Title      F8:Words      F10:Holdings
```

meaning. First, they require that patrons pay attention to the soft labels. Second, they prevent patrons from using function keys as a matter of habit. Conflicting function keys are the result of poor design; they often startle a patron by doing sharply different things at different times.

Function Keys and Menus

Function keys should be equivalent to commands and should not be used to make menu selections.

Some online systems use function keys rather than regular numbers or letters to make arbitrary numbered choices from a menu. Although function keys can't possibly be confused with text or commands with this type of usage, connecting function keys with menus creates at least one of three problems:

1. Function keys are not available for specific commands because they are dedicated to making menu choices.
2. Function keys serve different purposes at different times, making them more difficult to use.
3. The keyboard has a large number of function keys, some for menu choices and some for commands, resulting in an overly complex keyboard.

Function Keys and Commands

A function key should echo a word or phrase on the screen. That word or phrase should perform the same function as the function key, for those who prefer to type in commands.

A system that feeds back commands when it receives function keys will serve workstation and dial-in users, and will retain clear feedback on the screen. Good design would include the following points for the case where a labeled HELP key on public terminals is equivalent to key F1 on workstations and dial-in systems:

- When F1 is pressed, the text string HELP should appear on the screen on the command line.
- Software to support dial-up or workstation searching should have F1:HELP as part of a constant 25th line, assuming that the software recognizes and acts on F1.
- The keyed string HELP (followed by ENTER) should work exactly the same as the F1 function key.

Good design calls for consistent application of these principles. If the access system uses a Standard Command Language syntax for search statements such as *find title hiroshima* and uses labeled function keys to begin common searches, that is, has a key labeled TITLE, then a patron pressing TITLE should see the string FIND TITLE __ appear on the screen, with the cursor placed at the underscore.

Patron access systems should not use special keystrokes other than function keys to shorten or replace commands.

Combinations of CTRL and other keys, or ALT and other keys, can speed command entry for some typists. Such key combinations require more training than function keys or words and also dismay new users. Patrons using their own workstations or dialing up can be expected to create their own abbreviated commands, but those commands appear to be standard keyed commands when received by the patron access system.

The proposed Standard Command Language allows any command to be abbreviated to three characters and for some commands to be abbreviated to a single character. Given those conditions, special key combinations do not appear necessary and will certainly confuse users.

Overuse of Function Keys

The best uses for function keys are to assure patrons that they are in control. START, STOP, BACKUP, and some form of ESCAPE or NEW SEARCH function all establish that control. Other uses for function keys require careful thought because they are easily overused.

Function keys will not speed up most patron access functions. New users will look at on-screen suggestions and will be less distracted if they do not need to find function keys in the process. Experienced users can key a two- or three-word command sequence faster than they can follow a two-step or three-step function key sequence.

Pointing Devices

Pointing devices have potential to improve patron access, particularly when searching for related items. Pointing devices should be used carefully in system designs, should be equivalent to each other in functionality and should provide clear feedback. Pointing devices are not suitable as the primary or sole input devices for patron access systems.

A *pointing device* is any method for moving the cursor, or a special expanded cursor, to a specific point on the screen. A pointing device may also make it possible to define the range of a "cursor" or highlighted area of the screen. Pointing devices include cursor arrow keys, mouse, trackball, touch screen, light pen or anything else that the computer can translate to either a vector (physical direction and distance) or to points on the screen.

Several uses for pointing seem feasible:

- selecting an option from a menu or next-option set
- selecting one item from a multiple-item screen in order to display that item in a more complete form
- selecting a heading or term from a browsing screen in order to search that heading or term
- pointing out a name, title, series or subject within a bibliographic display in order to search for other items with the same access point
- selecting an access point as above, but defining the area selected in order to do a broader search, e.g., pointing to *Civilization, Modern—20th Century* but changing that to *Civilization, Modern* as a desired search
- pointing to a previously keyed command in order to edit and reissue it, to correct a misspelling, modify a search, etc.

Pointing devices can help those uneasy with a keyboard. Pointing within a bibliographic display provides a powerful enhancement for subject and related-item searching. Editing functions seem more problematic, though any good patron access system should allow users to retrieve and edit the most recent command.

Arguments against pointing include the relative imprecision of most pointing devices, the system overhead required to interpret pointing and the additional complexity that pointing adds to a keyboard-based system. Where numbered or abbreviated choices are available, such choices may be faster and more explicit than pointing.

Any system that relies solely on pointing will require many steps to show a known item, making the catalog less useful. Lack of a keyboard also eliminates sophisticated searching techniques, making the catalog less powerful. As a result, such a system serves primarily new users and does not serve them very well. While such a system may serve as an addition to a card catalog, it seems unsuitable as a replacement.

Touch screens have real advantages as pointing devices, but only as an extension to a keyboard.

A *touch screen* is a terminal display that can also be used as an input device, by allowing the user to touch (or, in some cases, almost touch) points on the screen. Patron access systems can use touch screens in two basic ways:

- *in place of* keyboards, with all patron input coming from the touch screen
- *in addition to* keyboards, with screen touching serving as a direct pointing mechanism

Touch screens have some built-in problems. First, they gather dirt and grime much faster than do other other display devices, making displays harder to read. Second, touch screens may suffer damage more often than other terminals. Third, fingers are too big to register an accurate column and row placement; as a result, touching a screen does not yield a precise result in all cases. At best, most touch screens deal with two-column-by-two-row areas. And finally, touch screens will almost always require more steps to achieve a specific result than will keyboard entry.

Keyboardless Touch Terminals

A keyboardless terminal cannot provide acceptable perform-ance for a good patron access system.

Some early patron access systems used touch terminals without keyboards. Recent experiments use nearly keyboardless terminals, providing only simple sets of function keys. Initially, keyboardless terminals appeared to have some advantages, particularly for patrons who might be intimidated by keyboards. In practice, however, any keyboardless system requires fairly complex menu structures and many selections from the screen, resulting in slow retrieval.

Long-term experience has not been positive. "Keyboard terminals . . . were much quicker in retrieving records if one knew the search specification, and provided greater flexibility in moving around the database. . . . Perhaps touch terminals would turn out to be just a fad, and once the general populace reached a certain level of expertise, no one would put up with the lengthy menu searches required with a large database."[3] Keyboardless touch screens provide unacceptable performance for known-item searches, and seem incapable of providing more advanced searches.

Touch Screen with Keyboard

Theoretically, a patron should be able to touch a desired option or text string faster and more definitely than pointing through other methods. However, touching does not provide exact location in most cases. It isn't clear that pointing at an access point is faster than moving a cursor to that point with cursor arrows. What does seem clear is that a "miss" (a case in which the terminal reads the touch as being a line above or below the desired line) is annoying.

When a touch screen is only an alternative to a keyboard, problems of accuracy may be less significant. Command options can be arranged so that touches will be recognized properly. Any library contemplating touch screens should carry out extensive experimentation, but such screens do represent one clear way to point at something on the screen and select it.

Voice Input

*Voice input has no place in public terminals for online cata-
logs except to serve patrons with special needs.*

Futurists suggest that keyboards will fade away as computers
learn to recognize speech. For private workstations, voice recognition
may eventually be significant as an input technique. But for now and the
foreseeable future, the technique has no use in public terminals. The
following questions need to be answered before voice input will be a
realistic possibility:

- Can voice input systems recognize the full range of tones,
  accents and speaking patterns, including people with colds or
  other problems causing speech difficulties?
- In a public setting, how will a terminal distinguish the speaker
  actually using the terminal from others in the area?
- How will a terminal distinguish explicit patron access commands from other conversation by the user or others?
- Is it possible to state search commands explicitly and unambiguously with speech, even with the best possible recognition?
- How can patrons maintain any semblance of privacy when using
  voice input?
- Do patrons actually have any desire to talk to a computer?

One possible use for voice input is discussed toward the end of
this chapter.

DISPLAY AND RESPONSE

*Patrons control the online catalog through input devices; the
catalog responds through a display. Other response devices
may be used in some special situations, but most communication back to the patron will be in the form of letters and
numbers on a terminal screen.*

Most present displays use monochrome cathode ray terminals
(CRTs), a mature technology offering excellent clarity at reasonable
prices. While CRTs may continue to dominate the display field for

several more years, display and response issues have nothing to do with CRTs as such. In 1986, other technologies offer quality that equals or surpasses the quality of CRTs, but usually at a significantly higher price. If electroluminescent displays (ELDs) or plasma displays become competitive in price, none of the issues raised here preclude their use in patron access. If liquid crystal diode (LCD) displays satisfy design criteria, they could be appropriate. To date, LCD displays have not yielded sufficient legibility.

Beeping and Other Audible Responses

In general, public terminals should not beep at patrons. Mistaken keystrokes and other common errors should not cause beeps.

Beeps have been, and could be, used when a patron's keystrokes produce one of the following:

- keystrokes not recognized by the system, including cases where a key should be legal but doesn't match a current pattern (e.g., choosing "8" when only seven numbered choices appear)
- incomplete or incorrect commands
- command problems repeated several times in succession
- searches with no results
- system problems, such as overly large results or temporary communications errors
- user problems, such as lack of activity for 9 minutes, where 10 minutes will cause blanking

The positive result of beeping is making the patron aware that something is happening. That appears to be the only positive result, since a beep is an extremely ambiguous communication. A soft beep in connection with a repeated error, with a suggestion on the display to consult a librarian, may be a useful device in a situation where the patron appears to be totally confused.

Beeping can have several negative results. Although it is intended to alert a patron to a problem, a beep can be heard several feet away in a relatively quiet library. To new or uneasy patrons, a beep may seem like a signal to all the other users that someone is using the catalog incorrectly. Negative connotations such as this will not inspire comfort or encourage the new patron to work through problems and achieve results. Beeping also reduces privacy, in feeling if not in fact.

Beeping for an unrecognized keystroke—without displaying the keystroke—not only says that the patron is at fault, but fails to tell the patron what error has been made. Nervous patrons tend to develop thick fingers. If every slip of a finger results in a beep without an indication of what key was incorrectly pressed, patrons will become more uneasy and learn to avoid the online catalog.

Finally, beeping is an annoyance, to the patron and to other library users. Occasional beeps disrupt concentration at the terminal, at shelves or at nearby reading tables. Frequent beeps make an area useless for any intellectual effort.

Patrons need to maintain a sense of control, which may mean making their own mistakes and learning from them. If a patron makes the same mistake several times, a soft beep and suggestion to consult a librarian may be justified. Even in this worst case, the suggestion to consult a librarian may be more productive if it is made silently.

Display Quality

Displays must be legible to be useful. Patrons will not use terminals constantly and can't be expected to learn the peculiarities of a particular character set. Displays must be clear and unambiguous.

Legibility involves a combination of screen size, screen design and character design. Character design and screen size must be balanced to achieve crisp, clear letters and numbers. Screens must be designed and placed so that information is not obscured by glare or reflection. Where such placement is impossible, glare filters should be used.

Almost all displays use small dots, lines or squares to make up characters; each dot is a *picture element* or *pixel*. Most displays provide the same space for each character—a cell containing a fixed number of pixels that can be used for the character or for spacing between characters and lines. Cell size and character size are usually defined by number of pixels per row and number of rows per cell. "An 8-by-10 character matrix within a 9-by-12 cell" means that each character position includes 12 rows of 9 pixels each, measuring from text line to text line and character to character, and that each character can use up to 10 rows of 8 pixels each.

All else being equal, a cell with more pixels will produce more legible characters. The minimum for clear, readable characters appears to be 7-by-9 characters within 8-by-10 cells. Some very legible displays use those numbers but, more commonly, the cell is 9-by-12 or 9-by-14. Some displays use higher densities, yielding characters that seem to consist of solid lines even when viewed close up.

Bigger screens aren't necessarily better. When viewed at a normal working distance (roughly 18 inches, possibly less at some public terminals), letters should be perceived as letters, and should blend naturally into words.

A character design that yields legible letters on a 12-inch screen may yield somewhat "dotty" letters on a 14-inch screen, resulting in less clarity. Privacy is also more of an issue with larger screens, making terminal placement and workstation design more difficult.

Display quality is fundamental to a successful online catalog; only a few critical points are mentioned here. Clear, legible displays need not be expensive because good terminals are available for $500 or less.

Character Legibility

Each character used in a public terminal must be distinct and clear. Patrons must be able to distinguish any character from any other character at a glance and without significant possibility of error.

Character designs should be clear and familiar. Lowercase *g, j, p, q* and *y* should have true descenders going below the normal line, as should the comma and semicolon. Lower case letters *a, c, e, m, n, o, r, s, u, v, w, x, z* should all be the same height. Lower case *i* and *j* should have the dot slightly higher; *b, d, f, h, l, t* should be higher still, though not necessarily all the same height. Most character sets use a constant height for all capital letters and numbers. Lowercase letters should be lowercase, not small capital letters.

Any useful public display terminal should make close pairs distinct. The close pairs most likely to appear in patron access systems are

I	T
0	8
1	1
0	O
m	n
u	w
u	v
w	v
[	(
]	)

Some other close pairs should not even be close. If any characters below can be confused, the display is much too poor to be considered for use:

i	j
g	q
;	:
,	.
2	Z
b	6
-	—

No display will meet the needs of all patrons; those with visual difficulties may always need special assistance or special terminals. By paying attention to the way characters work together, designers and librarians can ensure that most patrons will be able to read displays correctly.

Diacritics and Special Characters

Most patrons don't need diacritics or special characters at most terminals in most libraries. Some scholars do require diacritics and special characters.

Three types of special characters need attention:

- diacritics or special marks that appear above or below characters
- special characters within the USMARC character set, including modified Roman characters and a few non-Roman characters

- non-Roman characters, including other alphabets such as Cyrillic and Hebrew, and other scripts such as those used for Chinese, Japanese and Korean

Most items in most libraries in the United States have no special characters. Most patrons in most libraries in the United States have no need for special characters. Even so, professional standards appear to call for proper display of all diacritics and characters on all public terminals. Most libraries use catalog cards that contain such characters and assume that patrons not understanding them will at least not be injured by them. Unfortunately, proper display of diacritics and special characters on terminals is more complex than proper printing on catalog cards.

As noted earlier, each character position on a terminal has a certain number of picture elements available to make up a character. In order to display diacritics properly and display regular characters consistently, a terminal must use either fewer picture elements for alphabetic characters or more picture elements for each character position. In the first case, the legibility of the character set will suffer—in order to serve special needs, the library reduces quality of service for all patrons. In the second case, terminals used will be significantly more expensive and other aspects of the system may need to be upgraded.

Most current technical processing terminals, such as those used by WLN, OCLC and RLIN, avoid this problem by displaying diacritics as separate characters. That solution may not be appropriate for public use. Displaying an umlaut before (or after) an "o" is unconventional, and patrons will have no way of knowing whether the diacritic is attached to the letter preceding or following it.

Vietnamese diacritics represent a special problem. Two marks frequently attach to a single letter, requiring even more picture elements to provide clear display. A terminal providing proper display of Vietnamese entries and retaining good clarity for alphabetic text requires extremely high information density, not currently available at a reasonable price.

If public terminals do not display special characters, equivalent standard characters should be displayed instead.

Special characters represent a different problem. While good quality terminals have enough pixels to handle most special characters, the terminal must be capable of generating those characters. This becomes more of a problem for low-cost terminals and for dial-up and workstation users. Most special characters have Roman equivalents, but the Roman equivalents may be more than one character each. In extreme cases, the Roman equivalents are as much as five characters long (the Greek *alpha* and *gamma*).

Public terminals should display either all diacritics or none. Systems that display Western European and Latin American diacritics but ignore Vietnamese and other diacritics imply value judgments that will offend patrons in some libraries.

Computer output microform vendors and some microcomputer makers have moved to character sets that provide precombined character-diacritic combinations, but only for the major Western European and Latin American languages. Terminals providing such combinations may avoid some of the problems mentioned above, but will require software filtering to make sure that the proper combinations appear and that unsupported diacritics are eliminated.

Support for the "major" diacritics raises another issue, a serious one at least for public libraries in certain areas. What constitutes major, and why does one non-English literature receive preferential treatment over another? If diacritic support is limited, Vietnamese will probably be the first language to go even though some libraries serve a population with more Vietnamese than any other ethnic group.

Non-Roman characters represent a whole range of problems, depending on the script involved. Some go from right to left rather than from left to right; some require much more detailed displays than Roman characters; some involve tens of thousands of character images. Most libraries may choose to ignore non-Roman characters except for special collections in special locations. Fortunately, most current non-Roman cataloging provides romanized access points, providing some access to the materials.

Most large public libraries, and most academic libraries, should plan to provide display of diacritics and special characters at some terminals eventually. The characters should be retained in the database so that they will be available when better display equipment is more feasible economically. Terminals that will display diacritics and special characters clearly, while retaining clear display of regular characters, should become less expensive and more readily available over the next few years. For now, libraries may be justified in suppressing diacritics on most or all public terminals.

Special Display Features

---

*Special display features should be used sparingly. Sparse use
is effective use.*

Special display features include reverse video, capitalization, half
or double intensity, color, graphics, boldface, underlining, different
character fonts and blinking. Most patron access systems will use a
limited number of special display features, and a good case can be made
for such discretionary use.

Special features can serve or distract the patron. One special
display feature can call special attention to something on the screen.
Two special display features used together cleverly can improve the
effectiveness of the display. When five or six special features appear
together, any specific highlight tends to be lost in a confusion of
features. The simplest term for this confusion, used throughout this
discussion, is the *arcade effect*, in which the screen begins to look more
like a video game than a means for communication.

The most effective tools for evaluating special display features are
good taste and common sense. Consider dial-up users (if the catalog
will support them), consider your own reactions when spending more
than two or three minutes at a display, consider the needs of the large
color-blind population and consider the purposes of the patron access
system. With the exception of blinking, each feature mentioned below
has some possible uses, but any display combining all the features
seems likely to suffer from the arcade effect.

Reverse Video

---

*Reverse video—dark characters on a light background—can
effectively highlight text on a screen. Excessive use of reverse
video, particularly full-intensity reverse video, can cause problems. The screen becomes filled with too much light, making
text difficult to read and causing strain on the eyes.*

On a monochrome terminal, reverse (or inverse) video offers a
negative image, dark where regular letters are light, light where regular

letters are dark. For typical amber terminals, reverse letters are black on amber background; for typical green terminals, reverse letters are dark grey or black on a light green background.
Reverse video can be used

- to highlight choices, particularly in connection with pointing
- for labels in bibliographic displays
- for access points that caused a record to be retrieved
- for messages and other special text

Reverse video seems particularly appropriate to highlight choices. A moving band of reverse video controlled by cursor arrows or pointers provides a direct connection between command and response.

Half-intensity display and capitalization work well in combination with reverse video. Half-intensity bands of light containing capitalized words in dark letters produce clear labels and will not conflict with use of a movable, full-intensity reverse video strip to select options from the screen.

Capitalization

Text in ALL CAPITAL LETTERS will help to highlight labels and may be appropriate for titles within bibliographic displays.

Citations displayed entirely in capital letters are much more difficult to read, as are messages displayed all uppercase. Capital letters do serve to call attention to something, but overuse reduces legibility.

Use of capital letters to highlight the title within a brief unlabeled display is somewhat traditional, and seems to work well. Figures 5.3 and 5.4 illustrate that use in multiple-item displays and single-item partially labeled displays. Whether such use makes sense within a patron access system will depend on the library and on other needs. If the title always appears first or if the title is labeled, capitalization seems redundant.

Capital letters may also be effective to highlight the field used to retrieve an item, but only if titles do not normally appear in capital letters.

Figure 5.3: Multiple-Item Display with Capitalized Titles

```
Your search: FIN WORD PLAGIARISM                              MULTIPLE
     Finds: 13 items.                                     Items 1 to 6
-----------------------------------------------------------------------

  1. Casewit, Curtis W. KEEP IT LEGAL : (Sacramento, CA : Creative Book Co.,
     [1976]

  2. Douglas, John, 1721-1807. MILTON VINDICATED FROM THE CHARGE OF PLAGIARISM :
     (London : Printed for A. Miller ..., 1751.)

  3. Grier, Samuel L. A TOOL FOR DETECTING PLAGIARISM IN PASCAL PROGRAMS
     [Microform] / (1980.)

  4. Johnston, Dan. DESIGN PROTECTION : (London : Design Council : 1978)

  5. LEGAL ASPECTS OF PLAGIARISM / (Topeka, Kansas : National Organization on
     Legal Problems of Education, c1985.)

  6. Lindey, Alexander. PLAGIARISM AND ORIGINALITY / (New York : Harper, c1952)
------------------------------------------------------------CONTINUED-----------
NEXT ACTIONS:     Key: D1-D5 to Display an item     + for Next Screen
                       F to Find other items        ? for Help
                       Q to Quit
NEXT ACTION? +_
```

Intensity Variations

Half-intensity (dim) text may be useful for labels, particularly when combined with reverse video. Double-intensity (very bright), bold and underscored text should be used rarely, if at all.

Many terminals can display text at more than one intensity. Some terminals display normal and dim (half-intensity) text, some display normal and bright (double-intensity) text and some can display all three. Most terminals can add a form of intensity by underlining text, and some modern terminals can display text in **boldface**.

Half-intensity text is useful for background information, such as field labels and next-action choices. Double-intensity text could be useful for problem statements or to highlight what the user has keyed. Excessive use of double intensity raises problems similar to excessive use of reverse video.

Most terminals do not display more than two levels effectively, and some terminals do not display more than one intensity level very

Figure 5.4: Single-Item Display with Capitalized Title

```
Your search: Folsom, Franklin#                              CITATION
       Finds: 1 item                                   Screen 1 of 2
--------------------------------------------------------------------------

        Folsom, Franklin, 1907-  AMERICA'S ANCIENT TREASURES : a
        guide to archaeological sites and museums in the United
        States and Canada / Franklin Folsom and Mary Elting
        Folsom ; illustrations by Rachel Folsom. 34d rev., enl.
        ed. Albuquerque : University of New Mexico Press, c1983.
        xxviii, 420 p. : ill. ; 26 cm.

     SUBJECTS: Indians of North America--Museums--Guide-books.
               Indians of North America--Antiquities--Guide-books.
               United States--Antiquities--Guide-books.
               Canada--Antiquities--Guide-books.
               Archaeological museums and collections--United States--
               Guide-books.

 ------------------------------------------------------CONTINUED-----------
NEXT ACTIONS    Key: ? for Help            + to see the next screen
                     L to see a Longer display  - to see the previous screen
                     F to Find other items  Q to Quit
NEXT ACTION? +_
```

clearly. Different intensities, particularly when combined with reverse video, lead to an arcade effect. Boldface and underscoring fall into the same category as varied intensities: useful in small doses, distracting when overused. Boldface and double intensity may actually be the same device in most terminals. Underscores cause an additional problem—because they take up one of the pixels normally used to separate lines. As a result, lines may tend to merge in a display.

Blinking

Blinking text will distract and irritate patrons. Nothing on the display should blink except for the cursor, and the cursor should blink slowly.

Many terminals use a blinking cursor. That may be unavoidable, and can help to show where the cursor is located. If the cursor is an underscore rather than a solid inverse block, it should blink so that it does not disappear into the background. Other than the cursor, blinking seems inappropriate except for true emergency situations or irreparable problems. Blinking is an irritant, particularly for the patron trying to decide what to do next.

Color

Color has no proven effective use in online catalogs. Color can distract and lead to an arcade effect more rapidly than most other special features. Color displays should not be used unless the characters are as well defined as they are on monochrome displays.

Color terminals have appeared recently all over exhibit halls at library conferences, indicating that vendors believe color will attract people into a booth. It does not demonstrate that color has any real use in patron access.

Color raises a series of questions and balances. As of 1986, economics and the need for clear characters argue strongly against color displays. In future years, the question may become more complex.

At present, a color display can be either somewhat more expensive than a monochrome display and much less readable, or as readable as a monochrome display and much more expensive. At present, no clear research exists to show effective use of color within an online catalog or to suggest what uses of color would be effective.

Color can highlight, but such uses as red background for the vendor's name (to take one example seen at an exhibit) seem not only useless but ludicrous. Color can also distract, even when used sparingly, and particularly when color comes at the expense of character quality.

Some 8% of men suffer a degree of color blindness, as do a few women. A terminal that uses color for any significant function, either on the screen or on function keys, represents a disservice to a substantial number of library patrons.

If a terminal has two "B" keys, one colored red, and offers the instruction *Press the red B key*, that terminal is offering ambiguous instructions to color-blind users. If the instruction is *Press the red key* and the red key has no label, the instruction might as well be in ancient Greek to such users.

Graphics

Lines and boxes can help to separate areas of the display. Icons (symbols used in place of words or phrases) and other graphics have no demonstrated use in online catalogs.

Horizontal lines or rows of dashes provide clear separation between feedback, text and command option portions of a display. Online catalogs could use windows—temporary display areas set off as boxes—to provide help and other special feedback.

Icons and other graphics are of questionable value. Despite claims of some microcomputer companies and users, most icons represent a learned vocabulary just as much as words. Samplings of icons used in various systems usually show a high percentage that make no immediate sense; some icon-based systems acknowledge this problem by placing words beneath the icons.

Most patrons will use an online system to find bibliographic and status information, which will be in words. Words represent the least ambiguous means of communication, and represent a vocabulary that people have already learned. Icons represent a new learned vocabulary that appears to offer no advantages.

Font Changes

Different typefaces or fonts can highlight or differentiate information. Any use of multiple fonts must be careful and conservative.

Terminals with multiple-font capabilities are rare in 1986 but will become more common over the next few years. Used carefully and sparingly, different fonts can lend subtle highlighting to different portions of a display. Fonts differing in weight, size or actual design can serve the same purposes as reverse video, capitalization or varying intensity. Used to excess, multiple fonts achieve an arcade effect as rapidly as do multiple colors. The screen can become a dazzling but illegible display of effects, with little room left for communication.

Any font used for public access must be clear and crisp. Communication must take precedence over style; clarity counts more than elegance. Those who design printed pages know that multiple fonts must be used sparingly to be effective. Those who design display screens must be even more careful. Displays are inherently less readable than print and must be treated with even more care.

Health and Safety

Those concerned with the health and safety issues of video display terminals should consult other sources: one good recent source on health and safety issues for terminals is an article by R. Bruce Miller in *Information Technology and Libraries*[4] and an extensive annotated bibliography of recent related material appears in the first *Library Hi Tech Bibliography*.[5]

Most potential health and safety issues concern those who use terminals many hours at a time. Patron access systems do not appear to pose a real or potential problem since few patrons will use a terminal for more than 15 or 20 minutes a day.

Special Needs

Special terminals can offer better service to partially sighted and blind patrons and to those unable to use standard keyboards.

Most public terminals will serve fully sighted patrons able to use a standard keyboard. But libraries serve other patrons as well, and microcomputer technology offers methods of serving those patrons in ways that card catalogs cannot.

Devices to serve special patrons are becoming available, and will be more common in coming years. Such devices require special care; very large screens or voice-response terminals abandon privacy in favor of special service. As of now, screens with large characters and terminals offering special input techniques are available, as are fairly satisfactory voice-output terminals. Terminals producing other forms of output, including braille, should also be available. Input will be a problem for years to come because voice input techniques are still primitive at best, but keyboards with braille keycaps are available.

TERMINAL STATIONS

Terminal stations should be designed for easy, productive use. Patrons need writing surfaces, proper lighting and privacy.

Analysts and writers are beginning to pay more attention to the problems of public terminal stations in libraries. Institutes and preconferences are addressing station design, and the professional literature should offer more advice over the new few years.

Some of the issues surrounding terminal stations are as follows:

- Writing surface. People need to make notes while working with an online catalog, and they may need to refer to other sources. Terminals should be placed on surfaces with sufficient writing area. People may need space either to the right or left of the keyboard.
- Light and glare. Terminal stations should have sufficient lighting for writing and reference, but should not be subject to glare or reflection. Glare problems can be reduced by choosing good terminals or adding glare screens, but windows and general lighting patterns must be considered when siting terminals.
- Privacy. Patrons should be able to search for materials they need without worrying about others looking over their shoulders. Terminal stations should be designed to encourage privacy and discourage eavesdropping. People use libraries to get information on all topics, including difficult and embarrassing topics. Online catalogs must assure privacy so that patrons can carry out their own searches.
- Location. There is no reason to restrict public terminals to the same locations formerly used by card catalogs. Librarians should determine where terminals will be most useful and should not be bound by tradition.
- Height. Screen angles, desk height and desk arrangement depend on expected use of a terminal. Most libraries should use at least two types of terminal workstations: some designed to be used by seated patrons and some designed to be used while standing.

SUMMARY

The terminal is the physical manifestation of the catalog. Good terminal design will encourage patrons to become more familiar with the catalog. Bad terminal design will encourage patrons to avoid the catalog whenever possible. Decisions must vary from library to library, but thoughtfulness and common sense will yield good input and display design for any library.

NOTES

1. Matthews, Joseph R. *Public Access to Online Catalogs: A Planning Guide for Managers*. Weston, CT: Online; 1982. p. 33.

2. Hildreth, Charles R. *Online Public Access Catalogs: The User Interface*. Dublin, OH: OCLC; 1982. p. 79.

3. *Online Catalog: The Inside Story*. William E. Post; Peter G. Watson, eds. Chico, CA: Ryan Research International; 1983. p. 110.

4. Miller, R. Bruce. "Radiation, Ergonomics, Ion Depletion, and VDTs: Healthful Use of Visual Display Terminals." *Information Technology and Libraries*. 2(2): 151–158; 1983 June.

5. Hurlebaus, Alice J. [and others]. "Video Display Terminal Hazards and Ergonomic Issues: A Bibliography, 1981–1985." *Library Hi Tech Bibliography*. Ann Arbor, MI: Pierian Press; 1986. v. 1, p. 149–159.

6

Printers, Workstations and Dial-In Use

Carefully chosen printers, either attached to public terminals or as offline devices, can make online catalogs distinctly more useful.

Within universities, patrons may be using very powerful micro-computers or scholar's workstations; such workstations may provide ways to support functions not easily supportable from public terminals. Workstations may be attached to a campus-wide area network, a local area network or direct communications lines. Libraries can use this type of workstation at reference desks, for staff work and for other purposes.

Any contemporary online catalog should provide the option of supporting access from dial-in and network microcomputers. Since such computers may cover a broad range of capabilities and equipment, libraries must give special consideration to the task of supporting them.

PRINTERS

Printers enhance public access but can also cause problems. They can provide patrons with exact call numbers to ease book retrieval and bibliography preparation, but printers also make noise, can be difficult to maintain and can produce listings that are barely readable.

Patrons will appreciate the ability to print their searches. Eliminating the need to write down search results reduces the risk of error and saves time, which can be a significant factor for some patrons such as those building bibliographies. Printers can eliminate problems but can also cause problems of their own.

Making a Selection

Printers designed for public use should be quiet, compact and easy to use. They should provide good print quality and good paper, be durable and fast, and be inexpensive to purchase, run and maintain.

The right printers can improve patron access. The wrong printers will make the library less useful for patrons and librarians. Following are some points to consider when evaluating printers for patron access:

- Noise. Most printers are too noisy to use in open library areas without adding acoustic hoods, which substantially increase the cost and space required and make printers more difficult to use. Although no current models are wholly silent, nonimpact printers (including thermal, ink jet and laser printers) are relatively quiet.
- Space. Printers can be bulky, and they require space for paper input and output. If each terminal has a printer, space may be a problem. Compact printers are available but unfortunately are easy to steal from parts of the library less heavily used. Printers shared by many terminals reduce the space problem.
- Ease and convenience. Patron access printers must be easy to use, with simple controls and few options.
- Print quality. Listings must be legible enough so that most patrons can read them easily. If online systems print bibliographies, the listings should stay legible indefinitely. Many thermal and dot-matrix printers produce listings that are only marginally readable. Failure to maintain ribbons (for those printers that use ribbons) may also reduce legibility.
- Paper quality. The paper used for listings should not be unpleasant to the touch and should be suitable for annotation. People tend to make notes on listings.
- Cost of operation. Printers differ widely in operating costs. Thermal printers use either expensive paper or expensive ribbons. Some other printers use expensive ribbons or have high per-page costs. If patrons typically print the equivalent of one or two screens, some printers will make it possible to tear off the results without wasting a page; other printers will require an extra page feed before the listing can be retrieved. Some printers use significantly more electricity than others.

- Normal maintenance. Most printers require frequent attention to adjust and replace paper, replace ribbons and clear print jams. Some are more trouble-prone than others.
- Durability. Some printers tend to jam easily or to break down with heavy use. Many low-cost printers are intended for light duty; these may be suitable for some library locations but not for others.
- Price. Printers can cost as little as $150 and as much as $7000 or more.
- Speed. Commonly available printers range from 10 characters per second to 500. At 10 characters per second, a printer may take 3 minutes to duplicate a full screeen. Although printer speed is not a crucial factor for most libraries, the slowest printers will aggravate noise problems because they print for such a long time.
- Privacy. Shared printers may pose questions of privacy.

No single recommendation will work for all libraries. Some brief notes on common printer varieties may help show how the criteria above work out in practice.

Impact Dot-Matrix Printers

This type of printer uses rows of metal pins to print on plain paper using ribbons. Most popular printers for microcomputers are the impact dot-matrix variety. They can be fast, cheap, durable and compact and they can provide adequate print quality. Well-designed tractor feeds can keep normal maintenance requirements low, although many dot-matrix printers require constant attention. Fanfold paper is not expensive, even if libraries choose the attractive "laser-perforated" variety. Dot-matrix printers tend to be noisy, however, and some use fairly expensive ribbons. If libraries try to economize on ribbons, the print becomes illegible.

Thermal Printers

Thermal printers also use rows of metal points, but the points are heated, either to form an image on special paper or to transfer ink from a special ribbon to plain paper. Thermal printers with keyboards have been widely used in libraries as searching terminals for online databases. Thermal printers have a justified reputation for poor-quality print with very little noise. They can be inexpensive and compact but are expensive to use. Thermal paper is expensive and generally unpleasant to the touch, and thermal transfer ribbons (allowing use of plain paper) are extremely expensive, as much as 10 to 20 cents per page. Some modern thermal printers provide good print quality, but the cost of operation and difficulties of thermal paper must be balanced against the low noise of thermal printers.

Daisy-Wheel Printers

With plastic or metal wheels to print on plain paper, daisy-wheel printers use fully formed characters rather than dots. They are too slow and too noisy for most patron access use and ribbons can be expensive. As long as ribbons are changed frequently, daisy-wheel printers provide excellent print quality. Thimble printers have the same virtues and problems as daisy-wheel printers. Golf-ball printers (similar to IBM Selectric typewriters) are even slower and not much quieter.

Laser Printers

Combining desktop photocopier mechanisms, low-powered lasers and extensive electronics, laser printers print very high-quality images on sheets of paper at high speeds, usually six-to-eight pages a minute. Laser printers provide excellent quality, good speed, relatively low-cost operation and exceptional ease of use. Noise levels are low but tend to be constant, essentially the sound of a photocopier. Unfortunately, prices are presently quite high—around $2000. Low-volume laser printers use standard offset bond paper, the same as that used in plain-paper copiers. This feature keeps paper costs quite low and makes it easy to give the patrons just the sheet they need, but since most laser printers hold only 100 sheets at a time, the staff must keep the printer supplied. Most laser printers in the $2000 to $4000 price range are designed for light duty, no more than 300 single-spaced pages a day.

Ink-Jet Printers

Ink-jet printers use rows of nozzles to spray dots of ink on special paper, yielding fairly good print quality with very little noise. At present, they may provide the best possibility for patron access terminals, particularly when libraries choose to provide one printer for each terminal. Such printers are almost as quiet as thermal printers, as fast as most impact dot-matrix printers, very compact and can be quite inexpensive ($400 or less at discount). Ink-jet paper is not as easy to write on as regular paper but is much better than thermal paper and only slighly more expensive than regular paper. Print quality is good, normal operating expense and maintenance should both be very low and the printers are very easy to use. Ink-jet printers are not flawless. The ink cartridges can clog, some mechanisms are complex, the paper is slightly unusual, the paper can jam if not handled properly and some people may find the soft, high-pitched sound of an ink jet-mechanism annoying.

Printing Options

Online catalogs should provide printing for screen images, bibliographies and one-line-per-item "pick lists" for finding items on the shelves.

A *screen dump* is the simplest form of printing to provide and to explain. A PRINT SCREEN or PRINT key creates a printed image of whatever is on the screen when the key is pressed. For many libraries, that simple function may provide all the print support needed. Some terminals support a PRINT SCREEN function locally (i.e., without involving the online catalog itself).

A *pick list* is a compact listing, preferably one line per item, containing call number, location and enough of author and title to identify an item. If offered as a printing choice or optional display, such a list can serve the patron needing something to take to the stacks. Pick lists eliminate the weakest link in the catalog-to-book retrieval chain—copying down the call number. If a system provides a pick list, some careful design will be required to let users know that the list is available, how to ask for it and how to accumulate and sort a set of search results in order to create a useful list.

Bibliographies serve researchers and other patrons. Those using workstations will be served better by downloading records and reformatting them into desired bibliographies, using a suitable software package. Libraries wishing to print bibliographies must decide on a standard form for the entries and should offer some limited range of sort orders for the result. One good neutral form for bibliographies is that specified by American National Standard Z39.29. Libraries may also wish to consider some other widely supported form, such as the *Chicago Manual of Style* form.

Pick lists and bibliographies both work best when online catalogs provide a way for patrons to store search results selectively and sort those results. Chapter 9 discusses storing and sorting search results in more detail.

Central (offline) printing reduces noise and control problems but increases staff workload, causes privacy problems and generally reduces the value of immediate printing.

All the options above assume local printing, where the printer is at or near the terminal. Libraries may also provide printing offline, using one or more central printers. This option offers several advantages. A higher-speed and noisier printer can be kept in an isolated area, thereby reducing noise problems. Such a printer may also provide better quality at a lower cost per page compared to other small printers. Finally, offline printing lets the library control printing levels, preventing excessive use of a facility.

The disadvantages of offline printing are increased staff workload, loss of immediacy and loss of privacy. Offline printing requires that staff monitor the printer, separate listings, prepare the listings for distribution and distribute them in some manner. This workload may well raise the costs of offline printing above those of immediate printers. Offline printing also raises privacy questions. Will a patron be willing to use offline printing for a bibliography on a sensitive subject such as herpes or terrorism? For most libraries, the costs and dangers of offline printing may outweight the benefits.

WORKSTATIONS

A workstation should provide all the functions of a public terminal but should also provide special functions that take advantage of its power.

A *workstation* is a powerful microcomputer, connected to some network or other system providing access to such resources as the library's online catalog. Many universities and colleges anticipate that faculty members and other scholars will use such workstations as ways to access and manipulate various sources of information. Libraries may also use workstations at reference desks or for other uses. Workstations should provide access to the online catalog but should also provide gateways to many other sources of information.

Some workstation functions will be transparent to the online catalog and need not be considered in designing the catalog. For example, any workstation should be able to print online catalog screens or save them for use in documents by using background software.

Display and Input

Workstation users should be able to define their own preferred display formats, within limits. They should also be able to use special input devices not available at public terminals. If a workstation user prefers a mouse to cursor control keys, or wishes to establish dozens of special function keys to speed use of the catalog, the results should be transparent to the online catalog. If the workstation can capture catalog information and deal with it locally, workstation users should also be able to define their own preferred sort sequences.

Downloading

Workstation users should be able to download—to transfer bibliographic records in MARC format for later use in bibliographies and special databases. Transfer capabilities should be controlled to avoid ownership and copyright problems.

If the patron access system can pass search results to the workstation in MARC format, the workstation user can design a completely customized display. This reduces the computing load on the online catalog, but increases communications load when multiple-item results are passed in MARC format.

Several questions need to be addressed when considering downloading. For example:

- What protocols should be used for downloading?
- Should result sets be downloaded automatically, only on explicit request or based on user profiles stored by the workstation?
- Should searches always yield downloaded records or should formatted screens and result sets be used as well?
- Is software available, or will it be, to manipulate downloaded

MARC records? Are there database managers, parsers, languages, etc., that can accommodate MARC?
- Will downloading raise problems of copyright, ownership of information, fair use and payment for services?

Protocols for requesting and passing MARC records to workstations should be defined in a standard way. One starting point is Open Systems Interconnect (OSI), as defined in the Linked Systems Project (LSP) protocols; these will probably be used for connections between online catalogs. If the same protocols are used for workstation downloading, the online catalog can maintain a single consistent methodology.

The last question is a serious one. A library that makes downloading in MARC form generally available could avoid paying record usage fees for cataloging and retrospective conversion and might cause other problems as well. If downloading is limited to workstations that are on a local area network, these problems may be avoided.

Downloading won't do much good unless workstations have software that can manipulate USMARC.

Very little current microcomputer software can handle MARC records properly. Suitable software should be developed as workstations develop. With suitable software, users can prepare a wide variety of custom reports from downloaded catalog records, making the online catalog an integral part of their work.

Downloaded records cease to have current status information as soon as they are downloaded. While such records can be useful for bibliographies and other functions, they do not replace direct access to the online system.

Individualizing the Catalog

Workstations should be able to provide a level of individual preference not available at public terminals.

Some customization will take place at the workstation without the knowledge of the library. The library can ask to be informed or it can develop techniques to cope with the problems that will inevitably arise when a patron complains of malfunctions and the problem is in the patron's undocumented custom software rather than in the patron access system.

In addition to special displays and different sorting order, workstations might provide the following:

- User profiles. These are stored on the workstation to specify such things as preferred default display and special one-key command equivalents. If users have profiles on their own computers, privacy questions are not relevant.
- Gateway services. These services make it easy to search other databases within an institution or outside the institution, including locally mounted databases (possibly stored on optical disc). Ideally, the workstation should make it possible to use a single set of search techniques on many sources of information by translating search requests and results internally.
- Stored searches. These special requests should be run during off-peak hours, returning the results to the patron. This function may make very large or difficult searches possible without ruining response for other users, if scholars are willing to prepare searches with one-day turnaround.
- Selective Dissemination of Information (SDI). These standing search profiles run periodically against new additions to the catalog, and results are returned to the workstation.

The last three services are at least as valuable for staff use and at reference desks as for university faculty members. The last special service makes the workstation an agent of the patron and can provide useful results to the patron without significantly increasing the load on the system. SDI profiles would presumably be run at times in which little or no searching was taking place (2 a.m. to 4 a.m. on Sunday morning, for instance), making good use of otherwise idle computer capacity. SDI can be provided as a service without workstations, but workstations can eliminate the problems of formatting, printing and distributing search results.

Distributing the Load

Workstations should make it possible to limit searches by almost any element in a bibliographic record.

Workstations can limit searches only after records are downloaded. Clever design can make the complex array of USMARC codes and elements accessible to the patron, at least to some degree. There is no reason why a patron should not be able to search for all items related to William Shakespeare with publication dates between 1950 and 1965 that either have indexes or are stereophonic recordings in French. That may be a peculiar request, but that is not for the library to determine.

As CD ROM and other optical disc technologies penetrate libraries, the possibility of library catalog subsets mounted at the workstation will grow. Such subsets will not provide status information and cannot replace the central catalog, but they could handle some searching requirements without using the central catalog.

DIAL-IN TERMINALS AND COMPUTERS

Libraries should support dial-in use from home computers, which may not have the same features as public terminals.

Home computers offer a considerable range of capabilities, but some will not provide as many display features as public terminals. While nearly all home computers and telecommunications programs use ASCII as a standard for characters, there are no widespread standards for special characters or for special display features. The command string that initiates reverse video on one computer may do something entirely different, or nothing at all, on another computer. Dial-in support requires that special display features not be *critical* to patron access design, or that some clear equivalent be available.

Most home computers have function keys; few, if any, will have function keys labeled as they would be at public terminals. That problem speaks to the need for command equivalents for all function keys, but it also suggests that prompts should refer to the text on a key rather than to the key itself. *Press BACKUP to restore the previous search* is a better prompt than *Press the BACKUP key to restore the previous search.*

Not all home computers display 80 characters per line or have 24 lines available. Libraries may consider restricting dial-in support to systems with at least that minimum.

Should libraries provide software to improve dial-in use? Such software will be a substantial service for patrons who can use it, but it may pose problems of maintenance and discrimination. Discrimination arises because home computers, even those with 24 lines of 80 characters each, employ a wide range of operating systems. For a library to support all or nearly all of its computer-owning patrons, it would need to make the software available not only in CP/M and PC-DOS versions, but also in versions for Apple II, Macintosh, Commodore 64 and Amiga, Atari 800 and 520 ST/1040ST, Radio Shack TRS-80, and probably others.

This type of support may be unreasonable, and staff support to answer questions may also be unreasonable. Any decision to simplify the problem by offering only Apple or only MS-DOS versions will ignore a large percentage of home computer owners. If special software is available, it should not be *required* for dial-in access unless it can be offered in a range of versions sufficient to support the great majority of patrons who wish to use dial-in access.

7

Commands and Menus

Menus and commands must be designed to work with patrons since they are the vehicles that enable patrons to use online catalogs. Some patron access systems provide only menus, with no free choices and no commands. Others rely entirely on commands, with no menus or sets of options. Most patron access systems use a combination of the two. This chapter deals with specific aspects of menu and command design, parsing and truncation.

MENUS VERSUS COMMANDS: THE BASIC DICHOTOMY

Online systems that rely completely on menus or, conversely, that expect commands but do not display options, do not serve patrons well.

Before considering the merits of menu-driven and command-driven systems, the following terms must be defined:

- A menu is a set of choices that can be selected only by keying numbers or letters, by touching a screen or by moving a cursor.
- A command is any keyed instruction other than a direct menu choice.
- An option is a display that offers command possibilities and may also offer the alternative of keying a number or letter or pointing at an option.
- A completion is keyed text that completes a request begun from a menu.

117

Figure 7.1 shows a menu screen. The only possible choices are numbers. If the online catalog accepts SU followed by a subject instead of 1, and ST or STOP instead of 5, it is no longer a pure menu screen, but an option screen.

The primary distinction between menus and commands is that menus consist of complete choices and leave no alternatives other than those on the screen. Commands may or may not involve information other than what is displayed as a set of options.

Patron access systems can follow any one of four patterns:

1. Menu-driven. In a completely menu-driven system the patron never keys any textual information. Pure menu-driven systems limit search speed and flexibility, and cannot provide Boolean logic or fast known-item searching.
2. Command-driven. The most extreme command-driven systems provide a command prompt (an arrow, the word *Command:* or something similar) but never display possible command options. Pure command-driven systems require trained users and will mystify new or occasional catalog users.
3. Menu-driven with keyed completions. Most menu-driven online catalogs fall into this hybrid category. Figure 7.1 is a partial screen from one such system, presenting a pure menu. Figure 7.2 shows the result of choosing the number 2 from the menu—a screen requesting a keyed completion. Hybrid systems—those that are menu-driven with keyed completions—

Figure 7.1: Hybrid System, Pure Menu Screen

```
CHOOSE ONE OF THE FOLLOWING:

   1 = SUBJECT SEARCH
   2 = PERSONAL AUTHOR SEARCH
   3 = SERIES, ORGANIZATION, CONFERENCE NAME OR CALL NUMBER SEARCH
   4 = TITLE SEARCH
   5 = STOP THIS SEARCH

SELECT(1=SUBJECT,2=AUTHOR,3=SERIES/CALL#,4=TITLE,5=STOP):2
:                                                                    :
:                                                                    :
```

Figure 7.2: Hybrid System, Completion Screen

```
AUTHOR SEARCH - TYPE AUTHOR'S NAME (STARTING WITH LAST NAME)
:_
:                                                                    :
:                                                                    :
```

can carry out all possible online catalog functions but require more screens and more steps than command-driven systems.

4. Command-driven with displayed options. Any good command-driven system will fall into this category. Every screen will show some options, never leaving the patron without guidance. If options are numbered and the numbers serve as menu choices, the system functions both as a hybrid system and as a command-driven system. Figure 7.3 shows part of a screen from this type of system; a command-driven system with displayed options provides fast, flexible searching coupled with guidance for new users.

Figure 7.3: Command System with Options

```
SEARCH OPTIONS
                                        EXAMPLE

SUbject: Subjects or Topics             find su anthropology*
NAme:    Personal name                  find na asimov, isaac
TItle:   Beginning of title             find ti deer park*
COrp:    Corporation or conference      find co thor power*
SEries:  Series name                    find se nameless detective
CAll:    Call number                    find ca hd1000*

QUIT, HELP, START always work           *: followed by anything

Command:
:
:                                                              :
                                                               :
```

Many writers regard menus as friendly and feel that menu-driven hybrid systems are better than command-driven systems. The Council on Library Resources (CLR) study of online catalog use did not show positive results for menu-driven systems, either pure or hybrid. As one report from that study notes, "The aggregate report presented tentative evidence indicating that menu-driven interfaces for online catalogs were disadvantageous from the point of view of survey respondents. . . . Menus are not necessarily easier to use than command-driven systems, and . . . menu designs should be studied and tested carefully."[1]

Conversational Systems

Conversational online systems, which ask patrons a series of questions in order to prepare a search, force slow access and will frustrate experienced users.

To date, the only conversational online systems have actually been hybrid menu-command systems with very extensive prompting and very few choices at most points. A complete beginner may appreciate being prompted through each step of a search, though even a novice may be surprised that the first question after requesting a title search is *Is this title a periodical?* (as it is in one such system). If a conversational system allows immediate exit into direct command entry, the system may serve a useful, if very elementary, tutorial function. Otherwise, the system will serve raw beginners and annoy all other users, including beginners doing their second or third search.

Providing a conversational system as the only patron access system, or even as the primary system, may be a step backward from the card catalog. If a conversational system will obey direct commands, it functions as a pure command system without displayed options. The conversational mode will slow down all but the newest searchers and will offend many patrons.

As most users of microcomputer software can attest, it is indeed possible to oversimplify. While an interactive "natural language" approach may be user-friendly in one sense, it is decidedly user-hostile for most purposes. If conversational systems are placed alongside well-designed command-driven systems with the same user population and underlying database, independent research (not carried out by designers of either system) should help to show which system leads to better and faster results and more satisfied users. It seems almost certain that, once the novelty of the conversational system wears off, virtually all patrons will desert it for the command-driven system.

Opening Choices

If an online system supports both menu-driven and command-driven modes, patrons should be able to choose a mode at the opening screen. Patrons should also be able to switch modes at any point.

If users must choose a mode of operation, that choice should be offered at an early point and should be very clear. At the same time, the opening screen should offer as much power as possible to the experienced searcher and to the patron wanting information on a known item.

Good online systems do not require separate modes in order to combine ease and power. A command-driven catalog can provide opening options that function as menu choices. If the system will also accept direct commands at that point, experienced users can proceed rapidly while new users work through menus.

Those online systems that offer distinctly separated command and menu modes seem to irritate users. The command modes in such catalogs tend not to offer enough assistance, while the menu modes tend to be slow and cumbersome for searching.

OPTION SCREEN DESIGN

Menus and option displays should be terse and clear. Most such displays should contain no more than 300 characters.

Common sense and studies suggest that patrons can understand small amounts of text on a screen more rapidly than they can understand large amounts of text. Clear, unambiguous choices require analysis and experimentation.

Quantity and Usefulness of Options

In general, option and menu displays should offer no more than nine options, preferably no more than seven. Any set of options should be complete, even if one of the options is "More Options."

Psychological studies show that "a person can store roughly seven, plus or minus two, 'chunks' of information in short-term memory for a few moments."[2] Similarly, people can choose from a small set of options much more rapidly than from a large set.

Complete online catalogs will have more than nine options at some points. Should such systems display all the options, or use other techniques? When considering option sets, designers should be aware of the virtues of simplicity. Can a complex set of options be displayed as layers of simple options? Can this be done so that experienced users can key complete commands immediately while inexperienced users step through two or three menu layers?

Consider your own reaction when facing a screen that displays 15 or 20 choices. You must read through the entire screen to determine what best suits your needs. If the screen shows only seven to nine clearly worded choices, one of which may be *More Options,* you will probably make a decision much faster, as you can deal with the complete set at one time, and generally at a single glance.

Option sets should not preclude reasonable alternatives, which may mean that apparently redundant options appear occasionally. Few interactive experiences are more disturbing than seeing a list of options that does not include *Other Choices,* and wanting to do something that is not on the screen but that you know is supported.

Distinctive Options

Options should be distinct and unambiguous.

Subtle semantic distinctions should be ignored in on-screen options whenever possible. That seems so obvious that some counterexamples may be needed, all taken from existing systems:

- One system uses two function keys, one labeled SEARCH, the other labeled FIND. The first begins word searching, the second begins author/title and serial title searching.
- Another system has TOPIC as one search option and AUTHOR/SUBJECT as another.
- Another system has two indexes, one called SU for "Subject," another TE for "Term/Topic." The distinction between *topic* and *subject* is mysterious at best.

As designers of these sytems will point out, the instruction leaflet for each system explains the differences clearly. But in each case, unambiguous words could be used to avoid the problem altogether.

Layered Options and Sub-Menus

Sets of options should be presented either as ordered groups, with most likely options appearing first, or as layered groups, with some options leading to sub-options. In either case, a patron should be able to enter any command at any point, whether or not it is a displayed option.

A sophisticated patron access system may contain two or three dozen indexes, and even simpler systems may have more than nine options at some points. If we accept nine as a desirable maximum number of options for one screen, we are faced with the problem of grouping or layering options in meaningful ways.

Figures 7.4 through 7.8 show three possible ways of showing an unusually complex set of index possibilities. Figure 7.4 puts all the options on one screen, grouping similar options on the same lines. By most standards, Figure 7.4 includes too many choices and is difficult to decipher.

Figures 7.5 and 7.6 show the first and second partial screens for an ordered set of options. Figure 7.5 shows the most common searches, or at least those that the library would prefer patrons to use. Figure 7.6

Figure 7.4: Overcrowded Options Screen

```
Commands Available: Key at least the capitalized letters        COMHELP
To search, key Find, the index, and your search, e.g. "f pe asimov, isaac"
Use * to end a search if it may be incomplete, e.g. "fin title roots*"
Use two indexes to combine them, e.g. "f pe asimov, isaac & t robots*"


NAme                PErson (exact)      COmpany (exact)     CWord:Company word
CTerm:Company Term  PUblisher (exact)   PWord:Pub. Word     PTerm:Pub. Term


Title (exact)       TWord:Title Word    TTerm:Title Term    RElated Title
SEries (exact)      SEWord:Series Word  SETerm:Series Term


SUbject (exact)     SUWord:Subject Word SUTerm:Subject Term
Word (anywhere)     TErm (anywhere)     CNTerm: contents term
CNWord:Contents Word


CAll number         ISBn                ISSn                STRn
GOvernment doc. no. CODen               GEOgraphic code


QUALIFIERS - USE ONLY AFTER "&"
COUntry             Language            Year                Format


Backup              Help                Quit                STart over

Command:_
```

Figure 7.5: Ordered Options, First Screen

```
:                                                                     :
:                                                                     :
------------------------------------------------------------------------
Find:     Name:   Personal or other name TTerm:   Any portion of title
          Title:  Exact title            SUTerm:  Any portion of subject
          SUbject: Exact subject         SEries:  Series name
          CAll:   Call number            More:    More finding options
Command:_
```

Figure 7.6: Ordered Options, Screen Following Figure 7.5

```
 ---------------------------------------------------------------------
 :                                                                   :
 :                                                                   :
 | -------------------------------------------------------------------
 |Find:    COmpany:  Company or conf. name   PErson: Exact personal name
 |         PUblisher: Publisher's name       TErm:   Term in any field
 |         TWord:    Word(s) in title        More:   More finding options
 |Command:_
```

Figure 7.7: Layered Options, First Screen

```
 ---------------------------------------------------------------------
 :                                                                   :
 :                                                                   :
 | -------------------------------------------------------------------
 |Find:   Name:     Personal or other name   Title: Exact title
 |        SUbject:  Exact subject             CAll:  Call number
 |        SEries:   Series statement          TErm:  Term in any field
 |Command:find t_
```

Figure 7.8: Layered Options, Result of "Find T" on Figure 7.7

```
 ---------------------------------------------------------------------
 :                                                                   :
 :                                                                   :
 | -------------------------------------------------------------------
 |Title search options:
 |     Title: exact title         e.g. "find title online public acc*"
 |     TTerm: term within title    e.g. "find tterm art history"
 |     TWord: word(s) within title e.g. "find tword chromaticism"
 |     TRel:  related title        e.g. "find trel time magazine*"
 |Command:find t_
```

shows less commonly used or more difficult searches. An ordered arrangement means that most searches will use options from the first screen.

Figures 7.7 and 7.8 show similar screens, but for layered options. Figure 7.8 will appear when a patron keys F T OR FIND T, then keys nothing else for a second or two. The system offers more title-related options.

None of these figures is ideal or even close to it, but the ordered and layered option sets do appear easier to use than Figure 7.4, without sacrificing power or flexibility.

If options are numbered, a system may accept numbers as equivalent to commands.

Some people prefer numbers to commands, even if the commands are as short as the numbers. Figure 7.9 shows a numbered version of Figure 7.5. When numbers are used instead of commands, the system should respond by showing the command. Figure 7.10 shows one way that feedback can be provided in a case where the command must be completed.

Commands from Menus and Menus from Commands

A good menu-driven system allows direct command entry, even if the command keyed is not a menu option on the current screen. Direct command entry will work only if menu choices cannot be confused with commands. Where menu choices are numbers, no confusion is possible as long as all commands are alphabetic.

Figure 7.11 is an example of a menu screen explicitly allowing command entry. If a system maintains menu-driven and command-driven modes, entering a command from a menu screen should shift the system directly to the command-driven mode.

Figure 7.9: Ordered Options with Numbered Alternative

```
┌─────────────────────────────────────────────────────────────────────┐
:                                                                     :
: ------------------------------------------------------------------- :
Find:  1.  Name:     Personal or other name
       2.  Title:    Exact title
       3.  SUbject:  Exact subject
       4.  TTerm:    Any portion of title
       5.  SUTerm:   Any portion of subject
       6.  CAll:     Call number
       7.  More:     More finding options
Enter number or command:4
└─────────────────────────────────────────────────────────────────────┘
```

Figure 7.10: Response Screen from Figure 7.9

```
┌─────────────────────────────────────────────────────────────────────┐
You keyed: 4 FIND TTERM
Please complete the Title Term search below
-----------------------------------------------------------------------

A Title Term can be any phrase occurring within a title.

"Find tterm economic crisis" will retrieve any title containing the phrase
"economic crisis".
:                                                                     :
:                                                                     :
: ------------------------------------------------------------------- :
Other options:     Help                        Quit
                   STart over                  Backup
Command: Find TTerm _
└─────────────────────────────────────────────────────────────────────┘
```

Figure 7.11: Menu Screen with Explicit Command Alternative

```
:                                                          :
:                                                          :
Key a number and press [RETURN] to search by:

    1      Name of a person
    2      Title
    3      Subject
    4      Series
    5      Call number
    6      Name of corporation or conference

or enter a direct search or any other command.

HELP and QUIT always work.

Choice or command:_
```

If a system has both menus and commands, menus should be available from the command-driven mode on request or when apparently needed. In other words, it should be as easy to "back down" from command to menu mode as it is to move up from menus to commands. A good system will always display option sets in any case, making this assertion an inherent part of the design.

SYNTAX AND PARSING: UNDERSTANDING COMMANDS

A good command language uses familiar terms and syntax. A good language does not require prior training or trap occasional users, but it does reward experience and encourage fast, effective use.

Commands should be imperative sentences with as much flexibility for word order as possible. If the system can assume a particular verb without any ambiguity, it should do so. Thus, for example, if a screen shows multiple numbered search results and a patron keys 4, the system should be able to infer *display* as an implicit verb, acting as though the patron had keyed DISPLAY 4.

The Standard Command Language

The proposed Standard Command Language, dpZ39.58, offers a good model syntax for command-driven patron access systems. The syntax used in the proposed language, discussed in Chapter 4, is a familiar one already used in most command-driven systems. Commands consist of a verb (one or more letters) and an object. The object may consist of a single term, a combination of an index name and a term, or two or more terms or index/term combinations connected by Boolean operators or other qualifiers. That simple, straightforward syntax appears to offer a good combination of terseness, flexibility and clarity.

A good command language accepts abbreviations as well as words.

The commands that follow are all taken from the draft Standard Command Language and illustrate the syntax and some of the verbs. Required portions of verbs appear in CAPITALS. Optional portions appear in lower case, as do objects.

EXPlain subject heading
STOp
CHOose scores, recordings
FINd ti radiation not ti solar
FINd su (catalog or catalogue) and library
BACk 5
SCAn au orwell
RELate educational counseling
DISplay 1–3 short
PRInt 5–12 au,ti,su
SORt ti pd
SHOw cost

The standard also calls for single-letter abbreviations to be acceptable when they are not ambiguous. Of the verbs illustrated above, *B, C, F* and *P* would be acceptable synonyms for *BACk, CHOose, FINd* and *PRInt. D* is not a synonym for *DISplay* because of two other verbs, *DELete* and *DEFine.*
    The verbs above are all familiar, but the effect of some may not be obvious. BACK steps backward through sets of results or other lists, either by a specified number of items or pages or by a default amount. The equivalent command to move forward is MORE. RELATE asks for terms logically related to the object. SCAN in equivalent to BROWSE

in some systems. It provides access to a heading file or to some other list of search terms and allows free movement within that list or file.

Punctuation and Case

A good command language does not depend on punctuation or case for normal operation, but it may use distinctive punctuation for speed.

New users should be able to separate command elements with blanks. Users should not be penalized for forgetting (or not knowing) the rules for equal signs, slashes, commas or other normal punctuation. Truncation and command chaining (discussed below) should use punctuation that does not normally appear in text. Just as the parser should generally ignore punctuation, commands should never be dependent on uppercase or lowercase keying. Requiring specific capitalization adds a needless burden to keying.

The following commands should all do exactly the same thing:

FIND TI SU BEHAVIOR
Find TI,SU BEHAVIOR
fin ti,SU Behavior
f   su   ti   behavior

In each case, the system should retrieve items with *behavior* (with or without capital letters) in either a title or subject, assuming that the system defines *ti* as a title word index and *su* as a subject word index. That insensitivity to case, multiple blanks, use of commas and capitalization is specified in the proposed Standard Command Language. The proposal does require some blanks. The commands FTI,SUB-EHAVIOR and *fti su behavior* are not acceptable because the parts of the command are not separated.

The proposed Standard Command Language is not perfect and may be refined before it is adopted. Three symbols are defined for specific uses, at least two of which may cause difficulties:

- The semicolon is used to separate stacked or chained commands. For example, FIN AU PYNCHON, THOMAS;DIS ALL LON would find works by Thomas Pynchon and proceed to show them in a long display. Few patrons will use chained commands, and semicolons do appear in text. As a result, patrons may key semicolons as part of search arguments. This book recommends the reverse slash \ as a better separator for chained commands, since it is not likely to appear in text. The proposed standard uses the reverse slash as an abbreviation for *not*.

- The question mark is used as a truncation symbol. DIAGNOS? will match any word beginning *diagnos*. This choice has two problems. First, question marks do appear in text. Second, the question mark has a standard use among millions of microcomputer users, but it represents a single character mask, not a truncation symbol. This, DIAGNOS? would be expected to match *diagnose* but not *diagnosis*. The common truncation symbol for microcomputer users is the asterisk, which is also used for truncation in several existing online systems.
- The pound sign # is used as a single-character wildcard or masking symbol. WOM#N will match *woman* and *women*. Pound signs rarely occur in text, so this usage may not pose problems. However, the question mark may be a more widely used symbol for single-character masking. While question marks appear in text, they never appear in the middle of a word.

These problems are explained as examples of the thought required in designing a command syntax. They are not meant as criticisms of the proposed Standard Command Language.

Flexible Order

A command language should accept portions of a command in any order if the meaning is not ambiguous.

A command language should be able to treat DIS MED 1–4 and DIS 1–4 MED as equivalent commands. A preferred order should be used in all examples and training material, but a system should be able to carry out a command that can have only one meaning.

Consistency

A good command language is consistent throughout the patron access system.

Verbs and modifiers should have the same meaning and the same syntax should be used throughout the system. That permits a patron to enter any command from any point and speeds learning because patrons can keep using the same patterns.

Synonyms

A sophisticated patron access system may be able to accept synonyms for commands or index names, but synonyms may be more troublesome than useful.

An online catalog that conforms to the Standard Command Language could conceivably accept any or all of the options in Figure 7.12. A system that accepts synonyms is more user-friendly because a patron can begin by using a familiar vocabulary. Use of synonyms can also cause problems. Few word pairs in English are precise synonyms and the same word may be a plausible synonym for two different command verbs. If a patron uses a synonym, the system should have some way to display the standard verb, but must also display what was actually keyed. Finally, no recognized synonym can ever be used to define a new function or a new index.

Figure 7.12: Possible Synonyms for Verbs and Index Names

```
VERB OR INDEX        POSSIBLE SYNONYMS

DISplay              View, See, [name of display without verb]
FINd                 Get, Search, Locate, [name of index without verb]
HELp                 ?
SCAn                 Browse
MORe                 Forward, +, Next
BACk                 Previous, -

AUthor               NAme, PErson
SUbject              TOpic, ABout
```

Chaining Commands

Patrons should be able to issue a sequence of commands at one time, using a distinctive symbol to separate them.

Chaining and *stacking* both refer to the process by which several commands may be entered as a group, with the system carrying the commands out in sequence. Most patrons may never need or use command chaining, but the technique can be useful for experienced patrons who wish to skip past certain displays in order to complete work faster.

Accidental chaining will confuse patrons, particularly if the accident turns an otherwise good command into an error. If the symbol used for chaining is also found in text, this can happen. For example, if the forward slash separates chained commands, the search FIND TITLE MORNINGSTAR/EVENINGSTAR (where *Morningstar/Eveningstar* is the name of a book) may result in a message such as EVENINGSTAR: *Not a recognized command.*

Simple miskeying may cause problems with any symbol, but some symbols are more troublesome than others. The semicolon, used by Dialog and recommended in the draft Standard Command Language, shares a key with the colon on most keyboards and looks much like a colon. Semicolons may not be very common in searches, but colons will be. When the search FIND TITLE THE 80'S; A LOOK BACK results in an error message A LOOK BACK: *Not a recognized command,* the patron may need help to understand what has happened.

The best symbol to separate commands is one that neither appears in text nor shares a key with a character that appears in text. Ideally, the symbol should have some mnemonic value—it should look like a connector or separator. The two best possibilities, characters that share a key on most keyboards, are the vertical bar | and the backslash \. The vertical bar is commonly used to mean *OR* in Boolean logic, making the backslash a better choice.

If a chain of commands fails because a command is incorrect or inappropriate, the screen should show the results of successful commands and present the remaining commands for editing. If the final command is redundant, it should be ignored.

Miskeying within chained commands should be handled as gracefully as possible. The chain FIND TITLE WAR AND PIECE\ DISPLAY ALL BRIEF will fail because the library has no items titled "war and piece." A system might show the search with no results and offer *DISPLAY ALL BRIEF* for editing, or might offer the complete chain for editing given the point at which failure occurred. The complete chain of commands offers the patron more flexibility.

If a library has *Patron Access: Issues for Online Catalogs* and provides automatic single-record display when a search retrieves a single item, the chain FIND TITLE PATRON ACCESS: IS-SUES?\DISPLAY ALL should *not* be treated as a failure. DISPLAY ALL may be meaningless, but can be ignored without causing difficulty. In this case, "ALL" is a single result and the system displays that automatically—but since the system is doing what the patron has asked for, there is no reason to suggest any problem.

COMMAND ERRORS

Patrons should be able to edit commands that fail.

If screen design places executed commands near the top of the screen and uses the bottom of the screen to accept new commands, failed commands (and partially failed commands) should appear in both places. Figure 7.13 shows a possible example and also shows some of the difficulty of editing support. This is not recommended as an example of good design.

An advanced patron access system may be able to correct some command errors but any corrections may reduce the patron's sense of control. Many command problems arise from differences in vocabulary or incomplete commands. Advanced parsing routines, possibly involving elements of artificial intelligence, may be able to derive valid commands from a wide variety of keyed commands.

Figure 7.13: Possible Command Editing Screen

```
Your command: FIMD TITLE FOUNDATION'S EDGE*              PARSE ERR
begins with FIMD -- not recognized as a command or index name.
Please edit and resend or key a new command.
------------------------------------------------------------------
:                                                                :
:                                                                :
The left and right arrow keys may be used to move the cursor.
Use DEL to delete characters or BACKSPACE to delete previous characters.
Key characters to insert new text.
Press ESC key to escape from current command and start over.

------------------------------------------------------------------
Command: _fimd title foundation's edge*
```

The error in Figure 7.13 is simple misspelling. A patron access system could easily make the correction displayed in Figure 7.14. That level of correction, involving a dictionary of command terms and some type of phonetic or spelling-similarity analysis routine, may be desirable.

Figure 7.15 represents another simple correction, one that may also be desirable. The assumption here may not be correct for a catalog that uses the Standard Command Language. The patron may wish to see titles in the alphabetic vicinity of ROOTS; the proper verb may be SCAN rather than FIND.

The correction in Figure 7.16 is also fairly simple, but it also involves some assumptions. GET is assumed to be a synonym for FIND, and the system assumes that the patron wants only titles consisting of *foundations edge* with no additional words or subtitle.

Figure 7.14: Error Correction Results

```
Your command: FIMD TITLE FOUNDATION'S EDGE* was interpreted as        BRIEF
  the command  Find Title FOUNDATIONS EDGE*
Result: 1 item                        BRIEF display - Screen 1 of 1
------------------------------------------------------------------------
:                                                                      :
:                                                                      :
```

Figure 7.15: Very Simple Error Correction

```
Your command: TI ROOTS* was interpreted as                            MUL
  the command  Find Title ROOTS*
Result: 20 items                  MULTIPLE display - Records 1 to 7
:                                                                      :
:                                                                      :
```

Figure 7.16: Fairly Simple Error Correction

```
Your command: GET TITLE FOUNDATION'S EDGE was interpreted as          BRIEF
  the command  Find Title FOUNDATIONS EDGE
Result: 1 item                        BRIEF display - Screen 1 of 1
:                                                                      :
:                                                                      :
```

Assumptions become more questionable as the corrections become more ambitious. Figure 7.17 illustrates an attempt to assign missing index names, based on the word *by* in the search string. This level of correction may be too ambitious, although it will usually produce the desired results. The same routines would be able to take MYTHICAL

Figure 7.17: Moderately Complex Error Correction

```
Your command: FIND MYTHICAL MAN MONTH BY BROOKS was interpreted as      MUL
 the command: Find Title MYTHICAL MAN MONTH & Name BROOKS
Result: 2 items                    MULTIPLE display - Records 1 to 2
 :                                                                     :
 :                                                                     :
```

MAN MONTH BY BROOKS, without FIND, and produce the same result.

The example in Figure 7.18 may presume too much, but is still within the capabilities of a moderately sophisticated command parsing system. Future catalogs may have even more sophisticated methods for deriving useful commands from what the patron keys.

When a patron access system corrects a patron's command, it must show the patron the original command and how it was changed.

All these examples have one thing in common: they show the patron what the system is assuming. If the system corrects a command and fails to inform the patron, the system is taking control away from the patron. Even with such feedback, advanced error correction may disturb users, particularly those who fear computers.

Figure 7.18: Complex Error Correction

```
Your command: ANYTHING ABOUT ABRAVANEL? was interpreted as      AUTH
 the command: Find Subject ABRAVANEL *
 :                                                             :
 :                                                             :
```

If a keyed command is ambiguous but falls within a small group of possibilities, the system should note the ambiguity and show the possibilities. Figure 7.19 shows a fairly simple example of an ambiguous command. In this example, the parser has suggested *tterm* as the most likely alternative. The underscore suggests that the cursor might be placed on or immediately after the problem.

At some point, attempts to correct an error or locate possible alternatives will fail. Some patron will key QWERTUIOP as a command, just to see what the system will do. (More probably, some patron will key a variety of obscenities to see what happens.) If a keyed command can't be interpreted at all, it should be presented for editing

Figure 7.19: Ambiguous Command Error

```
Your command: FIND TR ART HISTORY                          PARSE  ERR
requests the TR index, which does not exist.
Please modify the index and resubmit the command, or key another command.
:                                                                       :
:                                                                       :
Title indexes: use at least the capitalized letters
    Title - complete title, truncate with *
    TTerm - any portion of a title
    TWord - one or more words within a title

Command: find tterm_ art history
```

along with a simply nonjudgmental message. If the same command is repeated, the system should present a help screen and eliminate the command.

TRUNCATION

Explicit truncation, signaled by a truncation symbol, should always be supported. Implicit truncation, where no symbol appears, should be avoided except for browsing.

Most online catalogs support truncation, but more use implicit truncation than explicit truncation. *Implicit truncation* views every search as a partial search and *explicit truncation* requires a specific character to mean "and anything else." To use a simple example, FIND WORD CAT will yield items with the word *catalog* if implicit truncation is supported. Without implicit truncation, *catalog* won't be retrieved, but neither will *cats*.

Any catalog that routes some or all searches to browse screens offers the equivalent of implicit truncation, but without the normal dangers of implicit truncation. A search to a browse screen is really a pointer. In a patron access system with browsable subject headings, SCAN SUBJECT CAT will properly yield a screen containing subject headings beginning with *Cat,* whether or not *Cat* itself appears as a subject.

Implicit truncation outside of browse screens involves giving patrons results they may not expect. In the example used here, it makes *cat* nearly useless as a word search, since the vocabulary beginning with those three letters is so large.

> *Explicit truncation poses three problems: it is difficult to learn and understand, truncation characters must be chosen carefully and truncation must be handled consistently in all indexes.*

People find truncation difficult to use and understand. The CLR studies suggest that "truncation is very nearly a universal problem for users."[3] That problem becomes worse if the truncation characters are not chosen carefully. If a truncation character also appears in text, patrons may accidentally issue truncated searches yielding unexpected results. Current systems use the pound sign #, dollar sign $, question mark?, at sign @, plus sign + and asterisk * for truncation, with no one symbol dominating the field. The Standard Command Language uses the question mark for truncation, with the pound sign used to represent any single letter. As discussed earlier, these symbols may be less desirable than others. The asterisk, at sign and pound sign seem least likely to be found in normal text strings.

If certain indexes do not permit truncation, patrons may become totally frustrated by the tool. The worst possible situation uses an explicit truncation symbol in some indexes and treats the same symbol as part of text in other indexes. As a result, a truncated search in certain indexes will yield no result, because no index entries contain the truncation symbol. That combination will trap novices and experts alike and is an example of unusually poor design.

NOTES

1. Lawrence, Gary S. [and others]. *University of California Users Look at Melvyl: Results of a Survey of Users of the University of California Prototype Online Union Catalog.* Berkeley, CA: Division of Library Automation; 1983 June 3. p. 122.

2. Borgmann, Christine L. "Psychological Factors in Online Catalog Use, or Why Users Fail." *Training Users of Online Public Access Catalogs.* Washington, DC: Council on Library Resources; 1983 July 23–24. p. 27.

3. *Using Online Catalogs.* Joseph R. Matthews; Gary S. Lawrence; Douglas K. Ferguson, eds. New York: Neal-Schuman; 1983. p. 132.

8

Feedback and Help

A patron access system should provide enough feedback to keep patrons informed and in control, but it should not drown them in excessive feedback. Some forms of feedback such as signposts, echoing, menus and option sets have already been considered; this chapter considers some other forms of feedback, namely, prompting for the most likely next step, search amplification and help screens or windows.

GENERAL PRINCIPLES OF FEEDBACK

A good patron access system responds to all commands, menu choices and function keys. The nature and extent of that response helps to determine the quality of patron access.

Feedback can be defined as all messages provided by the system in response to user input, other than search results. Some of the design guidelines for MELVYL, the intercampus partial online catalog of the University of California, serve as a good introduction to feedback issues:

> The user should always be able to understand the results of a request and what actions can be taken next. System responses should be consistent. Similar requests should always have similar results. The user must not be frustrated by lack of response or burdened with too much explanation. Brief messages should be limited to a line or two; fuller explanations should fit on one screen. System messages should be clear, concise, and informative; they should be neither intimidating nor condescending. Specialized library or computer jargon should be avoided.[1]

Placement and Consistency

Feedback should always be present and should always appear in the same area of the screen.

Many patron access systems (and most illustrations in this book) put feedback at the top of the screen, with options and command lines at the bottom. Some analysts believe that command lines make more sense at the top and that feedback should be close to the command lines. Whatever placement is chosen, it should be consistent so that the patron can predict where information will appear and can ignore unnecessary information.

Consistent placement need not mean wholly consistent size. The feedback section or window can change size as needed. Moving from a screen with 3 areas of 3 lines, 15 lines and 6 lines respectively to another with 5 lines, 14 lines and 5 lines should not disrupt the patron's confidence or concentration as long as the areas are still in the same order and contain all the necessary information.

Display Labels and Status Lines

Every display should be identified by a term in the upper right or lower right corner. This identification will help patrons find their way through a system and describe problems if any should arise. Some patron access systems include a status line within the feedback area or at the bottom of the screen; Figure 8.1 illustrates such a status line. While the illustration is simpler than some, the information shown is typical. Except for the name of the screen, the contents of the status line do not help the patron while using the online catalog.

A status line may be helpful, however, when patrons produce listings that consist of screen images. If patrons gather citations from several different systems at different times, the date, time and system identification can help them track down the source of a listing.

Figure 8.1: Simple Status Line

```
:                                                                    :
:                                                                    :
Terminal A401      Patron Access      02/08/88 12:57 pm      Screen: STARTING
```

Brevity and Clarity

Feedback should be crisp, except when help is asked for. While coded error messages are undesirable, a single phrase is almost always clearer than a multiline sentence or paragraph.

Some feedback is too terse, some feedback is too wordy. An overly terse version of the boxed statement above is *Keep it short.* An overly verbose version would go on for pages.

Consider the problem of telling patrons how to use truncation when building a subject search. The examples that follow show five different ways to explain this process:

1. Add * to truncate.
2. Key a * to retrieve all subjects beginning with your search. Example: COMPUTER*.
3. Key a * after your search unless you are keying a complete subject heading and only want to retrieve that heading.
4. If you are unsure of the complete form of the subject heading you wish to search, or wish to search for all subject headings beginning with your search, you may add an asterisk (*) at the end of your search. The asterisk means "and anything that follows."
5. Subject searches may use explicit right truncation in order to broaden the scope of the search. An asterisk keyed at the end of a search will cause the system to accept any subjects that begin with the search, no matter what text follows the searched string. Thus, right truncation will retrieve all subject subdivisions for your search, as well as the subject itself. Right truncation may result in a slower search, but unless you are sure of the exact form of a subject heading, you should use it.

The first version will mystify new patrons. The last version is much too long to serve as part of a prompt for completing a subject search, though some statement along the same lines might be useful to EXPLAIN * or EXPLAIN TRUNCATE. The second or third version, has better wording, and will serve libraries better than either extreme.

Libraries that listen to their users have discovered some problems with excessive feedback and prompting. "Originally, prompts appeared at the beginning of each search, but these turned out to be too wordy, bored patrons, and slowed down experienced patrons, staff, and the system. Help nessages are now used instead with a minimum number of prompts."[2] While some feedback should always be present, it is possible to present too much.

Feedback should be clear and unambiguous. A patron should always know why feedback has appeared, what the message is trying to say and how to respond to the message.

Clear feedback requires careful design. Messages should be studied for their open and hidden meanings, for vocabulary level and for the balance between clarity and brevity.

Feedback from Menus

When a system allows numbered menu choices and keyed commands, feedback should include the number and its textual equivalent. Figure 8.2 shows a possible response from a menu choice, where 3 was the choice to search subjects. The choice 3, which could have been keyed as FIND SUBJECT, is displayed as an echoed command on the top line along with the message that accompanied it on the preceding menu. The command equivalent FIND SUBJECT appears as the beginning of a new command. The middle of the screen offers brief advice and examples to help the patron complete the command.

The clear virtue of this form of feedback is that it maintains a consistent command model of the catalog. Menus are presented as "training wheels" and are easy to ignore after the first few searches. As patrons complete the command in Figure 8.2, they become accustomed to the faster, more direct command form. Some would argue that this type of system is less user friendly than a more conversational, heavily prompted model. A different view of user friendliness, one assumed in

Figure 8.2: Possible Command Feedback from Menu Choice

```
Your choice: 3 Subject Search                                           SUBSRCH
Fill in the subject desired on the Command: line.
------------------------------------------------------------------------------
:                                                                             :
:                                                                             :
Add a '*' after your search unless you are keying a complete subject.
Example:  find subject archeology* -- to find all subject headings beginning
    with "archeology"
------------------------------------------------------------------------------
Key your text at the flashing line.  Use arrows to edit.
Press [ENTER] when done.  You may key a new command at any point.
Command: find subject _
```

this book, is that user-friendly systems help the user to become more powerful.

PROMPTING

Prompting is a special form of feedback, offering an action as a prekeyed command string or as a highlighted option. When a prompted command appears, all the patron needs to do is press ENTER.

Prompting the Most Likely Action

A patron access system should prompt the action most likely to be taken next, when such an action can be determined.

Prompting the most likely action saves time and keystrokes and leads the patron toward desired results. The problem with such prompting is determining the most probable next action. Some cases are reasonably clear-cut. For example, if a search retrieves more than a screenful of items and the first response is a screen that gives only the size of the result, chances are that the patron will want to view the result. *Display all brief,* or some equivalent prompt, will accommodate most patrons. Displayed options may include brief instructions on narrowing the search. Similarly, once the first screen has been displayed, *More* becomes a natural prompt.

Most cases aren't that well defined. Should a system always offer some prompt, or should a prompt appear only when a "most likely" action seems reasonably clear? The former decision, to always offer a prompt, yields a consistent access system but may mean prompting a choice with little to recommend it.

Prompting the Authorized Form

Where authority files are available and a patron has searched for an alternate form, the system should prompt for the form used by the library but should not automatically search that form and display the result.

Patrons who key one name and retrieve another may not understand where the result came from. Unexpected search results usually happen when a system maintains an internal authority file and uses that file to redirect searches automatically. As will be discussed in Chapter 9, a more sensible result of a name search is a browsable heading screen. When an alternate form has been entered, the screen should show an appropriate cross-reference to the form actually used by the library—the *authorized form*.

The next action seems highly probable whether or not the search leads to a browsable heading screen. Most probably, the patron will choose to retrieve items based on the authorized form. With a browsable heading screen, a system may either provide a prompt at the bottom of a screen full of headings, highlight the authorized entry as referred to from the search entry with an appropriate option to search the highlighted line, or prompt the number of the authorized form on the command line. In any case, the patron need only press ENTER in order to retrieve items for the authorized form.

Prompting for Related Works

Patrons should have easy ways to search for items with the same subject, author, series or uniform title as a displayed item.

Experienced library users will look up a known book in order to find subject headings by which to search for unknown books; the same technique can work for author or series searching. Several patron access systems offer ways to search for related works, but not as prompted actions. At least one patron access system offers the option of "finding items like this one." This is a form of next-action prompting, but it can be ineffective because of the ambiguity surrounding the term "like."

The problem with offering a search for related works as a prompt is that most items have several access points, any of which may be "like" that item. One crude solution is to take the first subject entry and perform a subject search. But are all books with the same first subject entry necessarily "like" each other?

Clever designers and analysts may be able to find some potential for next-action prompting to search for related works, but there are some pitfalls.

Overriding a Prompt

Prompts should be suggestions, not requirements. A user must always be able to override a prompted command.

A forced prompt is a way of taking a patron through two screens for the price of one and should have no place in any modern patron access system. When the system requires that a patron take a specific step, the system seizes control from the patron. No screen should *require* that a patron press ENTER rather than keying a new command. Forced actions make sense in some tutorials but have no place within a patron access system.

EXPLAINING SEARCH RESULTS

Detailed messages explaining the results of searches can overwhelm the user but should be available on request. Too much explanation may be worse than none at all.

Frequently, the patron access system has more information about a search than just the number of items finally retrieved. Systems that give patrons all available information may generate excessive feedback that slows down patrons and confuses rather than enlightens. On the other hand, explanations of search results can help patrons to understand complex searches or to evaluate the results of a search.

The work *communist* will probably appear in names, subjects, series and titles. It may also appear in entries for films, books, sound recordings (of several varieties) and other types of material. Displays that show the items retrieved for each type of material and those that show occurrences in each field or index may be useful. A display combining the two types could require two or three screens and give more information than a patron can handle.

Expanding Boolean Search Results

Expanded results for Boolean searches provide too much information for most patrons.

Most people find Boolean searching difficult. Expanded results, showing the results of each part of a Boolean search, may help to explain what happens in a Boolean search. Unfortunately, such expansion requires more computer power and will result in long, complex displays for any Boolean search involving more than two terms.

Several patron access systems provide expanded information during the course of a Boolean search. Figures 8.3 through 8.7 show portions of screens from existing systems. Each example works in a way that is different from the others, and each has its own problems.

Figure 8.3 gives flawed information. Read literally, the display implies that the search S = LIFE would retrieve five items, a highly unlikely result. The display is almost certainly saying that only five items have *california* and *pioneer* as subject words, and that all five of those have *california* and *pioneer* and *life*. This is very different information. As displayed, this expansion is wrong and misleading. Expanded results for Boolean searches must be stated accurately to avoid misleading patrons.

Figure 8.3: Boolean Explanation, First Example

```
Enter your search here: S=CALIFORNIA PIONEER LIFE

SUBJECT:  CALIFORNIA                        141 matches
          PIONEER                           5 matches
          LIFE                              5 matches

Type "L" for a brief List or "D" for a Detailed display:
  :                                                        :
  :                                                        :
```

Figure 8.4 combines two forms of feedback. It expands the Boolean search and also shows results by index for each term. It provides correct information and a great deal of it. The problems with the display are twofold. First, it uses arcane symbols and repetitive information. Second, it simply provides too much information for most patrons. For some specialized uses, however, Figure 8.4 might be considered an excellent form of feedback.

Figure 8.5 demonstrates several problems, among them anthropomorphism and cuteness. It also fails to complete the process— what happened to *states?* The leading zeros in the results seem poor as well, but at least the actual expansion is correct. Taken as a whole, the display is confusing. If the system changed the order of words for a quicker search, then why does it say *UNITED is a long one?* Most patrons do not care how a search is done, as long as it is done. The second line of Figure 8.5 is pointless, except as yet another way of filling time while the system grinds away. The fact that two lines out of six serve as apologies for the system suggests either performance problems or compulsive chattiness, neither of which is appropriate for an online catalog.

Figure 8.6 provides correct information, but the second line from the top and the last line assume that the patron is thoroughly familiar with Boolean logic. A patron access system that informs a patron that *ANDS were assumed for missing Boolean operators* is making some surprising assumptions about the patron. Most patrons will not understand Boolean logic or will understand it vaguely; therefore, the jargon of Boolean searching should not be part of system displays. The suggestion to AND WITH ADDITIONAL WORD(S) OR USE LIMITING COMMAND TO REDUCE SEARCH RESULTS will leave all but the most expert users stumped. My first reaction to the line was "and what?" Only after looking closely for a verb did I conclude that *and* is the verb in the first clause.

And is not a verb in any common (nontechnical) dictionary, not even in those dictionaries that recognize its use as a logical operator.

Figure 8.4: Boolean Explanation, Second Example

```
IR? weather forecasting satellites
Name/Series      a$WEATHER        360
Title            t$WEATHER        511
Subject          s$WEATHER        883
S01    Keyword:WEATHER                  00:06  1338 Records  (08662)
Name/Series      a$FORECASTING      6
Title            t$FORECASTING    173
Subject          s$FORECASTING    815
S02    Keyword:FORECASTING               00:09   845 Records  (07817)
Name/Series      a$SATELLITES       3
Title            t$SATELLITES      66
Subject          s$SATELLITES     490
S03    Keyword:SATELLITES                00:10   516 Records  (07301)
S04    (S01 AND S03)                     00:11    36 Records  (07265)
S05    WEATHER FORECASTING SATELLITES    00:11    16 Records  (07249)
:                                                                     :
:                                                                     :
```

Figure 8.5: Boolean Explanation, Third Example

```
>UNITED STATES TENNIS
I am changing the order of your words for a quicker search...
TENNIS 00045 BOOKS
patience--UNITED is a long one...
TENNIS + UNITED 00004 BOOKS
PREPARING YOUR DISPLAY--HOLD ON...
:                                                   :
:                                                   :
```

Figure 8.6: Boolean Explanation, Fourth Example

```
>AT AMERICAN LIBRARY ASSOCIATION
ANDS WERE ASSUMED FOR MISSING BOOLEAN OPERATORS
3806   RECORD MATCHES AFTER TERM AMERICAN
 272   RECORD MATCHES AFTER TERM LIBRARY
 252   RECORDS MATCHED THE SEARCH
TYPE KI 1-20 TO DISPLAY FIRST 20 RECORDS (or)
AND WITH ADDITIONAL WORD(s) OR USE LIMITING COMMAND TO REDUCE SEARCH RESULTS
```

Presenting it as a verb indicates excessive use of jargon, even for most technical discussions. Using *or* in the same sentence—but this time as a conjunction, not a verb—compounds the problem. Taken as a whole, the message serves to convince patrons that they are not sophisticated enough to use the catalog. (The messages also suffer from excessive use of capitalization, making the display in Figure 8.6 hard to read.)

Figure 8.7 is both terse and correct, but it presents information in an odd sequence. It also uses the term *Boolean logic* needlessly and presents all feedback in capital letters. Expanded result information should be presented in a logical order. Figure 8.7 could be significantly improved with a few simple changes that are reflected in Figure 8.8.

Figure 8.7: Boolean Explanation, Fifth Example

```
CURRENT SEARCH bro su california industry
TOTAL SEARCH RESULTS - 56
BOOLEAN LOGIC - 1&2
    CALIFORNIA        TERM APPEARS IN 5701 SUBJECT HEADINGS
    INDUSTRY          TERM APPEARS IN 1922 SUBJECT HEADINGS
```

Figure 8.8: Boolean Explanation, Modified Version of Fifth Example

```
Current Search: BRO SU CALIFORNIA INDUSTRY

The term CALIFORNIA    appears in 5701 subject headings
The term INDUSTRY      appears in 1922 subject headings

The terms CALIFORNIA INDUSTRY appear in 56 subject headings
```

The examples in Figures 8.3 through 8.7 do not exhaust ways of presenting expanded information for Boolean searches, but they do show the problems that arise. Carefully designed result information can be useful as a form of assistance. Patrons using word indexes or combining author and title searches will probably generate Boolean searches without knowing that they are doing so. In such cases, any use of the term *Boolean* will confuse patrons, and the extensive feedback required to expand a three-term or four-term search will overwhelm them. Full expansions, where the results of each term and each combination appear, may also require substantially more computer power than is needed to produce the final result.

Dynamic Count of Results

A count of retrieved items, displayed while a search is in progress, may help patrons to avoid difficult searches. Such a count is most useful if patrons have an easy way to interrupt a long search.

At least one current patron access system displays a changing number (a count of retrieved items) as a search is in progress. If that number is clearly explained, it can alert a patron that the search is too general or involves too much work. It also tells the patron that the computer is doing something. When patrons accidentally issue bad searches, they should be able to stop the searches using some function key, preferably one that is shown as a command option or next to the changing number.

Result Summary by Index or Field

A display showing the number of items retrieved through each index or field, for a search involving multiple indexes or fields, can help some patrons use the results. Figure 8.4 provides results by index as well as by expanding the Boolean search. Figure 8.9 shows another way of displaying results by field or index. In this case, the Word index retrieves items from several specific indexes: NAme, TItle, SUbject and SEries. The display shows the specific results and permits the patron to choose which ones to see.

Result summaries by index or field pose two problems. First, as with other explanations of results, the summaries add another screen and require another command to display actual results. Second, result summaries may pose problems with system consistency.

Figure 8.9: Functional Index Expansion Screen

```
Your command: FIND WORD COMMUNIST                               SUMMARY
finds results in several different fields.
-----------------------------------------------------------------------


The word COMMUNIST appears in:

 #   FIELD       RESULT

 1.  Name            62 Names
 2.  Title        > 500 Titles    (more than 500)
 3.  Subject      147 Subjects
 4.  Series         22 Series
 5.  All         > 500 Items



_____
NEXT ACTIONs: Key one or more numbers or field names to select fields.
              AND to add more words to your search
              HELP for more information
              [ENTER] to display all items retrieved

Command: ALL_
```

---

*A result summary should not be presented when a search
yields a single result or when the patron cannot act on the
information.*

The logic of absolute consistency requires that any multiple-index
search or multiple-field index return a result summary, even if the
search retrieves only one item. A counterargument is that absolute
consistency and foolish consistency are essentially the same thing.
When the total result is one item, any intermediate screen wastes the
patron's time and does not serve anyone well.

Result Summary by Type of Material

---

*A display showing how many books, sound recordings, films,
etc., were found for a search will help patrons looking for
specific materials. Such a display should appear only if the
search retrieves more than one type of material.*

Figure 8.10 shows a possible result summary, showing results by
type of material. For most libraries and most patrons, such a summary
will be more helpful than any other search explanation.

A patron who wants to borrow the Beatles film *Help!* on videocassette will probably not be satisfied with the sound recording, a book about the film or a 16mm film. A patron looking for Beethoven's Fifth Symphony on compact disc is unlikely to have any interest in the musical score. On the other hand, a patron doing research on Martin Luther King will be interested in the fact that a library has 2 cassettes and 3 videocassettes with *King, Martin Luther, Jr.* as an entry, as well as 20 books.

A summary by type of material should be as specific as the library's own information. Figure 8.10 shows only one line for videocassettes; if a library has Beta, VHS and 8mm cassettes, separate lines for each type may be appropriate. Any summary by type of material should include only positive results. The lines below do not serve a patron well:

#	FORMAT	ITEMS
1.	Books	2
2.	Periodicals	0
3.	LP Records	0
4.	Compact Discs	0
5.	Cassette Tapes	0
6.	Musical Scores	0
7.	Videocassettes	1
8.	Computer Files	0

Figure 8.10: Possible Material Format Breakdown

```
Your command: FIND NAME BACH, JOHANN SEBASTIAN                    SUMMARY
retrieves 2326 items in several formats.
-----------------------------------------------------------------------


Items available include:

#   FORMAT          ITEMS

1.  Books            423
2.  LP Records      1209
3.  Compact Discs    257
4.  Cassette Tapes   403
5.  Musical Scores    22
6.  Videocassettes    12


NEXT ACTIONs: Key one or more numbers to select formats.
             AND to add more words to your search
             HELP for more information
             [ENTER] to display all items retrieved

Command: ALL_
```

The pertinent information—that the library has two books and one videocassette satisfying the search—is lost in the list of formats with no results.

HELP AND EXPLANATIONS

Patrons should be able to ask for assistance at any point while using an online catalog. The first level of assistance should come from the online catalog itself.

Patrons can become confused while searching, or they may want to know more about some aspect of a patron access system. Most libraries will not have librarians near each public terminal, and many patrons will be reluctant to ask librarians for help. While the assistance offered by a patron access system can never replace help from a librarian completely, the system should be able to satisfy many requests for help.

Feedback, displayed options and other messages discussed earlier all work to keep the patron informed and in control. The services discussed here appear when patrons ask for them or when patrons make the same mistake repeatedly.

Forms of assistance should include context-sensitive help, explanations of any part of the system and information about the current searching session.

Using the command words in the proposed Standard Command Language, the three forms of assistance can be summarized as follows:

- HELP provides assistance or instruction specifically related to what the patron is doing at the time. In other words, HELP is context-sensitive.
- EXPLAIN provides information about an aspect of the patron access system. EXPLAIN TITLE should provide a brief tutorial on the TITLE index, and EXPLAIN EXPLAIN should tell the patron how EXPLAIN works.
- SHOW provides information on the state of the search session. SHOW SEARCH should repeat the current search. If a patron can restrict all searching to certain forms of material, SHOW FORMATS should show the list of formats selected.

The verbs HELP, EXPLAIN, and SHOW may not be inherently superior to any other alternatives, but will be used throughout the rest of this chapter to provide a known vocabulary. The three categories viewed as a group are called *aid,* as in *aid text* or *aid screens.*

Aid text should be prepared as carefully as other messages and should be consistent with other messages.

Whether aid text appears as a full screen or as a window opening up within an existing display, it must adhere to the same criteria as other text and follow these guidelines:

- Be concise, preferably less than 600 characters long.
- Be clear, direct and positive, keeping the patron in control.
- Avoid library or computer jargon.
- Use the same terminology as the rest of the access system.
- Avoid anthropomorphism (the catalog isn't an "I").
- Be nonjudgmental and do not assume that the patron is in trouble.
- Do not talk down to the user.
- Avoid excessive humor.

Surprisingly often, patron access systems with clear, terse feedback fill every line of HELP and EXPLAIN screens with text. Frequently, the essential information in a screen full of text can be edited into half as many words, assuring faster reading and better understanding. Some aid screens appear as if those writing the screens saw an empty 24-line space and felt compelled to fill it. When those who prepare aid text understand that sparse screens communicate more effectively than full screens, they write briefer text.

Aid screens should be self-contained. No single topic should require more than one screen.

A 24-line screen has room for at least 300 words—about as many as fit on a full page of this book. It should be possible to explain any single topic within a single screen, at least at the level of detail present at a public terminal. A patron should be able to get more information from additional screens, but no single topic should require more than one screen. HELP text should rarely require more than 100 words, or 30% of a full screen.

HELP and EXPLAIN text must be clear and effective. Aid screens should not be afterthoughts, and should be written and edited at least as carefully as other written materials for the catalog.

Windows and Screens

HELP should appear in windows opened within an existing display, if a system can support that feature.

Most existing patron access systems respond to calls for help or explanation by presenting separate assistance screens. A separate screen eliminates any distractions and makes it possible to use fairly long explanations while keeping screen density low.

But clearing the screen removes the existing context. If a user has accidentally pressed a HELP key instead of an adjacent function key, seeing a familiar screen organization replaced by a block of text will be startling, even if the text is clear. Context-sensitive help can be simplified and shortened if the context remains visible.

A window opened in the existing display may take one of three forms:

- A box may open up, partly obliterating other portions of the display, to show the requested information.
- The center segment of the screen may be replaced by the requested information, leaving the top (how the patron got here) and bottom (where the patron can go) unmodified.
- An assistance segment may be added, probably below an abbreviated top segment.

The term "window" is sometimes reserved for the first alternative, a graphic box opening over other information which reveals the other information when it is closed. This technique provides the most obvious indication that the previous display is still available, if patrons actually understand the window overlay.

HELP messages should be short, should relate directly to an existing display and should fit within a three to eight-line window, particularly since part of the existing display will still be available.

EXPLAIN and SHOW messages should use the full screen and follow the same organization as any other screen.

EXPLAIN messages will frequently be much longer than HELP messages and may have nothing to do with the previous display. The context of the display from which EXPLAIN or SHOW was requested may be irrelevant and should have no bearing on the text of the aid screen.

The overall system context should be retained at all times, meaning that EXPLAIN and SHOW displays should be organized into the same three segments as other displays (assuming that displays are organized in three parts). The top segment should be very short but show the keyed command, and the bottom segment should show some possible next actions.

Leaving Aid Screens

Patrons should always be able to press ENTER from an aid screen or window and return to the previous display. Patrons should also be able to key any other command without returning to the previous display.

A surprising number of patron access systems fail to leave aid screens gracefully or consistently. An aid screen is part of the access system but can normally be assumed to be an *interruption* in the flow of control.

Patron access systems can fail in one of two ways. Perhaps the most unsettling is when a system loses track of the patron's place. If a patron is displaying the 45th through 52nd items of a 120-item result and asks for HELP, the patron should be returned to the same 45th through 52nd items—not to the first 7 items in the result, not to the 53rd item, not to a new search prompt and certainly not to some entirely different place in the system.

More commonly, patron access systems fail to maintain consistency. EXPLAIN screens accept commands, but interpret them as requests for more explanations rather than as direct commands. This may make it easy to get more information on a topic, but it makes it more difficult to achieve desired results.

Patrons should be able to get assistance readily. They should also be able to get on with their work rapidly and smoothly.

A patron access system can and should assume that the patron will usually want to return to the previous display. That option should always be offered and should only require pressing ENTER. But it should not be the only option. In some cases, a HELP message or EXPLAIN screen tells the patron enough so that the patron wants to do something different. Carrying out this option should be as straightforward as entering a command from any other display.

Help: Immediate Assistance

HELP should always be available, preferably by pressing a HELP key.

Designers can't always predict the points at which patrons may feel lost or uncertain. A labeled HELP key assures patrons that help is always available. When such a key is present, it should always be active if the keyboard is active. A HELP key reassures; if the patron presses the key and nothing happens, that reassurance turns to frustration.

A keyed question mark *?* or the word *help* should also produce help. The keyed text *help* should work only as a separate command. If a patron keys FIND TITLE and is uncertain what to do next, FIND TITLE HELP is not a reasonable way to get help—it makes the Beatles film and sound recording *Help!* impossible to retrieve by title.

Some relevant HELP message should be available at every point and at every command. That doesn't necessarily mean that the text will relate directly to the actual keystrokes keyed prior to HELP. It does mean that the patron access system should never return messages like *No help available for this screen* or, worse, *No help available*.

Context-sensitive help may be difficult to develop, and it is possible to become too sensitive to context. A HELP request from a title search should relate to title searches, not only to the peculiarities of the particular search request. Good HELP text should allow most patrons to correct their own mistakes, but should not be so specific that it further confuses patrons who are already partly lost. Any HELP screen or window should offer some way to get more information, probably by mentioning the EXPLAIN command or its equivalent.

Repeated mistakes can be interpreted as calls for help.

More than one system also provides a context-sensitive HELP message when a user makes the same mistake three times. That technique may even be reasonable after the mistake is made twice. If HELP text appears within the existing display rather than as a replacement for the display, patrons with problems will receive help rapidly, while those who have accidentally keyed the same command twice will not have their work disrupted.

Explain: Online Tutorials

Brief lessons on any aspect of a patron access system should always be available but should never be required.

Most patrons won't go to classes on the catalog. Few patrons will read an extended print tutorial and most don't want an extended online tutorial. Online tutorials provide a critical training mechanism, but must be designed to work with the patron. If possible, tutorials should consist of self-contained screens on specific topics rather than extensive sets of screens where the patron is forced through the series.

Good explanations require sophisticated design. If an online tutorial is simply online access to the printed documentation, it will not serve patrons as well as it should. Writing self-contained screens that link together well and provide as much information (or as little) as the patron needs can be much more difficult than writing good printed tutorials. Written materials can reasonably take several pages to provide a clear explanation of a complex topic. Offering the same information online may require several screens, frustrating and infuriating the patron who wants a quick explanation.

Online tutorials represent little overhead for a system and considerable value for the user. Even if a specific tutorial is used only once or twice a year, it will probably require only as much disk space as one bibliographic record and call for only a single index entry. Good online tutorials offer an inexpensive way to educate users when they want to be educated.

Show: Session Information Screens

Patrons should be able to see a summary of specific information on their current search session. If systems have too few user-selected options to make such a screen useful, it need not be provided.

Most patron access systems will not have many options that patrons can set. A SHOW facility will be more valuable for technical processing and other views of an online system but may also be helpful to patrons.

A SHOW screen can include search results that have been stored, files selected (if patrons can select files), formats selected and any other items that are specific to the patron's session. SHOW might also be used to provide search expansions on request.

NOTES

1. Radke, Barbara S. [and others]. "The User-Friendly Catalog: Patron Access to MELVYL." *Information Technology and Libraries.* 1(4): 1982 December. p. 360.

2. *Training Users of Online Public Access Catalogs.* Washington, DC: Council on Library Resources; 1983 July. p. 51.

9

Retrieval and Browsing

A patron comes to an online catalog with a need for information; sometimes that need is specific, sometimes it is not yet defined. This chapter and the next discuss the ways that a patron access system can help a patron locate that information.

RETRIEVAL

"The catalog should: enable a person to find a book of which either the author, the title, or the subject is known; show what the library has by a given author, on a given subject, or in a given kind of literature; assist in the choice of a book as to its edition—bibliographically, as to its character—literary or topical." [Charles Ammi Cutter, 1876]

Good retrieval requires both *recall*—the ability to find everything needed—and *precision*—the ability to find only what is wanted.

Recall

Recall is the power to find *everything* a patron needs. Patron access systems improve recall by normalizing searches and indexes. Recall is also improved by providing an easy way to find related works. Word indexes that incorporate many fields can also improve recall, as can other expanded indexes.

Normalizing Searches and Indexes

Searches and index entries should be normalized so that patrons need not know the exact capitalizaton, punctuation or special characters used in the bibliographic data. Normalization improves recall by allowing a patron to key text strings without too much concern for precise form. Patron access systems (and the database engines that support them) should incorporate several types of normalization, which are discussed below.

The searches *FIND TITLE MARC for Library Use, find title Marc for library use* and *find title MARC FOR LIBRARY USE* should all be treated as the same search. A search for the word *roots* should retrieve *roots, Roots* and *ROOTS.* In almost every online catalog, users should not have to worry about capitalization when keying a search, or about how an entry is capitalized.

As patron access systems progress, detailed research projects may identify situations in which case-sensitive searching tools would be useful. Even if such situations exist, the possible gain in precision seems far outweighed by the burden that case-sensitive searching and indexing places on the patron.

Punctuation, initial articles and some connective words, and distinctions between upper and lower case should be ignored in searching.

All searches within each numbered group below should be considered identical by the system.

1. Find title the people no different flesh
   find title The People: No Different Flesh
   find title PEOPLE: NO DIFFERENT FLESH
2. FIND TITLE GRAVITYS RAINBOW
   find title Gravity's Rainbow
3. Find title 20,000 Leagues Under The Sea
   find title 20000 leagues under the sea
4. FIND TITLE Gladiator-At-Law
   find title gladiator at law
5. Find Title The Sot-Weed Factor
   Find title Sot Weed Factor
   Find title sotweed factor
6. Find title Waldo & Magic, Inc.
   find title waldo and magic inc
7. Find title THE MOST OF S.J. PERELMAN
   find title the most of sj perelman
   find title most of s.j. perelman

find title most of s j perelman
find title most s.j. perelman

Any competent patron access system will handle the first three examples properly, stripping initial articles and punctuation out of indexed terms and out of searches. The last four examples may pose more difficulties. Examples 4 and 5 show one problem in normalizing punctuation: is a hyphen equivalent to a blank, or to nothing? Ideally, either should be acceptable, but that may mean that the title must be indexed twice—in the fourth example, under both SOTWEED FACTOR and SOT WEED FACTOR.

Example 6 should pose no difficulties for titles in English, but it does create problems for libraries with many foreign language titles. Should an item containing an ampersand be indexed with the ampersand, with *and* in its place and with the proper language equivalent (*et* for French, *und* for German, etc.)? That requires not only three index entries but a proper language-based table to provide the equivalent words.

Periods may pose a problem, as may other punctuation that can be considered equivalent to nothing or to a blank. A patron access system that will find the desired item based on any of the five versions in example 7 provides better recall capabilities than a catalog that fails with some of the versions.

Current cataloging policies solve some of these problems by requiring multiple versions of the same access point. However, retrospective conversion records and records created in earlier years are unlikely to have the multiple access points.

For searching, special characters should be translated to well-understood standard alphabetic equivalents. Diacritics should be ignored.

The ampersand may be the most common special character with an alphabetic equivalent. Other such characters include the slashed o, the thorn, the Greek beta and the *AE* digraph. Public terminals may not have keys for such special characters. Patrons should be able to assume that alphabetic equivalents will retrieve items properly.

One problem is the lack of a single set of standard alphabetic equivalents to special characters. No formal standard exists and no research has been done on existence of a de facto standard—or lack thereof. This problem may be addressed in the near future by the

Technical Standards for Library Automation (TESLA) Committee of ALA's Library and Information Technology Association (LITA), which has begun an investigation into this and other problems of index normalization.

One significant problem can arise when diacritics are ignored in indexes and in searches. Names and titles that contain vowels with umlauts sometimes appear with the umlaut replaced by an *e* following the vowel. If a patron enters a search including the *e*—as in, for example, *Uebersetzung*—the search may fail. The replacement of an umlaut with a trailing *e* is by no means universal and is wrong in many cases, particularly when the mark is not an umlaut but a diaeresis (as over the *e* in *Brontë*).

The problem can be avoided by indexing terms twice, with and without a trailing *e*. No other solution will provide good recall, since patrons may key the added *e* without being aware of its significance.

Searches must be treated in the same way that index entries are treated. Patrons should not be penalized for normalized searches or for exact searches.

Normalization works properly only if the same methods apply to searches and to indexes. If the database engine translates a slash / to a blank when building an index entry, but strips out the slash (not leaving a blank) when processing a search, exact searches will fail. Patrons should never be penalized for keying an exact form. Keying an initial article, using precise capitalization or inserting periods after initials should not cause a search to fail.

Related Works

Patrons should be able to retrieve additional material based on what they find initially. Patrons should be able to retrieve items matching any specified heading or access point within a displayed bibliographic record.

One of the most powerful tools to increase recall is the ability to retrieve related works—items with the same subject heading, series, author or uniform title as a displayed work.

Figure 9.1 shows a display that provides easy retrieval of related works. The command RELATED 3 asks for all items with the subject heading *Eskimos—Canada*. Figure 9.2 is another example, using a traditional cardlike display. FIND SUBJECT 2 will retrieve items with the subject heading *Man—Influence of environment*. In either case, the command could lead to a browsable subject heading display in the area of the subject heading noted, or could lead directly to a multiple-item bibliographic display.

Experienced catalog users have long used a similar technique to locate subjects in a card catalog. If the user knows the title of one book in a field, subject tracings on that card can lead to other books. An online catalog can provide much faster and more powerful retrieval of related works.

Figure 9.1: Bibliographic Display Supporting Related Work Search

```
            FULL DISPLAY              ITEM 1 (OF 1)

     Mowat, Farley.
        People of the deer / Farley Mowat ; drawings by Samuel Bryant -- New York
     Pyramid Books, 1968, c1952.

     PHYSICAL FORM  303 p. : ill. ; 18 cm.
     SERIES         (A Pyramid book.)

     NOTES       LCN: 52005023

     ENTRY     OTHER ENTRIES THAT MAY BE SEARCHED
       1         AUTHOR       Mowat, Farley.
       2         SERIES       A Pyramid book.
       3         SUBJECT      ESKIMOS--Canada

       LOCATION              CALL NUMBER          HOLDINGS
       College Library       E0099 E7 M86         copy 1
         Ethnic Area Rm 3250

     END OF DISPLAY
     ----------------------------------------------------------------
     >RELATED 3
```

Figure 9.2: Display with Related Work Search

```
 Alive man!
 Shepherd, Roy J.
    Alive man!, The physiology of physical activity. / by Roy J. Shephard.
 Springfield, Ill., Thomas, [1972].
    xiv, 607 p. illus. 24 cm.
    Includes bibliographies.
    1. Exercise -- Physiological effect. 2. Man -- Influence of environment.
 3. Physical fitness.
 Call#: QP301.S47
    East Library Second Floor
 - - - - - - - - - - - - - - - - - - - - - - - - - - - - - - - - - - - -
 >>>
 >>> FIN SUB 2
```

Precision

A searching system is precise if it avoids extraneous results.

Precision is the ability to retrieve *only* the items wanted or needed. The primary tools for high precision are sufficient indexes, varied indexes, Boolean search capabilities and the ability to refine an existing search without starting over. Good feedback from the system can also help, as Karen Markey suggests: "OPACs could suggest to searchers, whose input access points result in 100 or more items, to reduce the number of postings by entering another keyword or phrase and combining these results with the results of the previously input search statement."[1]

Two specific capabilities that may also help to improve precision—the ability to narrow searches by MARC fields and the ability to limit searches by coded elements—involve some difficulties and possible dangers.

Narrowing Fields Within Searches

Some patrons in some circumstances can clearly benefit by narrowing the MARC fields on which a search operates. Overly narrow indexes will not serve most patrons well in most circumstances.

Name and title indexes typically include several different fields and may include subfields from quite a few fields. Some systems provide a few large indexes covering many fields. Title indexes frequently include series statements and title portions of added entries. Name indexes may even include personal name subject entries.

Including multiple fields within an index improves recall and makes the system easier to use. Indexes covering single fields or smaller groups improve precision if the fields can be described clearly.

Fields can be described within technical processing in a clear, unambiguous manner: MARC tags. A search statement such as FIND TITLE (240–245) MAKING OF A REVOLUTION or FIND AUTHOR (100) ASIMOV, ISAAC can be as precise or broad as needed, with parenthetical lists of fields applied as part of the searching process.

MARC tags are too obscure for most patron use. The distinction between a main entry and an added entry is always difficult to explain to a patron and MARC tags simply add another layer of jargon. Those indexes that cross *types* of entries should allow limiting, however.

The capability to limit searches by specific MARC tags may not serve patrons. The ability to search only series statements or to exclude them from title searches will serve them, however, if the limits can be expressed clearly. One solution is to provide multiple indexes, where the indexes may actually constitute index limits internally. For example, a search FIND SERIES EARLY AMERICAN IMPRINTS might actually be carried out internally as *find title (400–490, 800–830) early american imprints.*

Limiting Results by Coded Elements

Patrons should be able to limit searches by requiring that items meet certain coded criteria such as language, country of publication and date of publication.

A library should be able to specify certain control fields and other MARC elements that can be used for limiting. Systems typically use one of two methods to limit results, both of which are transparent to the patron. The first method indexes the elements available for limiting; the second scans each record in a result to see whether it matches limiting criteria.

The second method is slower but more flexible. Both methods raise the same problems for a public access system:

- How can limiting elements be specified by patrons not familiar with MARC? Should the specification of coded elements involve internal translations (so a patron's *english* translates to *eng*), a screen full of possible values or some other methodolgy?
- What limiting elements make sense for public terminal support?
- Do the same limiting elements make sense for all forms of material?
- Should options to limit searches appear for every search or only on request, and how extensive should the options be?

Can a patron access system make it easy to retrieve only those recordings of Beethoven's Ninth Symphony that are on compact disc? How can a patron access system support a researcher who needs editions of *Hamlet* produced between 1955 and 1982, in countries other than the United States and England, in languages other than English? The CLR study indicated that "*search limiting features,* including limiting by date, type of material, and other elements, are generally helpful but apparently make the online catalog appear more difficult to master."[2]

For those systems supporting workstations, the problems and questions may be somewhat different. If records derived from searches are sent to workstations in MARC form, workstation users should be able to use any conceivable combination of MARC elements to narrow the result set if they can specify what those elements are.

The best use of search limiting is to reduce a large result set. Limiting should not be offered or performed until a search yields a large result.

One substantial danger with result limiting is overkill. In many cases, a patron will be served better by stepping through a large result set than by stepping through a complex limiting screen before issuing a search. Good sense enters into any design for result limiting. Search limiting makes no sense when an unlimited result includes 10 items, and it makes very little sense when the result includes 25 items or less.

BROWSING OR SCANNING

Most readers would rather browse than search, just as most library patrons want to find material more than they want to use catalogs.

Traditional libraries offer two very different sorts of browsing, each with a special value: browsing the shelf and browsing the catalog. Online catalogs may not offer the same type of browsing that a card catalog offers, but they can provide new and much more useful browsing tools.

Retrieval through browsing is significantly different from retrieval through direct search. On the one hand, the process is slower. First, the patron must enter the browsable file at some point by doing a search. Then, after browsing that file, the patron must take another action to retrieve specific items.

> *Online browsing is slower than direct retrieval, but gives patrons an overview of some aspect of the library in a way that direct retrieval cannot provide.*

A browsable subject file can help patrons understand how subject headings work and help them find narrower, broader or different subject headings that may be appropriate.

Browsing, for this book, is defined as access to an authority or heading file, with the ability to move freely backward or forward in the file. *Scanning* is a synonym for browsing, and SCAN is the verb recommended in the proposed Standard Command Language. In a command-driven system, browsing always begins with a search, possibly using a special verb. Unlike searches that are intended to retrieve items, searches that result in browses never fail. A browse-oriented search acts as a pointer to a file.

Browsing a heading or authority file is not the same as moving back and forth within a large set of results. The two actions may look alike and appear to function alike, but browsing should be open-ended whereas movement within a result set is constrained by the limits of that set. Systems that support subject word access may yield a screen that looks like a subject heading browse, but is actually a set of subject headings derived from a word search. A system may also include an author-title index that, when used, resembles a multiple-item result set but is actually a browsable file. The only clear distinction between the two is that movement within a browse file is limited only by the beginning and end of the alphabet and movement within a result set is limited by the bounds of the results.

Some aspects of browsing discussed below are also relevant for search results, where the results are headings rather than bibliographic items.

> *Browsing isn't the best answer for all retrieval.*

Some systems go too far by making all searches into browses. One system uses any search term only to display an appropriate portion of the proper file. Converting name and subject searches to browse requests may make sense; changing *all* searches into browses handicaps known-item searchers and constricts powerful searching techniques.

Browsing Subject, Name and Series Headings

> *The most valuable and most common browsable files are subject, name and series authority files. Even an online catalog that does not use full authority control should have heading files that can be browsed.*

Some systems send all name and subject searches to browse screens as a first step. This appears to be sensible, although a case can be made for retrieving actual results when a search yields a single heading. Patrons are certainly well served when subject or name searches that yield more than one heading, or those that yield no direct matches, result in a browsable authority screen.

> *Systems that route subject searches to heading files can make patrons aware of relationships among subject headings. Knowing these relationships enables patrons to narrow an overly broad search or widen an overly narrow search.*

Name searches that yield a single name pose a more difficult problem. For consistency, such searches should be routed through a browse screen with the matched name offered as a prompted retrieval. For maximum efficiency, however, the browse screen should probably be skipped completely. Neither solution seems clearly preferable.

> *All subject phrase searches should result in browsable heading screens, as should all name searches yielding no direct match, a reference to an authorized form or more than one match.*

A subject word search is likely to retrieve subject headings from various points within the heading file, which indicates that such a search should probably yield a heading result set. A patron can move back and forth within such a set, and the displays resemble those from a fully browsable file, but movement is limited to headings containing the word or words searched.

Browsing Other Indexes

Patrons can benefit from a browsable title file, which can incorporate series authorities. A browsable class number index might also be useful.

Many titles appear more than once, particularly uniform titles. A browsable title file will look like an authority file, but may not have any cross-references.

Call numbers, either Dewey Decimal or LC, can be a powerful browsing tool, especially if brief descriptions of the classification appear along with the call number range and number of items (postings). A very powerful system could support a hierarchical browse file in an intelligent manner, offering different levels of detail.

Figures 9.3 and 9.4 show two possible screens at the first and second levels of a hierarchical class/call number browsing file. The third level would offer narrower call number ranges. The fourth or fifth level would show actual call numbers, possibly with brief titles attached.

A browsable call number file offers a much more powerful electronic version of a shelf list, and offers a form of "shelf browsing" with the ability to work at any level of abstraction.

Figure 9.3: Hierarchical Class Browse, Top Level

```
You keyed: BROWSE CALL C                                     CLASS:1
Call Number Browse
-----------------------------------------------------------------------
  # CALL #              DESCRIPTION                            ITEMS
 1. C - CT              History: Auxiliary Sciences            12,792
 2. D - DX              History: Europe, Asia, Africa, etc.   221,738
 3. E                   History: US and American Exploration   19,372
 4. F                   History: State, Local, Other Americas  48,520
 5. G - GV              Geography, Anthropology, Recreation     33,461
 6. H - HX              Economics and Social Sciences          146,145
 7. J - JX              Political Science and International Law  37,258
 8. K - KZ              Law                                      3,404
 9. L - LT              Education                               35,256
10. N - NX              Arts                                    49,800
11. P - PZ              Language and Literature                209,647
12. Q - QR              Science                                 67,961
13. R - RZ              Medicine                                   650
14. S - SK              Agriculture                             19,651
-----------------------------------------------------------------------
NEXT ACTIONS    Key:   > # for more detail     ? for Help
                       + for next screen       F to Find something else
                       - for previous screen   Q to Quit
                       Press [ENTER] to perform action shown below
NEXT ACTION: > 1_
```

Figure 9.4: Hierarchical Class Browse, Second Level

```
You keyed: > 1   More detail for Class C-CT                    CLASS:2
Call Number Browse
--------------------------------------------------------------------------
  #   CALL #          DESCRIPTION                                ITEMS
 1. C                 History: General auxiliary sciences            1
 2. CB                History of Civilization and Culture        2,640
 3. CC                Archeology                                    736
 4. CD                Diplomatics, Archives, Seals                  650
 5. CE                Chronology                                    270
 6. CJ                Numismatics                                 1,944
 7. CN                Epigraphy                                     273
 8. CR                Heraldry                                      993
 9. CS                Genealogy                                   2,483
10. CT                Biography                                   2,802
11. D                 General History                            32,754
12. DA                England, Wales, Scotland, Ireland          21,613
13. DB                Austria, Hungary, Austrio-Hungary           9,442
14. DC                France                                     24,469
15. DD                Germany and Prussia                        17,011
--------------------------------------------------------------------------
NEXT ACTIONS    Key:  > # for more detail       ? for Help
                      + for next screen         F to Find something else
                      - for previous screen     Q to Quit
NEXT ACTION:_
```

Number of Items

Browsable heading files should always show the number of items that will be retrieved by each heading.

The number of items shown within a heading file work as relative values, to show what terms have many items attached and what terms represent only a few items. Thus, patrons can use heading files as a guide to determine the headings that might best suit their needs, easing the searching load on the system. In order to be useful, the number of items must be presented in a clear, meaningful way. The term *Items* is a precise name for the number of items and should replace the more common *Postings*.

Cross-References

Browsable heading files should include clearly worded cross-references.

In order to be useful cross-references must be clearly presented and be properly worded. Obviously, *x* and *sa* have no place in an online catalog. *See* and *see also* are better, though far from perfect.

Some recent studies have suggested that a majority of cross-references are redundant or otherwise unnecessary in online catalogs. Such studies make certain assumptions about how people will search online catalogs and seem to find fault in information being available in more than one way. A well-worded cross-reference is useful, however, because it provides specific information about a bibliographic relationship and assures the patron that the relationship is known and intentional.

Presentation of Browsing Screens

Browsing screens may be denser than other screens and should be arranged in columns to make them readable.

Heading and other browsing screens typically involve four or five elements:

- line number for quick searching
- heading or entry
- cross-references, which may have their own following line numbers
- descriptions of the entries for special files such as class indexes
- postings or numbers of bibliographic records that a search on the heading will retrieve

Browsing screens tend to be dense, with one heading on each line where possible. Despite the general argument that no more than seven to nine choices should be available at one time, high density is appropriate for heading files.

Each browsing screen should be numbered from "1."

A browsable index is different from a large result set, and while an argument for continuous numbering may make sense for result sets, it does not seem sensible for browsing.

Continuous numbering requires one of three assumptions for a browsable file. The first assumption, numbering from the start, yields line numbers like *501307,* a clear nuisance for searching from the browse. The second assumption makes the searched entry point *1* and yields negative numbers if the patron asks for previous screens, presumably numbered downward from screen-bottom. The third assumption uses only positive numbers, but forbids patrons to back past the point of entry. None of these assumptions is reasonable. Numbering each screen from *1* may not always be convenient, but it is the only solution for browsing screens.

Headings and index entries should appear in upper and lower case, not as all capital letters.

Many existing systems show some or all index entries as normalized strings of capital letters. That saves disk space, but forces patrons to deal with a screen full of capital letters, an unnecessary nuisance.

Other items on a browse screen require thought and some experimentation. If postings appear at the far right on a screen, will patrons lose track of which numbers go with which headings? If postings appear before the headings, will two numbers side by side cause confusion? How should references be presented—with succeeding whole numbers, with decimal numbers, indented? Should *see also* references be listed as part of the browsing screen or only displayed through a separate command?

Location of the Searched Item

The searched item should be near the top of the first retrieved browse screen, but not at the top unless it is the first item in the index. If the searched item does not exist, a dummy listing (one with no postings) should appear.

Some online systems place the searched item in the middle of the screen, with several prior headings and several following. Some place the searched item on the third or fourth line of the screen. Some systems place the searched item at the top of the screen, as in Figures 9.3 and 9.4.

Some systems display a "zero postings" line in place of a nonexistent item, at its proper alphabetic position; others repeat the search but do not add a special line within the browse. Each arrangement has its advantages. Inserting two or three headings before the searched item clarifies the nature of the browsable screen. An artificial heading line for a search with no result helps to make the screen clearer.

Searching from a Browse Screen

Patrons should be able to select headings by number, ranges of numbers or highlighting, in order to retrieve items for those headings. A good retrieval system should accept commands such as DISPLAY 1, 3–5, 7, rather than requiring the patron to key a complete search statement. Some systems treat browsing screens as the end point for searches. A patron wishing to see items for a particular heading must key the complete heading as part of a search—a requirement that is blatantly user-hostile. The programming and computer effort required to allow direct searching from a browsing screen are nominal, and the benefits are obvious.

STORED RESULTS

Patrons should be able to save results of searches selectively, combine those results and manipulate them. Patrons should be able to control result storage quickly and easily.

When patrons search a card catalog for several different items, they must handle each search independently, writing down any needed information. Many patron access systems work in the same way. Once a search is completed, its results disappear and are replaced by those of the next search. Online systems offer more power and flexibility than do card catalogs by allowing a patron to combine some or all of the results of several searches.

A patron retrieving 30 items in one search might issue a command such as SAVE 1–3, 6–8, 10 from the first multiple-item screen, or might simply say SAVE from certain single-item displays. Another related search might result in more items being saved. After several searches, the patron would save a group of items that could be sorted, printed and possibly transferred to diskette.

Storage and manipulation require some sophistication to present and to handle well. Different libraries will offer different levels of flexibility, depending on the patrons they serve. Although few libraries will provide patrons with tools for result handing that are as flexible or arcane as those used in online reference work, offering some sort of result storage and manipulation will inevitably serve patrons better.

Patrons should be able to sort stored results, print them as pick lists or as bibliographies, or hold them for downloading.

The patron access system should define a few ways to arrange results, such as alphabetized by main entry, alphabetized by title, alphabetized by first subject, or in reverse chronological order.

As discussed in Chapter 6, the two obvious choices for print formats are pick lists (one or two lines per item) and formatted bibliographies, but other choices may also make good sense for some libraries and some patrons.

Downloading may not be reasonable at a public terminal but should certainly be possible from dial-in computers and workstations. Some libraries may also wish to provide one or two microcomputer-based terminals to which result sets could be routed; that would allow the patron to bring a diskette and offload the results for later manipulation.

SUMMARY

Retrieval requires a balance between recall and precision. A system with good recall makes it easy to find all the information needed; a system with good precision makes it easy to avoid or eliminate unwanted information. The ideal online catalog provides both.

Browsing—scanning a set of headings from a given entry point that may not be present—is important for online catalogs and requires thoughtful design.

When a patron is looking for more than one book or when a user is doing bibliographic research, the ability to store results and manipulate them can make the catalog a more powerful tool. The catalog should make such storage and manipulation straightforward.

NOTES

1. Markey, Karen. *Subject Searching in Library Catalogs: Before and After the Introduction of Online Catalogs.* Dublin, OH: OCLC; 1984. p. 53.

2. *Using Online Catalogs.* Joseph R. Matthews; Gary S. Lawrence; Douglas K. Ferguson, eds. New York: Neal-Schuman; 1983. p. 132.

10

Searching

Patron access systems should cater to both the novice and the expert. They should also cater to users who need the call number and status of one specific title, without ignoring users with less well defined needs.

Some early online systems provided good service only to those patrons seeking specific items because subject access was not deemed very important. Attitudes have since changed and subject access is now incorporated into most systems. Unfortunately, some systems cater to subject access in ways that slow down patrons seeking specific items.

In this chapter I consider ways that catalogs assist or hinder known-item searching, issues relating to Boolean searching, some possible ways of dealing with "failed" searches (those that do not return any items) and issues involved in nonlocal searching.

SUBJECT SEARCHING

Search support should not favor subject access at the expense of known-item access. Tools should be provided to speed known-item searching and to make subject searching more productive.

Several sources have cited the Council on Library Resources (CLR) study of online catalog use to support the assertion that most users search by subject or topic. Some writers go on to suggest that patron access should favor subject searching, even if the result is slow, awkward access to known items. Some recent patron access systems do

173

precisely that and use access methods that require a patron to go through six or seven screens to get status and call number information for a proper citation.

There are at least two things wrong with such systems. First, intelligent system design should be able to accommodate new users and subject searchers without hampering fast access. Second, the statements are based on curious interpretations of a very limited study done very early in the history of online catalogs.

The CLR study was a landmark, pioneer effort; it provided, at best, a starting point for thought and discussion about online catalogs. It did not present answers or proven findings. Few of the libraries in the study returned enough samples to be statistically useful, and only two sizable samples came from online systems with complete databases. The CLR study does not support the claim that most searches are subject searches; it does, however, support the claim that subject searches are important, accounting for roughly one third of all searches.

Subject searching is critically important, and innovative subject search techniques can make online catalogs far more effective for such searching than card catalogs. Patrons use subject searches when they need help and are unsure what items they need.

Subject searching can be improved by a variety of tools and techniques, some of which are listed below:

- subject authority files with browsing, number of items and cross-references, so that patrons can see how formal subject headings work and what headings will yield large or small result sets
- word indexes to subject headings
- word and term (multiple word) indexes to titles, series and other entries, so that patrons may use topical words that are not used in LC subject headings
- call number indexes, and possibly call number indexes that can be searched by words from LC or Dewey classification schedules
- clear Boolean techniques to broaden and narrow searches
- related works searching—the ability to retrieve other items with the same subject heading as an item already retrieved
- searchable thesauri to allow patrons to use different vocabularies for subject searching

Any tool that improves searching for items other than known items will also improve subject searching; a few of the tools and techniques noted above serve subject searching specifically. In some modern online catalogs, the problem is finding a balance between subject searching and access to known items.

SEARCHING KNOWN ITEMS

Once a patron roughly understands library filing, the card catalog is an efficient tool to find the call number for a known item. A good online catalog shows the status of the item as well, providing better service to patrons who know what they want.

Many patrons ignore card catalogs when looking for known items. They go directly to book shelves, at least for fiction and some nonfiction items. These same patrons may use online catalogs if they are not cumbersome, and they will receive better service as a result. To be most effective for known-item searching, online catalogs should include circulation status information.

If patron access systems require more than two or three steps to find the status of a known item, many patrons will continue to go directly to the shelves, ignoring the catalog. An unused catalog serves nobody, and online catalogs with clumsy known-item access fail to serve a large number of library patrons.

Speed of Known-Item Search and Display

Known-item searching should be fast, easy and clear. It should result in a bibliographic and status display after no more than two commands. An author-title or title search that retrieves one item should automatically display that item.

Patrons with a specific item in mind don't want to carry on an extended dialogue with a patron access system. They want to find out where the item is and whether it is available, and probably want to spend as little time as possible at the catalog.

The known-item searcher doesn't ask much from the catalog and so the catalog shouldn't ask much from the patron. The faster and simpler the path from initial screen to record display, the better. Ideally, even a new user should be able to get to an item within two screens, if the user has a good citation.

Several systems display the same intermediate screen for all searches that yield results, no matter what the result set. For a single result, that screen may have messages such as *Your search retrieves 1 item. Key dis 1 to see first item.*

Other systems will show a display, but it will be a multiple-item display (even though there is only one item), lacking call number and status information.

Designers argue that this design ensures consistency and reassures the user. Given the high percentage of searches that can be expected to yield a single item or a very small group of items, it is an unnecessary and almost arrogant system feature to force patrons through intermediate screens in the interest of consistency. Systems that require six or seven steps to get to a known item represent a great leap backward from card catalogs.

Curiously, systems that require too many screens tend to be called user-friendly. A distinction should be made between user friendliness—providing assistance and guidance as needed—and hostility in the name of friendliness. Turning a one-step check on item status into an extended series of actions is hostile to patrons who want known items, no matter how easy the series of actions may be.

Author-Title Searches

Patron access systems should offer author-title searching as a primary option. Any author-title search should be assumed to be a known-item search yielding an item display.

Author-title searches represent the clearest way to find known items and patron access systems should provide clear ways to execute them. Author-title searches usually involve two indexes and somewhat more complex syntax than single-index searches.

Menu-driven systems with completion screens can prompt for author and title clearly, but they may require three screens to do so: one to choose the search, one to key the author and one to key the title. Systems that prompt both author and title completion lines on the same screen permit faster entry, though still not as fast as command-driven systems.

Many online systems use special punctuation to improve author-title searching. Commands such as FIND AT ASIMOV, ISAAC/ ROBOTS OF DAWN may work well if a clear example appears along with the index choice. Any such command has the usual problem of special punctuation: the punctuation must be learned and could possibly appear in a title. This is less of a problem for an author-title search, assuming the author appears first, since author's names rarely have slashes, colons or most other punctuation (except apostrophes, dashes and commas). Many systems use special syntax rules for author-title searches; all such systems rely on knowledgeable users or examples on the screen.

Clear, easy Boolean searching represents the most consistent support for author-title searching.

Any combined author-title search, including a Boolean search, raises some other questions:

- Should the title portion be treated as title words or as a title phrase?
- Should the author portion be treated as an exact name or as an approximate name?
- Should either or both portions be treated as though a truncation symbol appeared at the end of the search?

All of these questions deserve further analysis and research. One response to all three questions is that the search should be done first as a complete title phrase and exact name. If that search yields results, the results should be displayed. If not, the search should be reapplied with more lenient rules, such as changing the title portion to title words, changing the author portion to an approximate name or treating both arguments as truncated. That answer involves more work for the patron access system, but it should serve patrons better than any other solution.

Interpreting Searches

Patrons new to an online catalog are likely to key text strings that constitute known-item searches but don't follow the rules of the catalog. A forgiving parser may be able to interpret some of these text strings. Command parsing routines should interpret unknown commands as known-item searches, if such interpretation can be made unambiguously.

Figures 10.1 and 10.2 demonstrate possible parser interpretations, in each case leading to the same known-item search. Both figures assume moderately sophisticated command interpretation, but both should be possible.

Figure 10.1: Parser Interpretation of Known-Item Search, A

```
You keyed: BYZANTIUM BY A. MILLER -- interpreted as a search request:
FIND NAME MILLER, A. AND TITLE BYZANTIUM #
   Finds: 1 item
 :                                                                        :
 :                                                                        :
```

Figure 10.2: Parser Interpretation of Known-Item Search, B

```
You keyed: DO YOU HAVE ARTHUR MILLER'S BYZANTIUM? -- interpreted as:
FIND NAME MILLER, ARTHUR AND TITLE BYZANTIUM #
   Finds: 1 item
 :                                                                        :
 :                                                                        :
```

This level of interpretation will serve users if it works consistently, but it can lead to peculiar results if it does not work well. More advanced interpretation may be possible. Research, analysis and testing should help to show whether "friendly" command interpretation will help patrons or will simply waste computing resources.

Title Searches

When a title search yields a single result, it should be treated as a known item. The single record should be displayed immediately, even if the system would otherwise default to a title browse.

This is an issue only in catalogs that have title browse screens or in catalogs that force every title search through an intermediate screen. Quite possibly, more known-item searches will be title searches than author-title searches. Title searches can be keyed more quickly and easily than author-title searches and patrons remember titles more accurately than they remember authors.

> *Subject and author searches that result in single bibliographic items should not be treated as known-item searches.*

Patrons wanting known items will not usually use subject searches. Patrons who happen to key a subject that has only one posting may well be unaware of subject relationships. A well-designed subject browse will show those relationships and help patrons find the best approach. In many cases, the reason for the single result is that the patron is using an overly specific subject.

Displaying Known Items

> *When a known item is retrieved, the first display should include location, circulation status and call number.*

Patrons with known needs should be able to get in, get their information and get out. Showing the needed information on the first display screen helps that process.

BOOLEAN LOGIC

> *A good patron access system supports Boolean logic. However, Boolean logic probably causes more difficulty in online systems than any other single feature.*

Boolean logic is the most powerful searching tool; it is also the most difficult to explain, understand and use. Even in the Research Libraries Information Network (RLIN)—a straightforward Boolean system designed for experienced users—Boolean logic causes more faulty searches than any other searching feature.

Patron access systems should be able to retain the power of logical *ands* and *ors,* while minimizing difficulties in Boolean searching. Computer techniques for handling Boolean searches are well known and unambiguous, if not always efficient; the problems with Boolean logic lie in the presentation. Undoubtedly, it is an area of online access wide open to future development.

> *Less sophisticated and less formidable terminology should be used in place of "Boolean logic" in displays of command options or in most HELP screens.*

One difficulty with Boolean searching is the term itself. Patrons can understand the ability to narrow or broaden searches, but will be put off by the term *Boolean* or the use of *and* as a verb. A message such as *Key & followed by one or more words to narrow your result* makes much more sense than AND WITH ADDITIONAL WORD(S) OR USE LIMITING COMMAND TO REDUCE SEARCH RESULTS.

This book presents no formula for superior presentation of Boolean searching. The points that follow address a few specific issues and may help to clarify some of the problems with Boolean searching. The issues discussed relate to the following questions:

- When should a patron access system assume that a search is a Boolean search?
- Should searches that involve multiple indexes be treated differently from those that involve a single index?
- Should patrons be able to add Boolean operators after issuing a search?

Searches Involving More than One Index

> *Patrons should be able to issue a search involving more than one index.*

When a patron explicitly keys a Boolean search involving multiple indexes, the only possible question is whether an *and* is a Boolean operator or part of a phrase. That may be a real question. If an online catalog has a NAME index and a TITLE index, the search FIND TITLE CRY HAVOC AND NAME OBLIVION could be a search for the title "Cry Havoc and Name Oblivion" or for the title "Cry Havoc" by an author named Oblivion.

Distinctive index names that are *not* words help to ease this problem, though some question will always remain. If a catalog uses *pe* for exact personal names and *tp* for titles, the search FIND TP PHYSICAL FITNESS AND PE REQUIREMENTS can be misinterpreted as a search for the title "Physical Fitness" by "Requirements."

These examples illustrate some problems with Boolean searches. Any system that permits Boolean searches from a single command line will result in a few misinterpretations and ambiguities. Some ambiguity is acceptable if the bulk of Boolean searches works correctly.

As long as index names cannot be mistaken for words, an implicit "and" should be assumed when a second index name appears in a search argument.

If a patron access system uses *au* for an author index and *tw* for a title word index, the search FIND AU VELIKOVSKY TW COLLISION should have the same effect as FIND AU VELIKOVSKY & TW COLLISION. It should be treated as a Boolean search retrieving all items with the word *collision* in a title field and the name *Velikovsky* in an author field.

The crucial question is whether or not index names can be mistaken for words. There will always be one or two cases where an index name will also appear as a word, but good choices for index names can make such cases rare.

Recognizing Boolean Operators

Patron access systems should not interpret "and," "or" or "not" as Boolean operators unless they are followed by an unambiguous index name.

Patron access systems may take one of three approaches to the words *and, or, not* and to searches using word indexes and involving multiple words:

1. Strict. If the search string for a word index contains more than one word and does not separate the words with &, | or &not, the search is assumed to be a phrase search. Strict interpretation assumes that the words *and, or, not* within searches are simply part of the text to be searched.
2. Mixed. Multiple words in a word search are assumed to represent a Boolean *and* search (i.e., a search that asks for items with all the words). The words *and, or, not* are recognized as Boolean operators within word searches but not within phrase

searches, except when explicit punctuation makes their role clear. (The search FIND TITLE "MAKE MINE MAGIC" AND NAME "BERKELEY, BUSBY" is quite clear.)

3. Liberal. The words *and, or, not* and the symbols &, | are always considered to be Boolean operators unless they appear between double quotes, which means that the search FIND TITLE WALDO & MAGIC, INC will fail unless it is rekeyed as FIND TITLE "WALDO & MAGIC, INC."

Good arguments can be made for each of the three approaches. The third leads to the most confusion (and may be the most widely used). The first or second approach will cause less confusion. The search FIND TITLE WAR AND PEACE should be identical to the search FIND TITLE "WAR AND PEACE."

Many users do not understand the effects of implicit Boolean *and*s within word indexes. A patron who keys FIND TW CIVIL WAR may expect to retrieve items containing the phrase *civil war*, not those with *civil* somewhere and *war* somewhere else.

Modifying a Search

Patrons should be able to use Boolean logic in order to broaden or narrow a search.

A patron should always be able to add *and xxx* after a search has been performed and should be able to undo the modification if the result is too small. If a system does not allow patrons to add Boolean terms after a search has begun, the system offers no reasonable way to reduce a result set. A system that requires patrons to rekey searches in order to modify them is user hostile and fails to use the power of the computer to remember what has been done.

Clarifying Boolean Searches

Boolean logic requires clever prompting, parsing and training because people have trouble with Boolean commands. What should a system do when a search can be interpreted as either a Boolean request or a mistakenly keyed phrase search? How should a parser interpret FIND TW WAR AND PEACE? Three possibilities exist:

- Treat the *and* as a Boolean operator.
- Assume the user actually intends a phrase search.
- Ask the patron to clarify the request (as in Figure 10.3).

Any one of the three possibilities will work, but none will work perfectly. Effective use of Boolean logic requires effective design and makes for powerful, flexible retrieval. To date, Boolean logic has caused problems in many systems that support it. The solution to these problems is surely not to abandon Boolean logic, but to improve Boolean searching from the patron's perspective.

FAILED SEARCHES

Searches fail for many reasons. Good design can help to ensure that searches will succeed if the needed items are in the collection and in the catalog.

The patron access system has failed when any one of the following occurs:

- A patron finds the system too confusing and will not use the catalog—a clear failure for patron access.
- A system does not provide the forms of access that a patron desires and the result is partial or complete searching failure.
- The system provides results that match the patron's explicit request but do not represent the best answer to the patron's real needs. When this happens, the system has failed in a manner not apparent to the patron.

The remainder of this chapter addresses two specific cases of searching failure, both showing the same result from the patron's perspective. In both cases, the patron's search is acceptable syntactically,

Figure 10.3: Possible Handling of Ambiguous Boolean Search

```
You keyed: FIND TW WAR AND PEACE
:                                                            :
:                                                            :
Your search is unclear.  Two possible interpretations:
1. find tw war and tw peace
2. find tp "war and peace#"

Please enter the number that expresses the search you want to issue,
or enter a new search.
NEXT ACTION:_
```

but the system does not return any items or headings. Zero results for correct searches happen for three reasons:

1. The search strategy is inadequate. If the patron enters a different search, the system will return useful results. Subject searches may be too specific; title word searches may involve too many words; author searches may have an incorrect form of the name.
2. The search strategy is correct, but the items desired are not in the library's collection.
3. The search strategy is correct and the library has items to meet the patron's needs, but those items are not represented in the online system or lack sufficient access points. Most libraries have some material that is never cataloged; retrospective conversion may yield records that do not have a full range of access points.

The suggestions that follow address the first case; the final portion of this chapter, "Nonlocal Searching," addresses the second case; and the first portion of Chapter 2 discusses aspects of the third case.

Different search strategies may require different actions for zero results:

The need to suggest search adjustments is especially acute when the search has found no matches. Depending on the nature of the search that failed, the system might offer a number of suggestions:

- Truncate, or truncate further.
- Use fewer key words connected by AND.
- Use more key words connected by OR.
- Change indexes.
- Change to broader terminology (for subject searches).[1]

Karen Markey offers several suggestions for failed or "null" searches:

- Null title search: suggest or guide author search.
- Null author search: suggest or guide title search.
- Null author-title search: suggest author or title.
- Allow matches "on any substantive title word."
- Use automatic truncation.
- Use spelling correction routine.
- Use name authorities to redirect searches to proper forms.[2]

Boolean Searches with No Results

When a Boolean search fails, a patron access system can show the results of searching each term, check the spelling of terms or return items that match some, but not all, of the search.

Boolean searches may fail because one of the elements has no matches or because the combination of the elements eliminates all matches. Five possible forms of assistance will each solve some of these problems but not others:

- A *Boolean summary screen* can be prepared, showing how many items each element of the search retrieves. Figure 10.4 shows such a screen, as do Figures 8.3 through 8.8. Figure 10.4 is probably the most helpful of the possible Boolean summaries but is also the most expensive to prepare: the results that are displayed will require much more computing time than the original search. A full summary screen may also be very long; a complete expansion of the search in Figure 10.4 would require a second screen.
- A *report of terms with no results* requires less computer power

Figure 10.4: Boolean Expansion for Zero Result

```
You keyed: FIND TW WEATHER FORECASTING SATELLITES AUSTRALIAN        BOOLHELP
Your search finds no items.
--------------------------------------------------------------------------
Portions of your search do find items.
 #        ITEMS       WORDS
 1.       1,338       WEATHER
 2.         845       FORECASTING
 3.         516       SATELLITES
 4.       2,396       AUSTRALIAN
 5.         275       WEATHER FORECASTING
 6.          36       WEATHER SATELLITES
 7.          25       WEATHER AUSTRALIAN
 8.          16       FORECASTING SATELLITES
 9.          25       FORECASTING AUSTRALIAN
10.           5       SATELLITES AUSTRALIAN
11.          16       WEATHER FORECASTING SATELLITES
12.          25       WEATHER FORECASTING AUSTRALIAN

--------------------------------------------------------------------------
NEXT ACTIONS:    Key: # (1-12) to perform one of the searches displayed.
                 F to Find something else    ? for Help
                 Q to Quit
NEXT ACTION:_
```

and will help patrons when the search includes a "bad" term. If a patron keys FIND TW WEATHER FORECASTING SATEL-ITES AUSTRALIAN, a screen saying *The term SATELITES does not appear in any item* alerts the patron to a problem.

- A *spelling check* of any terms with no results may help the patron more directly, by offering alternative spellings. Spelling checkers will help small public libraries much more than large academic libraries; as the size and complexity of a collection grow, including collections in foreign languages, a spelling checker may become nearly useless. Figure 10.5 shows a partial screen with the results of checking *satelites* through real spelling checkers.* Note that Figure 10.5 shows a different search from the one in Figure 10.4; in this case, a word has been misspelled.

Figure 10.5: Spelling Check for Zero Boolean Result

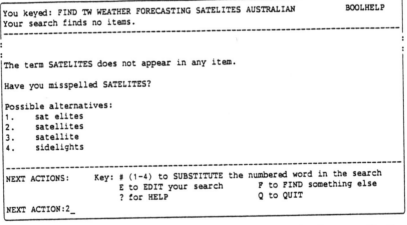

```
You keyed: FIND TW WEATHER FORECASTING SATELITES AUSTRALIAN        BOOLHELP
Your search finds no items.
------------------------------------------------------------------------
:                                                                        :
:                                                                        :
The term SATELITES does not appear in any item.

Have you misspelled SATELITES?

Possible alternatives:
1.    sat elites
2.    satellites
3.    satellite
4.    sidelights

------------------------------------------------------------------------
NEXT ACTIONS:     Key: # (1-4) to SUBSTITUTE the numbered word in the search
                       E to EDIT your search      F to FIND something else
                       ? for HELP                 Q to QUIT
NEXT ACTION:2_
```

- *Transfer to a browsable term index* based on the first word in the search will probably confuse the patron, since it ignores the remainder of the search. It does offer some results, but the results may be useless.
- *Fuzzy matches* tell the patron that nothing satisfied all of the search, then display those results that come closest. For the search in Figure 10.5, a fuzzy match would yield the 16 items that match *weather forecasting satellites,* the 25 items that

*Terms suggested came from spelling checkers in The Final Word II and Word Perfect 4.1, both word processing systems for the IBM PC.

match *weather forecasting australian* and any items that match *weather satellites australian* or *forecasting satellites australian.* These items should be identified as matching three of the four items; the patron could proceed to see the hundreds of items that match two of the four terms. At least one patron access system shows fuzzy matches.

Phrase Searches with No Results

When a phrase search fails, a patron access system may suggest words instead of phrases, go to a browse screen or attempt a truncated version of the same search.

Phrase searches, for this discussion, are searches for all or part of a field, starting from the beginning. Unless truncated, phrase searches must match the complete field. Title, subject and series searches are usually phrase searches. If a phrase search routinely yields a browse screen, the patron always obtains results, even if the phrase actually searched does not retrieve any items.

If no browsable phrase index exists and if the patron has not used truncation, another possible solution is to return the result of a search using truncation. The search FIND TITLE CREWEL LYE may fail because the book was cataloged with *Crewel Lye: A Caustic Yarn* as a title. In that case, if the system does a second search using FIND TITLE CREWEL LYE*, the patron will achieve results—probably the desired results. In other cases, an automatic truncated search will not help the user. If the user keys FIND TITLE HELP! and the library has neither the Beatles film nor the sound recording of that name, an internal search *find title help** will return quite a few items beginning *Help,* and the patron must look through them to find that the wanted item is not present.

The only solution that does not require any work for the patron access system is to feed back a message suggesting that the patron try words instead of a phrase. The system could also initiate a word search using all the words keyed. (In the case of FIND TITLE CREWEL LYE, that alternative will probably yield the book wanted.)

If a patron access system has term indexes (those containing phrases of two or more words from anywhere within a field), it can suggest using them, or initiate an automatic search against them. This solution will help patrons who key FIND TITLE FIRE ON THE

MOON because they are unaware that the full title of Norman Mailer's book is *Of a Fire on the Moon*. Term indexes are discussed in more detail in Chapter 2.

Name Searches with No Results

Name searches should yield browse screens. If a catalog does not have a browsable name index or authority file, it should provide approximate name searching.

Browse screens are the best response to name searches; catalogs that use this technique do not need to provide approximate name searching or other techniques.

Since name searching is often imprecise, good algorithms for imprecise name searches need to be devised. Patrons may not know how the library cataloged a name and may not have a good citation. A patron could search for Asimov's books under ASIMOV, I because of uncertainty about the number of "a"s in *Isaac*. A patron might remember an author as *Curt Vonnegut* or *Kurt Vonnegut* without the *Jr.*, and a patron might search for *Piers Anthony Jacob*, the name under which Piers Anthony's books are copyrighted.

RLIN and some similar online systems allow both exact personal name searching and approximate searching. Approximate searching ignores all but the first letter of any first or middle names, and will match that letter with either a first initial or middle initial. Unfortunately, the algorithm is both too forgiving and not forgiving enough. It will retrieve *Isaac Asimov* given *Asimov, I.* If given *W. Crawford*, it will retrieve several authors, most of whom have a middle name beginning with *W*. The algorithm will not help those who search for *Curt Vonnegut* or *Piers Anthony Jacob*.

Spelling Checkers, Synonyms, Soundex and Artificial Intelligence

Revised searches based on spelling checkers, synonym tables, "sounds-like" searching or artificial intelligence routines may be useful.

Several special techniques offer possible alternatives to failed searches, particularly failed word and name searches.

Soundex is the name of an old technique for finding names that sound alike. It works by ignoring vowels within words and grouping together similar-sounding consonants (for instance, "f" and "v"). The algorithm is useless when the first letter in a word is wrong (it retains the first letter), but can bring together many other possibilities. Soundex was designed for proper names and works better for names than for words. Soundex poses two problems. First, it may pull together too many alternatives. Second, patrons will tend to assume that, if a Soundex search fails, the situation is hopeless. This is not necessarily true because the Soundex algorithm rejects many possible matches.

Modern spelling checkers can do a remarkably good job of suggesting correct alternatives to misspelled words, even in cases where the first letter has been omitted. As noted earlier, spelling checkers will be more helpful in smaller collections because of the extremely wide vocabulary in large collections.

Lists of synonyms, or online thesauri, can help a patron find different terms to use in a topical search. English has few true synonyms except for simple alternative spellings. Automatic retrieval of alternative spellings such as *catalog* and *catalogue* makes sense; automatic retrieval of words with similar meanings does not, but the ability to call up synonyms can help a searcher who is not obtaining results.

Research into artificial intelligence may yield useful tools for suggesting better searches, though the possibilities in online catalogs are so varied that such suggestions may not be very useful. In any case, one fundamental rule applies to suggestions based on artificial intelligence techniques, as to all the other techniques noted above: the patron must stay in control.

Searching alternatives should be offered to the user, not performed automatically. Search results should never surprise the patron because they are based on something other than the original search.

NONLOCAL SEARCHING

Library automation systems will have more and more links to other libraries and to nonlibrary resources. These complex networks can theoretically allow access to information on items held throughout the country or even the world.

Some searches fail because the library does not have the material.

Some patron access systems will have the ability to pass searches to other systems, possibly finding the material in another location.

Failed searches should not be passed automatically to other linked systems.

Any searching beyond the local library should be on request only, for three reasons:

- A search may fail for many reasons other than lack of an item.
- Most patrons do not wish to go elsewhere to retrieve an item, or to wait long enough to receive an item through interlibrary borrowing. In many cases, patrons have alternatives that are more acceptable.
- Nonlocal searching will almost certainly be much slower and more expensive than local searching. If the search is for an item that does not exist at all and a library has access to extended nonlocal links, considerable quantities of processing power and telecommunications may be expended before the last link in the chain reports that the search does not return any results.

Libraries should carefully evaluate when nonlocal searches are warranted and whether such searches should be done directly by patrons or by librarians only.

For some time to come, and possibly for an indefinite period, searches against other systems will have fewer options than local searches. If another system does not have a title word index, it is not possible to do a title word search. The patron access system must be able to explain that situation and to determine which searches can succeed on another system.

Nonlocal searching should use National Information Standards Organization (NISO) protocols, those originally developed by the Linked Systems Project (LSP).

Other protocols to link two systems from the same vendor may be cheaper or simpler, but the developing LSP/NISO protocols offer the only method to allow *any* library-related system to deal with any other library-related system on a computer-to-computer basis. The protocols are designed to be independent of any given computer or system, and have growing support within the library community, including the vendor community.

SUMMARY

A good patron access system can help new patrons, while providing fast access to known items and fast retrieval for experienced searchers. An online system that shows the current status of items offers more useful information than a card catalog and is likely to have even more known-item searching. Balanced search support will serve all patrons well.

Boolean searching is at the heart of powerful online access, but the logic is difficult to learn and easy to misuse. Innovative techniques to make Boolean searching more workable will lead to better online catalogs. A variety of techniques may help patrons whose searches do not retrieve any items. One such technique is extended searching—the ability to search the catalogs of other libraries—but it should not be automatic.

NOTES

1. Corey, James F. "Search Retrieval Options." *Online Catalog Design Issues: A Series of Discussions.* Brian Aveney, ed. Washington, DC: Council on Library Resources; 1984 July. p. 43.

2. Markey, Karen. *Subject Searching in Library Catalogs: Before and After the Introduction of Online Catalogs.* Dublin, OH: OCLC; 1984. p. 135.

11

Display Issues

Patrons use online access systems to find items. The desired end result of most searches is an item in hand; this follows the last step at the catalog—viewing a display of bibliographic, holdings and status information. The quality of this display affects the overall usefulness of the patron access system.

Displays should be open, coherent, meaningful and useful.

The purpose of a bibliographic display is to convey information from the database to the patron. A display that adheres to the following principles will transfer that information to the patron rapidly and clearly:

- Overall context. System context should be maintained. Bibliographic displays should contain the same display elements as other screens, including command options and previous-action signposts.
- Internal context. A series of items should be displayed in a clear and meaningful order, as should elements within a single item.
- Openness. Displays should not be overly crowded so that patrons may scan information easily.
- Coherence. A patron should be able to deal with all aspects of an item without losing track of any given element. The easiest way to give a display this coherence is to fit items or series of items on one screen or on as few screens as possible.
- Meaningfulness. Patrons should be able to understand the information displayed.
- Completeness. Patrons should be able to see all the information they need. Different patrons need different amounts of information.

- Usefulness. Information should be displayed so that it is readily available for patrons to use when locating items or gathering bibliographic information.

Some of these principles have been suggested earlier in the book, as have other criteria important to display design. These criteria may be in conflict with each other. For example, open displays may require more screens to display an item, diminishing coherence. Some aspects of display design can be tested statistically, but more aspects require professional judgment tempered by extended experience.

Well-designed displays will communicate the information that a patron needs, even if the displays contain information that the patron does not need.

Most online systems give a library considerable flexibility in designing the bibliographic displays. Any contemporary online system should also be open to future change in fundamental apsects of design. As experience with online catalogs grows, and as the variety of well-designed online catalogs increases, ideas for effective bibliographic displays will change and develop further.

The Research Libraries Group, Inc. (RLG) has developed a system to test the effects of different display designs for online catalogs. The system receives a series of instructions for a display and prepares screen images for up to 400,000 bibliographic items representing current cataloging. Each display test generates sample screens to show how the design looks and produces a series of statistical measures to show how the design works (e.g., the percentage of items that fit on one screen and the density of the average screen).

An extended series of display tests was performed in early 1986 and the results of those tests are reported in *Bibliographic Displays in the Online Catalog.*[1] The book discusses the results of some 200 test runs and includes more than 300 sample screens; some statistical comments in this chapter and the next are taken from those tests.

OVERALL SCREEN DESIGN

Bibliographic display screens should follow the same overall design as other patron access screens.

Most examples in this book use a three-part screen that shows where patrons were (how they got here), where they are and where they can go. This is not the only possible model, but whatever model is chosen must be used consistently throughout the system. Some patron access systems provide good command options and feedback until a final result is displayed, at which point the patron is left with nothing but a simple command prompt such as *Command:* or ->.

The reasons for eliminating feedback and options on display screens seem clear enough. Most patrons will execute one, and only one, search. Once they reach a bibliographic display, they are done. Designs that eliminate most feedback and prompting leave more of the screen for bibliographic display. On the other hand, many patrons will not be satisfied with a single search result. Since bibliographic displays have no "most probable" next actions, patrons should be given some clues as to what they can do next. More important, the display should include a feedback section that shows the command and the search that led to the display.

Blank lines and spacing lines should be used to make biblio-graphic displays clear and easy to read.

Judicious use of blank lines helps to group related information and make it easy to identify. Unfortunately, blank lines and dashed lines used to set off the parts of the screen do add significantly to the space required to display a record.

Figures 11.1 and 11.2 show the same bibliographic item and the same top and bottom segments. Figure 11.2 is much easier to read and understand than Figure 11.1. Figure 11.3 shows the same item in a cardlike display. Most observers would consider Figure 11.2 easier to understand than Figure 11.3. Figure 11.3 uses much less space to show the same amount of information, but a patron would need knowledge of card catalog conventions in order to interpret the information.

Spacing forces significantly more items to second screens. Using the display in Figure 11.2, 59% of the records in a 400,000-record sample require more than one screen to show the bibliographic information and minimal holdings. Using the display in Figure 11.1, only 3% of the records require more than one screen.

Those are dramatically different numbers and typical of the balance between legibility and compactness that is a part of many display issues.

Figure 11.1: Labeled Display Without Vertical Spacing

```
Your search: Psalmen Davids fu#                      MEDIUM Display
     Finds: 1 record                                 Screen  1 of  3
        TITLE: Psalmen Davids fur Chor und Schlagzeug.  Anaklasis fur
               Streicherk und Schlagzeug.  Sonate fur Cello und Orchester.
               Fluorescences fur Orchester.  Stabat Mater fur 3
               a-capella-Chore.
    PUBLISHED: Wergo WER 60 020. [1965]
     MATERIAL: 1 disc. 33 1/3 rpm. stereo. 12 in.
        NAMES: Penderecki, Krsyzstof, 1933-
               Palm, Siegfried.
               Markowski, Andrzej, 1924-
               Filharmonia Stoleczna, Warsaw
               Panstwowa Filharmonia w Poznaniu.
       SERIES: Studio Reiha neuer Musik.
     SUBJECTS: Choruses, Sacred (Mixed voices) with instrumental ensemble.
               Psalms (Music)
               Percussion with string orchestra.
               Violoncello with orchestra.
               Orchestral music.
                                                      (CONTINUED)
NEXT ACTIONS:     Key: ? for help           + to see the next screen
                       L to see a Longer display  - to see the previous screen
                       F to Find other items  Q to Quit
NEXT ACTION?_
```

Figure 11.2: Labeled Display with Vertical Spacing

```
Your search: Psalmen Davids fu#                      MEDIUM Display
     Finds: 1 record                                 Screen  1 of  3
-----------------------------------------------------------------------
        TITLE: Psalmen Davids fur Chor und Schlagzeug.  Anaklasis fur
               Streicherk und Schlagzeug.  Sonate fur Cello und Orchester.
               Fluorescences fur Orchester.  Stabat Mater fur 3
               a-capella-Chore.
    PUBLISHED: Wergo WER 60 020. [1965]
     MATERIAL: 1 disc. 33 1/3 rpm. stereo. 12 in.

        NAMES: Penderecki, Krsyzstof, 1933-
               Palm, Siegfried.
               Markowski, Andrzej, 1924-
               Filharmonia Stoleczna, Warsaw
               Panstwowa Filharmonia w Poznaniu.


-------------------------------------------------CONTINUED-----------
NEXT ACTIONS:     Key: ? for help           + to see the next screen
                       L to see a Longer display  - to see the previous screen
                       F to Find other items  Q to Quit
NEXT ACTION?_
```

Figure 11.3: Cardlike Display with Some Vertical Spacing

```
Your search: Penderecki, Kryzys#                        MEDIUM Display
     Finds: 1 record                                  Screen  1 of  2
-----------------------------------------------------------------------

        Penderecki, Krsyzstof, 1933-
           Psalmen Davids fur Chor und Schlagzeug. Anaklasis fur
        Streicherk und Schlagzeug. Sonate fur Cello und Orchester.
        Fluorescences fur Orchester.  Stabat Mater fur 3
        a-capella-Chore. Wergo WER 60 020. [1965]
           1 disc. 33 1/3 rpm. stereo. 12 in.
        (Studio Reihe neuer Musik)
           1. Choruses, Sacred (Mixed voices) with instrumental
        ensemble.  2. Psalms (Music)  3. Percussion with string
        orchestra.  4. Violoncello with orchestra.  5. Orchestral
        music.  6. Chorusas, Sacred (Mixed voices), Unaccompanied.
        7. Stabat Mater dolorosa (Music).  I. Penderecki, Krzysztof,
        1933- Psalms of David. [Sound recording] 1965.
        II. Penderecki, Krzysztof, 1933- Anaklasis [Sound recording]

-------------------------------------------------------CONTINUED-----------
NEXT ACTIONS:    Key: ? for help            + to see the next screen
                      L to see a Longer display  - to see the previous screen
                      F to Find other items   Q to Quit

NEXT ACTION?_
```

PUNCTUATION AND CAPITALIZATION

ISBD Punctuation

ISBD punctuation neither helps nor hinders most patrons and should be displayed as it is stored.

Some librarians have complained of the "secret punctuation" that litters library cards. Nobody seems to have asked patrons whether that punctuation bothers them or whether they even notice it.

A patron access system can strip ISBD punctuation or, more plausibly, can remove the space before such punctuation and change some of the symbols. The testing program at RLG includes an option to do just that: test the ends of MARC fields and subfields, change a trailing slash "/" to a comma and remove the space before other punctuation. For simple cases, that process seems to yield slightly more attractive displays.

But ISBD punctuation does not appear only at the ends of subfields. In order to make all ISBD punctuation appear normal, a program must check all character strings for the distinctive ISBD space-symbol-space combinations such as " ; " and " /. " This check involves significant overhead for a very small gain in "normality." It isn't even clear that the slash should be changed to a comma or that any other punctuation mark is a good replacement for it in every circumstance.

Figures 11.4 and 11.5 show the descriptive portion of the same item, with and without ISBD punctuation at the ends of fields and subfields. When a group of items was printed with and without the modified punctuation, most observers did not notice the difference between the displays. Most of those who noticed it felt that it didn't make any difference.

Figure 11.4: Descriptive Elements with ISBD Punctuation

```
  :                                                                   :
  :                                                                   :
  |     TITLE: Whose house is it? / Alice L. Hopf ; illustrated by Leigh |
  |            Grant.                                                  |
  |     PUBLISHED: New York : Dodd, Mead, [1980]                       |
  |     MATERIAL: 63 p. : ill. ; 22 cm.                               |
  :                                                                   :
  :                                                                   :
```

Figure 11.5: Descriptive Elements with Modified Punctuation

```
  :                                                                   :
  :                                                                   :
  |     TITLE: Whose house is it?, Alice L. Hopf ; illustrated by Leigh |
  |            Grant.                                                  |
  |     PUBLISHED: New York: Dodd, Mead, [1980]                        |
  |     MATERIAL: 63 p.: ill.; 22 cm.                                 |
  :                                                                   :
  :                                                                   :
```

A refined version of the program could almost certainly do a better job of making ISBD punctuation look like ordinary punctuation. After the testing, however, it seems clear that the results would not be worthwhile because not much of a problem exists.

Capitalization

Bibliographic data should always appear in upper and lower case, except when capitalization is used for highlighting.

Some older patron access systems present all information in capital letters, making the information much more difficult to read and understand. For example, the first citation below is much more difficult to read than the second one:

SATIE, ERIK, 1866–1925. GYMNOPEDIES / ERIK SATIE ;
TWO ORCHESTRATED BY CLAUDE DEBUSSY ; EDITED BY PETER
DICKINSON. LONDON ; NEW YORK : EULENBURG, C1980.
1 MINIATURE SCORE (XI, 19 P.) ; 19 CM.

Satie, Erik, 1866–1925. Gymnopedies / Erik Satie ;
two orchestrated by Claude Debussy ; Edited by Peter
Dickinson. London ; New York : Eulenburg, c1980.
1 miniature score (xi, 19 p.) ; 19 cm.

Capitalization, however, can be effective for either of two cases: to highlight the access point within a retrieved record or to highlight the title within either a multiple-item display or an unlabeled descriptive paragraph. Figures 11.6 and 11.7 show capitalized titles within multiple-item and single-item displays.

Figure 11.6: Multiple-Item Display with Capitalized Titles

```
Your search: FIND TWORD PLAGIARISM                              MULTIPLE
       Finds: 13 items.                              Items 1 to 6
------------------------------------------------------------------------
 1. Casewit, Curtis W. KEEP IT LEGAL : (Sacramento, CA : Creative Book Co.,
    [1976]

 2. Douglas, John, 1721-1807. MILTON VINDICATED FROM THE CHARGE OF PLAGIARISM :
    (London : Printed for A. Miller ..., 1751.)

 3. Grier, Samuel L. A TOOL FOR DETECTING PLAGIARISM IN PASCAL PROGRAMS
    [Microform] / (1980.)

 4. Johnston, Dan. DESIGN PROTECTION : (London : Design Council : 1978)

 5. LEGAL ASPECTS OF PLAGIARISM / (Topeka, Kansas : National Organization on
    Legal Problems of Education, c1985.)

 6. Lindey, Alexander. PLAGIARISM AND ORIGINALITY / (New York : Harper, c1952)
------------------------------------------------------------CONTINUED------------
NEXT ACTIONS:    Key: D1-D5 to Display an item    + for Next Screen
                      F to Find other items       ? for Help
                      Q to Quit
NEXT ACTION? +_
```

Figure 11.7: Single-Item Display with Capitalized Title

```
Your search: Folsom, Franklin#                        CITATION
      Finds: 1 item                              Screen 1 of 2
------------------------------------------------------------------------

      Folsom, Franklin, 1907-  AMERICA'S ANCIENT TREASURES : a
      guide to archaeological sites and museums in the United
      States and Canada / Franklin Folsom and Mary Elting
      Folsom ; illustrations by Rachel Folsom. 34d rev., enl.
      ed. Albuquerque : University of New Mexico Press, c1983.
      xxviii, 420 p. : ill. ; 26 cm.
      Indians of North America--Museums--Guide-books.
      Indians of North America--Antiquities--Guide-books.
      United States--Antiquities--Guide-books.
      Canada--Antiquities--Guide-books.
      Archaeological museums and collections--United States--
      Guide-books.
      Archaeological museums and collections--Canada--Guide-books.

----------------------------------------------------CONTINUED-----------
NEXT ACTIONS    Key: ? for Help           + to see the next screen
                L to see a Longer display - to see the previous screen
                F to Find other items     Q to Quit
NEXT ACTION? +_
```

HOLDINGS AND STATUS

Patrons want to find items. Holdings should be presented along with bibliographic displays, preferably on the first screen displayed for an item. Compact holdings and status information can be more effective than extensive information.

The first screen should be designed to leave room for some holdings information, but it may not be reasonable to place extensive holdings on a normal bibliographic display.

Different types of libraries have different problems with holdings, and serials present even more problems than monographs. Medium-sized and large public libraries tend to have many copies of items, resulting in lengthy holdings displays even if only one line is needed for each copy. Research libraries tend to have single copies of most items. Any library may have problems with detailed holdings for serials and other complex items.

Extensive holdings require separate displays that have enough bibliographic information to identify the item. Segregating *all* holdings on special screens ignores the primary motive of most patrons in using online catalogs—to determine where an item is and how it can be obtained. At least some holdings information should appear on the single-item display that usually appears for an item (the default display).

Circulation Status

The call number and circulation status of an item should appear on the first screen of any normal single-item display. An item's status should be stated in words, not in codes.

Status information should be terse but clear and use intelligible vocabulary. Current circulation status is one vital element that card catalogs cannot provide but that online catalogs can and should. Design of good circulation status displays involves a difficult balance of completeness, correctness and space.

The patron needs immediate information on whether the item circulates, whether it is available and how to get it. Circulation status may involve additional details, such as the number of holds, when an item is due and when it can be recalled. That may be too much information for a single line, and it may be more information than most patrons need.

If the combination of call number, location and circulation status will fit on one line in several columns, a display summarizing the status of four copies will take only five lines (including labels for the columns). If extended information requires a second line, that same display requires nine lines, using most of the available space on a three-part screen. The problem becomes worse for items with more copies. Additionally, any multiple-line display of holdings/status information makes column labels more difficult, since the second line must be distinctly labeled and must not cause confusion with labels for the first line.

The circulation status should appear in upper and lower case, particularly if a location code on the same line is in capital letters.

Most early online access systems use all capital letters for status information and location names. The result is that the status display consists of almost all capital letters, making it look more like codes than like words. *On shelf* is easier to read than ON SHELF.

Librarians need to think through each element of the wording for circulation status. How specific should status information be, and what wording should be used? Existing systems use a variety of items such as *on shelf, no current loan, in* and *available* to indicate the same status. *On shelf* may promise more than the library can deliver. *Not charged out* is more neutral, if somewhat negative. An item labeled *on shelf* may not be shelved properly, may be on a return shelf or truck, or it may have been stolen. An argument in favor of *on shelf* is that it tells the patron that the item *should* be on the shelf. If it is not, the patron can pursue the matter further and may help the library to identify missing or stolen items.

When books are charged out, what term communicates that status most distinctly? *Charged out, checked out, on loan, circulating* and *out* are all plausible, as is *due date* followed by the due date. A library will probably have many other statuses, such as *lost, mending, on display* and, for academic libraries, *course reserve* or something similar. Regardless of the terms chosen for circulation status, clarity is essential.

Patrons will be served much better by catalogs that show the status of items, but no catalog can give perfectly accurate status information.

Should a library provide specific status information on books that are in the process of being reshelved? Changing status codes at each step in the operation would be time consuming, unless scanning devices that require little or no labor are used to update codes. One sensible solution is to deal with significant delays only. When a book goes out to be mended, that should be recorded. If a library shelves returned books in an accessible area for two or three days before reshelving, the library should consider using a status to indicate that area. If a library takes an average of two hours to get books back to the stacks, it should not bother with a status code for an intermediate area. A system could even "age" status codes automatically based on typical performance; that is, a book that has been checked in could have a status such as *sorting shelf* for a set number of hours, after which the status automatically changes to *on shelf* or *available*.

Call Number Placement and Format

Call numbers should appear along with location and status information. Multiple-line call numbers do not serve any useful purpose and may establish an inappropriate "online card catalog" metaphor.

A few patron access systems arrange call numbers in a multiple-line format, and some place call numbers at the top of bibliographic displays.

Call numbers at the top of displays are not usually accompanied by location and status codes. The result is that locational information is split on the screen. If a patron wants to retrieve an item, not just bibliographic information, then the call number is a finding tool and may be no more important than the branch or library name.

Multiple-line call numbers also split locational and status information, at least to some extent. The arguments in favor of multiple-line call numbers are that the arrangement is familiar and the arrangement makes it easier for a patron to copy call numbers and find them on book spines. Ideally, libraries should provide printers so that patrons can print out lists with call numbers and avoid writing them down. Familiarity may not be a virtue in this case; patron access systems should not be regarded as online card catalogs.

CARDLIKE DISPLAYS

Cardlike displays fit more information into a smaller space but may be substantially harder to understand than labeled displays.

Many proponents of online catalogs decry catalog cards as devices that serve librarians at the expense of patrons. In their view, catalog cards have never communicated effectively to patrons, and cardlike displays have no place in online systems. Some studies do show that patrons are not able to articulate the contents of a catalog card as well as a librarian. However, these studies have never clarified whether the problem is the way information is arranged or the fact that patrons simply do not care about some of the information.

Patrons benefit from cardlike formats in two ways: they pack large amounts of information into a small amount of space and they establish a familiar context for those patrons who are accustomed to card catalogs. The first issue is quite clear because card formats make efficient use of space. In RLG's testing of bibliographic displays using the same "medium" set of data elements (all access points but no notes), only 2% of a 400,000-record sample required more than one screen to show a traditional cardlike online display, including minimal holdings. Using the same elements but substituting a good labeled format for the cardlike one (including vertical spacing to group elements), 45% of the records required more than one screen. That's a major difference. The difference stems from the need for blank lines and the need to start each element on a new line in a labeled format. When the cardlike display was limited to 60 characters per line (the same as the labeled display, not including labels), and the blank lines were removed from the labeled display, the difference was much smaller, but still significant. Using the cardlike display, 8% of the items needed more than one screen; with the labeled display, 19% required more than one screen.

Cardlike and other unlabeled displays also avoid certain design pitfalls. Unlabeled elements cannot bear misleading labels and problems of library jargon (in labels) do not arise.

The questions are clear:

- Are patrons confused by cardlike displays?
- Does the compactness of cardlike displays justify their use, in spite of problems?

The statistical evidence is in, and librarians must make decisions based on that evidence and their own professional judgment.

CITATION-STYLE DISPLAYS

A display in the form of a bibliographic citation may be useful to accompany holdings displays or as the default display. Figure 11.8 illustrates a citation display. The main entry, title, edition, publication information and physical description appear as a single paragraph. Entries (including the main entry), subjects and notes may be displayed with labels or in a cardlike arrangement. Figure 11.8 uses labels (in this case, only one label).

The following problems arise when attempting to use citation displays based on standard cataloging:

- There is no standard citation format. ANSI Z39.29, *American National Standard for Bibliographic References,* constitutes a formal consensus standard for citations, but it includes several options and is not widely used. The most widely used style is that specified in *The Chicago Manual of Style.*
- Common citation styles use simpler punctuation than ISBD, and citation punctuation cannot be created easily (if at all) from ISBD punctuation.

Figure 11.8: Partial Entry Using Title Citation

```
Arie amorose. [Sound recording] Philips 9500 557 p1978. 1
disc. 33 1/3 rpm. stereo. 12 in.

NAMES: Baker, Janet.
       Marriner, Neville.
       Academy of St. Martin-in-the-fields.
```

- The title portion of a standard AACR2/MARC record includes information not present in the title portion of standard citations, and the main entry of a standard cataloging record for an item with multiple authors does not include the same information that would be in a standard citation.

The major virtues of citation style are compactness, familiarity and the ease of copying or downloading such citations for use in a bibliography. Compactness is a significant factor. Figure 11.9 includes the same information as Figure 11.8, in a fully labeled display. Full labeling makes the display clearer but requires significantly more space. Including the same medium level of elements, 59% of the items tested using the display in Figure 11.9 require more than one screen; 40% of those tested using the display in Figure 11.8 require more than one screen. Those percentages can be compared directly to the percentages cited for cardlike displays.

Figure 11.9: Partial Entry Using Labeling

```
    TITLE: Arie amorose. [Sound recording]
PUBLISHED: Philips 9500 557 p1978.
 MATERIAL: 1 disc. 33 1/3 rpm. stereo. 12 in.

    NAMES: Baker, Janet.
           Marriner, Neville.
           Academy of St. Martin-in-the-fields.
```

A citation paragraph can begin with a title or with a main entry. In the case of Figure 11.8, there is no difference because the sound recording has a title as its main entry. Figure 11.10 shows a title citation for a sound recording with a composer as main entry. That example shows a problem with omitting the main entry from the citation paragraph. While the display works well for most books, serials, films and maps, it does not work as well for sound recordings and scores, many of which have titles that are not distinctive.

LABELS

Labels should help patrons to find and understand information. If labels fail to make information clear, they simply waste space.

Labels can make bibliographic displays clearer and can identify information that might otherwise be mysterious to the patron. Labeled displays also take more space on the screen and require additional screens more often. Poorly chosen labels may do more to confuse patrons than to help them.

Location of Labels and Text

Labels should be right-justified and placed to the left of text, separated by a colon and a space or by several spaces.

Numerous possibilities exist for placing labels in a bibliographic display. A few of these follow:

Figure 11.10: Partial Entry with Title Citation, Sound Recording

```
            Suite no. 1 for 2 pianos, op. 5 (Fantasy). Suite no. 2 for
            2 pianos, op. 17. Desto DC-6431 [1969] 1 disc. 33 1/3
            rpm. stereo. 12 in.

     NAMES: Rachmaninoff, Sergei, 1873-1943.
            Holby, Lee.
            Mester, Jorge.
            Foster, Lawrence.
            Harkness Symphony Orchestra.
            London Symphony Orchestra.
            Harkness, Rebekah, arr.
            Holby, Lee, arr.
```

Figure 11.11: Labeled Display, Version 1

```
Your search: find title creative computing                    MEDIUM
    Finds: 1 item                                         Screen 1 of 1
------------------------------------------------------------------------

TITLE: Creative computing. EDITION: v. 1-   ; Nov./Dec.,1974-
PUBLISHED: [Morristown, N.J. Creative Computing, etc.] MATERIAL: v. ill. 29 cm.
SUBJECTS: Computers--Popular works--Periodicals. Games--Data processing--
Periodicals. Electronic data processing--Periodicals. Microcomputers--
Periodicals.




------------------------------------------------------------------------

NEXT ACTIONS      Key: ? for help              + to see the next screen
                       L to see a Longer display  - to see the previous screen
                       F to Find other items      Q to Quit

NEXT ACTION?_
```

- Labels are followed immediately by text, in block or paragraph form. Figure 11.11 illustrates this display, which is difficult to read.
- Labels are followed immediately by text, with each element on a new line. Figure 11.12 illustrates this display. The information is much easier to read than in Figure 11.11, but is still not very legible.
- Labels are left-justified and text begins on the next line. Figure 11.13 illustrates this display. The results are quite legible, but the information takes up an inordinate amount of room. Patrons who do not need the labels can hardly avoid them in this display.
- Labels are left-justified and left-justified text begins at a constant indentation. Figure 11.14 illustrates this display, which is probably the most common way to display labeled information. The information is clear and the display is legible.
- Labels are right-justified and are followed by left-justified text. Figure 11.15 illustrates this display, which is unusually clear and effective.

Figures 11.13, 11.14 and 11.15 are all clear and legible, but Figure 11.15 does the best job of combining legibility and compactness. Blank lines added before the group of subjects can make the display even

Figure 11.12: Labeled Display, Version 2

```
Your search: find title creative computing                    MEDIUM
        Finds: 1 item                                   Screen 1 of 1
--------------------------------------------------------------------

TITLE: Creative computing.
EDITION: v. 1-    ; Nov./Dec. 1974-
PUBLISHED: [Morristown, N.J. Creative Computing, etc.]
MATERIAL: v. ill. 29 cm.
SUBJECTS: Computers--Popular works--Periodicals.
Games--Data processing--Periodicals.
Electronic data processing--Periodicals.
Microcomputers--Periodicals.




--------------------------------------------------------------------
NEXT ACTIONS     Key: ? for help              + to see the next screen
                      L to see a Longer display  - to see the previous screen
                      F to Find other items    Q to Quit
NEXT ACTION?_
```

Figure 11.13: Labeled Display, Version 3

```
Your search: find title creative computing                    MEDIUM
        Finds: 1 item                                   Screen 1 of 1
--------------------------------------------------------------------

TITLE
  Creative computing.
EDITION
  v. 1-    ; Nov./Dec., 1974-
PUBLISHED
  [Morristown, N.J. Creative Computing, etc.]
MATERIAL
  v. ill. 29 cm.
SUBJECTS
  Computers--Popular works--Periodicals.
  Games--Data processing--Periodicals.
  Electronic data processing--Periodicals.
  Microcomputers--Periodicals.

--------------------------------------------------------------------
NEXT ACTIONS     Key: ? for help              + to see the next screen
                      L to see a Longer display  - to see the previous screen
                      F to Find other items    Q to Quit
NEXT ACTION?_
```

Figure 11.14: Labeled Display, Version 4

```
┌────────────────────────────────────────────────────────────────────────┐
│ Your search: find title creative computing                    MEDIUM     │
│     Finds: 1 item                                    Screen 1 of 1        │
│ ------------------------------------------------------------------------ │
│                                                                          │
│ TITLE:        Creative computing.                                        │
│ EDITION:      v. 1-    ; Nov./Dec. 1974-                                  │
│ PUBLISHED:    [Morristown, N.J. Creative Computing, etc.]                │
│ MATERIAL:     v. ill. 29 cm.                                             │
│ SUBJECTS:     Computers--Popular works--Periodicals.                     │
│               Games--Data processing--Periodicals.                       │
│               Electronic data processing--Periodicals.                   │
│               Microcomputers--Periodicals.                               │
│                                                                          │
│                                                                          │
│                                                                          │
│                                                                          │
│ ------------------------------------------------------------------------ │
│ NEXT ACTIONS    Key: ? for help               + to see the next screen    │
│                      L to see a Longer display - to see the previous screen│
│                      F to Find other items    Q to Quit                  │
│ NEXT ACTION?_                                                            │
└────────────────────────────────────────────────────────────────────────┘
```

Figure 11.15: Labeled Display, Version 5

```
┌────────────────────────────────────────────────────────────────────────┐
│ Your search: find title creative computing                    MEDIUM     │
│     Finds: 1 item                                    Screen 1 of 1        │
│ ------------------------------------------------------------------------ │
│                                                                          │
│          TITLE: Creative computing.                                      │
│        EDITION: v. 1-    ; Nov./Dec. 1974-                                │
│      PUBLISHED: [Morristown, N.J. Creative Computing, etc.]              │
│       MATERIAL: v. ill. 29 cm.                                           │
│       SUBJECTS: Computers--Popular works--Periodicals.                   │
│                 Games--Data processing--Periodicals.                     │
│                 Electronic data processing--Periodicals.                 │
│                 Microcomputers--Periodicals.                             │
│                                                                          │
│                                                                          │
│                                                                          │
│                                                                          │
│ ------------------------------------------------------------------------ │
│ NEXT ACTIONS    Key: ? for help               + to see the next screen    │
│                      L to see a Longer display - to see the previous screen│
│                      F to Find other items    Q to Quit                  │
│ NEXT ACTION?_                                                            │
└────────────────────────────────────────────────────────────────────────┘
```

more legible, and still leave it significantly more compact than Figure 11.13.

Labels and Fields

Any field labeled directly should start on a new line.

Some existing systems display more than one labeled textual field on a line. As illustrated in Figure 11.11, the results are neither attractive nor clear. Actually, most displays tend not to be quite as bad as Figure 11.11. More typically, systems save space by placing such elements as LCCN and ISBN on the same line with other elements. These labeled elements placed somewhere in the middle of a line, with no clear spatial consistency, tend to get lost. This may not matter for LCCN and ISBN, but if these items are so unimportant, why do they appear at all?

Any field that deserves its own label also deserves its own line. There are three significant exceptions to this statement—two of them clearly reasonable, the third more questionable:

- Holdings and status displays—where multiple elements should appear on each line—are usually columnar displays, with labels at the top of each column rather than fields labeled directly.
- One-line-per-item displays—either pick lists or other very compressed multiple-item displays—should have column labels and be in specific columns.
- Coded elements such as language and country codes are too short and too obscure to place on separate lines.

Coded elements are more likely to appear on a tagged MARC display than on a labeled display designed for patron use. As with LCCN and ISBN, the first question is why country and language codes should appear at all.

Labels should not be repeated for each occurrence of a type of field.

Some existing systems label each group of fields; some label each field and use the label SUBJECT before each of the four subjects in

Figure 11.15. Either method can work well and each has advantages and disadvantages.

By providing a label for each field, a patron access system avoids problems that occur when multiply-occurring fields break between screens. Labeling each field also avoids using a plural label when a field appears only once. Most items have only one author or name entry, but enough have more than one that a group label must be at least NAME(S) or AUTHOR(S).

Labeling each group leaves the screen more open and makes group locations more obvious. Most fields in most records require only a single line to display. Labeling each field can result in an almost solid column of labels. With fewer labels, each label stands out more distinctively.

Wording and Highlighting

Labels should be whole words or phrases, not abbreviations, should be in English and avoid library jargon and should be capitalized and possibly be in half-intensity reverse video.

Good labels are difficult to design without lapsing into library jargon, but the effort is worthwhile. Abbreviations are less clear than words and abbreviations of jargon may be the worst possible alternative. Displaying labels in all capital letters helps to separate them from bibliographic information. A similar effect can be obtained by using half-intensity and reverse video for the labels.

Cryptic abbreviations and library jargon may make labeled displays less effective than cardlike displays. The range of labels in current use is surprisingly wide and, in almost every case, given to abbreviations, library jargon or both. Labels observed in online catalogs include *Main entry, tracings, added entries,* SO, IM, CO, SUBJT, AAUTH and IMPRT. None of those is meaningful to patrons and one of them—SO—will mystify most librarians as well.

The most difficult issue in labeling may be main and added entries, particularly those added entries that include both author and title or title only. One possible solution is to separate name entries without titles from all added entries with titles, calling the first *Names* or *Authors* and the second *Works.* Publication information (imprint) and physical description both pose some problems, but the labels *Published* and *Material* appear to work well.

Partial Labeling

Within a group of labeled elements, each distinctive element must have a distinctive label.

Some existing systems use a cardlike or citation-style descriptive paragraph and label subjects and other access points. Such a mixture appears to work well. Fewer labels stand out better. Partial labeling makes the edition, publication information and physical description less obvious. It also saves space and avoids some troublesome labels.

Some systems use partial labeling in a different and troubling way. One online system uses the label IMPRINT but includes physical description. Another system uses the label *Title* and includes publication information and physical description. Another online catalog includes physical description under EDITION, and still another includes it under PUBLISHER. In each case, the absence of a label suggests that the information is somehow attached to the previous label; in no case is that suggestion legitimate.

Labels on Brief and Multiple-Item Displays

Brief and multiple-item displays may not require labels.

Figure 11.16 shows the same items as Figure 11.6, but with labels. One result is that only four items, instead of six, can be displayed on the screen even though one spacing line has been removed.

The best argument for labeling brief and multiple-item displays is consistency. If some displays use labels, all displays should use them. This is a good argument, but not an overwhelming one. Libraries and designers should consider the possibility that brief and multiple-item entries don't need labels.

Partially labeled displays may avoid the issue. If the first few elements (entry, title, edition, publication information and physical description) appear unlabeled in longer displays, then any subset of those elements should appear unlabeled for multiple-item and brief displays.

OTHER DISPLAY ISSUES

The two remaining issues in this chapter do not fall into any single category, but should be considered when designing and evaluating online systems.

Figure 11.16: Multiple-Item Display with Labels

```
Your search: FIND TWORD PLAGIARISM                              MULTIPLE
        Finds: 13 items.                                   Items 1 to 4
-----------------------------------------------------------------------
  1.    AUTHOR: Casewit, Curtis W.
         TITLE: Keep it legal! :
     PUBLISHED: Sacramento, California : Creative Book Co., [1976]

  2.    AUTHOR: Douglas, John, 1721-1807.
         TITLE: Milton vindicated from the charge of plagiarism :
     PUBLISHED: London : Printed for A. Miller ..., 1751.

  3.    AUTHOR: Grier, Samuel L.
         TITLE: A tool for detecting plagiarism in Pascal programs [Microform] /
     PUBLISHED: 1980.

  4.    AUTHOR: Johnston, Dan.
         TITLE: Design protection :
     PUBLISHED: London : Design Council : 1978

-----------------------------------------------------CONTINUED-----------
NEXT ACTIONS:      Key: D1-D5 to Display an item   + for Next Screen
                        F to Find other items      ? for Help
                        Q to Quit
NEXT ACTION? +_
```

Main Entries and Statements of Responsibility

Statements of responsibility do not always duplicate main entries and should appear in most bibliographic displays.

Some librarians complain of redundant statements of responsibility, with some justification. In many cases, if the main entry is displayed, the statement of responsibility is wholly redundant and could be omitted.

Unfortunately, that is not always the case. Statements of responsibility frequently include information on illustrators and editors that cannot be gathered easily from added entries. After extensive testing, RLG staff working on the Bibliographic Display project concluded that the statement of responsibility could not be omitted without losing information in a significant portion of items.

Another alternative that appears somewhat more promising is leaving off the main entry and including that field along with other NAME entries after the title. This alternative results in peculiar displays for some sound recordings and scores, but it works well for most other material.

Items Other than Books

The same display designs can be used for all forms of material, with the possible exception of archival and manuscript control information.

Multiple-item displays should almost certainly have the same minimal information for all forms of material. Medium and long displays pose more difficulties. Sound recordings pose special problems for display of added entries, and they need uniform titles and main entries more than most other materials (except scores). Visual materials and machine-readable data files pose few special problems in terms of display, though notes may be more important for these and other nonbook items than for books. Maps also work fairly well when displayed as if they were books. Serials involve more linking entries, usually treated as notes, than any other format and require more attention to extended holdings.

Archival materials pose extremely unusual problems and are unlikely to be integrated into most library catalogs. An archival control record may have more than 100 entries; hundreds of archival control records may have the same nondistinctive title. Given the length and complexity of such records, special display considerations may be needed.

NOTE

1. Crawford, Walt; Stovel, Lennie; Bales, Kathleen. *Bibliographic Displays in the Online Catalog.* White Plains, NY: Knowledge Industry Publications, Inc.; 1986.

12

Specific Displays:
Single and Multiple Items

Any good access system needs one or more multiple-item displays and one or more single-item displays. Multiple-item displays allow patrons to look through search results rapidly; single-item displays provide more information on individual items.

For any given system, designers must decide the following:

- how many different multiple-item and single-item displays to provide
- what information to include in each display
- how to arrange that information
- how to identify each display and what displays to provide by default
- for multiple-item displays (and sequential display of single items), what sequence to use for each display

MULTIPLE-ITEM DISPLAYS

Multiple-item displays show sets of items in a compact arrangement that allows patrons to look through a search result rapidly.

Multiple-item displays differ from browsable heading screens or heading result screens. Heading screens are always an intermediate step in searching; they should show the number of items for each heading and, where available, cross-references. On the other hand, multiple-item displays show actual bibliographic items and generally lead patrons to display one or more items individually.

Single-Line Displays

Displays with one line per item provide a quick overview of search results with very limited information. Such displays should be columnar.

Figure 12.1 illustrates a columnar single-line display for multiple items. The display provides up to 20 characters of author name and up to 50 characters of title information. Figure 12.1 shows items arranged alphabetically by main entry, which may cause some confusion with respect to lines 5 and 10 (those items with title main entries). Some systems display all title main entries at the beginning of a set of multiple items in an attempt to avoid confusion. Either solution may cause problems.

The display in Figure 12.1 is *not* identical to the *pick list* recommended in Chapter 7. A pick list includes location and call number, and has so little room for bibliographic information that most items will be severely truncated. (Assuming 5 characters for location and 20 for call number, with no line numbers, a 15-character field for authors will leave only 37 characters for title.)

Figure 12.2 shows the same items as Figure 12.1, but combines

Figure 12.1: Fully Columnar Single-Line Display

```
Your search: FIND TWORD PLAGIARISM                           OVERVIEW
        Finds: 13 items                               Items 1 to 12
        ------------------------------------------------------------------

    #  AUTHOR               TITLE                                     DATE
   ---- -------------------- ------------------------------------------ ----
    1. Casewit, Curtis W.   Keep it legal! :                          1976
    2. Douglas, John, 1721  Milton vindicated from the charges of plagiari... 1751
    3. Grier, Samuel L.     A tool for detecting plagiarism in PASCAL prog... 1980
    4. Johnston, Dan.       Design protection :                       1978
    5.                      Legal aspects of plagiarism /             1985
    6. Lindey, Alexander, 1 Plagiarism and originality /              1952
    7. Mayr, Roswithe.      The concept of love in Sidney and Spenser / 1978
    8. Noble, June.         Steal this plot :                         1985
    9. Salzman, Maurice.    Plagiarism, the "art" of stealing literary mat... 1931
   10.                      Sources, their use and acknowledgment :   1962
   11. Weber, Carl Jefferso Plagiarism and Thomas Hardy /             1937
   12. White, Harold Ogden. Plagiarism and imitation during the English re... 1936


   NEXT ACTIONS     Key: D1-D12 to Display an item   + for next screen
                         L1-L12 for Long display      ? for Help
                         F to Find something else     Q to Quit
   NEXT ACTION:+_
```

Figure 12.2: Partially Columnar Single-Line Display

```
Your search: FIND TWORD PLAGIARISM                              OVERVIEW
       Finds: 13 items                                    Items 1 to 12
----------------------------------------------------------------------

   #  AUTHOR AND TITLE                                              DATE
----  --------------------------------------------------------------  ----
   1. Casewit, Curtis W. Keep it legal! :                           1976
   2. Douglas, John, 1721-1807. Milton vindicated from the charges of pla... 1751
   3. Grier, Samuel L. A tool for detecting plagiarism in PASCAL programs... 1980
   4. Johnston, Dan. Design protection :                            1978
   5. Legal aspects of plagiarism /                                 1985
   6. Lindey, Alexander, 1896- Plagiarism and originality /         1952
   7. Mayr, Roswithe. The concept of love in Sidney and Spenser /   1978
   8. Noble, June. Steal this plot :                                1985
   9. Salzman, Maurice. Plagiarism, the "art" of stealing literary material, 1931
  10. Sources, their use and acknowledgment :                       1962
  11. Weber, Carl Jefferson, 1894-1966. Plagiarism and Thomas Hardy / 1937
  12. White, Harold Ogden. Plagiarism and imitation during the English re... 1936


----------------------------------------------------------------------
NEXT ACTIONS      Key: D1-D12 to Display an item    + for next screen
                       L1-L12 for Long display      ? for Help
                       F to Find something else     Q to Quit
NEXT ACTION:+_
```

author and title into a single column. The display shows more information but is less legible. Patrons who are looking for titles will find Figure 12.2 much harder to read. Certain design variations may make this type of display much more legible; capitalization of titles is one of many possibilities.

Do single-line displays make sense? That depends on the library and its needs. Placing 12 or more items on a screen certainly allows fast scanning of a result set. Though not illustrated here, a system with compact top and bottom segments could possibly place as many as 20 items on a screen. As shown in the two figures, single-line displays require frequent truncation. Figure 12.1 has four truncated titles and three truncated authors; Figure 12.2 still has four truncated titles.

How well does such truncated information serve patrons? That depends on the library, the patron and the search. Unfortunately, in those situations where additional information is needed most—when a search retrieves a large result with many similar items—the fast overview of single-line results will be most valuable.

Other than truncated information, the other significant drawback of single-line displays is screen density. Single-line displays are likely to have as many as 1200 characters on a screen and a density as high as 60%, which makes an extremely full screen.

Patrons would be well served by a single-line display that includes some indication of material form, such as videocassette, compact disc, cassette, LP, book or computer software. Unfortunately, MARC formats do not provide a single place where that information can be stored in clear, compact form. A library may find it difficult to devise a set of codes that make sense to patrons without taking up too much of a single line.

Multiple-Line Displays

Any multiple-line display should leave a blank line between bibliographic items. No more than four to seven items should display on a screen. Those bibliographic elements displayed should not be truncated except at the subfield level.

The second approach to multiple-item displays uses more than one line per item. Several versions of that approach are possible: labeled or unlabeled, with or without blank lines between items, and with complete fields or truncated fields. Two possibilities appear in Chapter 11, both using complete subfields (Figures 11.6 and 11.16).

Without spacing lines, multiple-line entries will be very difficult to read. With spacing lines, and assuming at least two lines per item, a screen will not have room for more than four to seven items. Blank spacing lines make the display easier to read and also reduce information density to less than 50% in most cases.

If the display includes full main entry and at least the complete short title, the patron should have enough information to decide whether to display a given item in a longer format. In some cases, the main entry and short title will require quite a few lines. Some government publications and early monographs require more than one screen to display main entry and short title.

Further information beyond author and title can reasonably appear in a multiple-line display. Publication information, or at least date of publication, will help patrons identify material. The physical description will help users of nonbook material, and the number of pages can help all patrons. Almost all the information in a bibliographic citation can be helpful. A citation-style display may be compact enough for multiple-item displays, even including all elements of a citation.

Item Sequence

Multiple items should always appear in a meaningful sequence (one that is obvious to the patron). The most obvious sequence is alphabetical by main entry or title, whichever appears first in the display.

Displays that show items in no sequence, or in a sequence that is not immediately clear, are a disservice to the patron. They hide any internal relationships within a set of results and force the patron to page through all the result sets to ascertain what is available.

Suggestions have been made that some results should appear in some sequence other than alphabetic order. Two sequences that have been suggested are *sorting by importance* and *sorting in reverse chronological order,* with the newest items appearing first.

Sorting by importance can be dismissed for almost any library. It requires that somebody determine the importance of each item, an almost impossible task and one that raises critical questions of intellectual freedom. Any patron would be puzzled by a display that shows items in a seemingly random order, and a message such as *The most important items appear first* will not help much. (Most patrons would probably respond that the computer has no business telling them what is important.)

If items appear in reverse chronological order, the date must appear at the left. Placing items in reverse chronological order will not guarantee that the best or most useful items appear at the beginning of a display.

Subject searching specialists have suggested that results of subject searches should be displayed so that the newest items appear first. Figure 12.3 shows the first screen of a single-line display for the subject *Evolution.* Charles Darwin's *On the Origin of Species* would appear on the ninth or tenth screen in a fairly large collection. A subject searcher would page through textbooks, popular treatments and tracts on "creation science" before getting to the classics in the field.

Patrons may not even realize that Figure 12.3 is in reverse chronological order. Even if the order is clear, it does not seem to be helpful to the patron in this case. Reverse chronological order calls for assump-

Figure 12.3: Subject Search Result in Reverse Chronological Order

```
Your search: FIND SUBJECT EVOLUTION                      OVERVIEW
     Finds: 258 1items                               Items 1 to 12
-------------------------------------------------------------------

 #  DATE AUTHOR                TITLE
---- ---- -------------------- -----------------------------------
 1. 1986 Delbruck, Max.        Mind from matter? :
 2. 1986 Kutter, G. Siegfried  The universe and life :
 3. 1986                       Let's discover the prehistoric world.
 4. 1986                       Multidomain proteins :
 5. 1986 Stein, Sara Bonnett.  The evolution book :
 6. 1985                       The biology of mutualism :
 7. 1985 Eldredge, Niles.      Unfinished synthesis :
 8. 1985                       Evolution at a crossroads :
 9. 1985                       Evolutionary case histories from the fossil re...
10. 1985                       The evolution of genome size :
11. 1985 Grant, Verne.        The evolutionary process :
12. 1985                       Morphometrics in evolutionary biology :

-------------------------------------------------------------------

NEXT ACTIONS       Key: D1-D12 to Display an item  + for next screen
                        L1-L12 for Long display     ? for Help
                        F to Find something else    Q to Quit
NEXT ACTION:+_
```

tions to be made that are suspect in the hard sciences and absolutely false in the humanities. The newest works in a field are not necessarily the best and do not necessarily deserve special emphasis. If patrons are interested only in recent works, they should be able to qualify a search by date of publication.

Ideally, patrons should be able to specify display sequences that suit their own needs. That requires some method of identifying a display sequence, which may mean understanding the structure of bibliographic records. A set of options such as the one below might be feasible:

Key a number from 1 to 5 to arrange results:
1. Alphabetically by title
2. Alphabetically by author
3. From newest to oldest
4. By language, English first, then alphabetically
5. By country, U.S. first, then alphabetically

Numbering

Results should be numbered continuously, beginning with "1," based on the order of display.

Existing patron access systems number items in one of three ways:

1. Numbers appear randomly, based on a hidden data element. The first screen might show numbers *3, 7, 1, 2, 8, 4* in that order from top to bottom.
2. Numbers are assigned sequentially, beginning with *1* for each screen (i.e., with *1* as the first number on each screen).
3. Numbers are assigned sequentially *throughout* a result set (with *1* as the first number on the first screen, *7* as the first number on the second screen—if six items display on the first screen—and so on).

The first case seems almost deliberately hostile to the patron. The second works well within a screen, but makes it difficult for a patron to navigate among screens or determine relative position within a result set. The third is perhaps the most sensible solution because it allows a patron to jump to the middle of a large set immediately, placing each screen in context.

The last item on one screen should not be repeated as the first item on the next screen for multiple-line displays. For single-line displays, the repeated line may provide continuity.

Repeating an item from one screen to the next will always help to maintain continuity, but the repeated item takes up too much space in multiple-line displays. In some cases, a repeated item may mean that only one or two new items appear on each screen.

SINGLE-ITEM DISPLAYS

Every patron access system should have at least two single-item displays, not including a tagged display. Many, perhaps most, libraries will find a third display useful.

For most patrons, success in using a patron access system means a single-item display. Different patrons may have different needs, and a single display may not be able to meet all those needs equally well.

Most designers seem to have arrived at the conclusion that a single display is not enough. Unfortunately, every additional display means more work for the system and more complexity for patrons, including a more difficult task of naming the displays and providing access to them. A system with five or more single-item displays has too many choices to provide good service.

The proposed Standard Common Command Language does not limit the number of displays, but does call for at least two displays—a short and a long one. Most patron access systems, and most patrons, will be well served by three ways to display single items:

- Brief with holdings. This display, equivalent to the Standard Command Language SHORT display, has enough bibliographic information to identify the item and has enough space on the screen for extensive location, call number and status information or for extensive serial holdings.
- Medium. This provides all the bibliographic and access information that the vast majority of patrons need or can use, including all access points, in a display that will usually fit on one screen with room for nominal holdings. It is probably the best default display for most libraries and will satisfy Standard Command Language specifications for a LONG display.
- Long. The long display provides all the information, no matter how obscure, that patrons at any level can understand or use. Predictably, records displayed in this arrangement will usually not fit on a single screen.

Some libraries may see no need for the long version or may wish to provide only a brief and long version, omitting the medium version. Depending on the library, its patrons and the way displays are designed, either of those decisions might be justified. These display types are discussed in detail later in the chapter.

Online catalogs should display enough information to satisfy all patrons, not just 90% of them. Eliminating less frequently used information is equivalent to eliminating less frequently used services and books.

The assertion has been made that an online catalog should display only those elements used by a majority of patrons. "For the most part [users] do not need to see the collation, imprint, series statements. . . . Include the entire bibliographic record in the database and enhance it (if possible) with table of contents and index information, but display only a brief form of the record to online catalog users."[1] Emily Fayen's suggestion is not the only one of its type, but is one of the clearest. If the last sentence of her statement went on to say *as a default display,* the argument would be over details. But her statement does not go on to suggest a more complete alternative display. The specific examples in Fayen's statement are discussed later in the chapter, but the question really is not one of specifics.

If online patron access systems are to replace card catalogs, they should be at least as informative as card catalogs. Online catalogs should enhance retrieval and provide more information, not reduce access to information. Such online library systems maintain complete information in their databases, for such uses as preparing complete displays for technical processing, and since there are no financial or other benefits in hiding bibliographic information from patrons, why not make it available?

A library should use a default display that patrons can understand and that will serve most of their needs, but should make complete information readily available to those who can use it.

There is nothing wrong with favoring the needs of the majority, though the reasons for omitting some elements do not stand up to examination. An overly complex default display may confuse some patrons. The problem is one of *only* serving the needs of the majority when the information needed to serve others is readily available.

Brief Display with Holdings

The simplest display should provide enough information to enable patrons to identify the item, locate the item and determine whether it is available.

Providing sufficient information to enable patrons to retrieve an item requires relatively brief bibliographic information combined with complete holdings and status information. Elements included in the simplest display should identify the item clearly, but need not provide subject headings and all entries for an item.

The authors of the book *Bibliographic Displays in the Online*

Catalog studied information suitable for a brief display, including information needed to identify nonbook material. Physical description is a key element to properly identify things other than books, and the publisher's name also helps to provide basic identification.

In order to properly identify library material including non-books, a brief display should include main entry, full title field (with statement of responsibility), publisher and date of publication, and physical description.

Three different displays with those elements were tested against 400,000 current cataloging items. All three tests use a 14-line display area, as do all the figures in this chapter. In every case, the results are quite satisfactory. Figure 12.4 illustrates a brief cardlike display; Figure 12.5 shows the same information in labeled form.

A brief display should provide ample room for holdings information. When tested against 400,000 bibliographic items, the cardlike display in Figure 12.4 had room for seven or more lines of holdings in 95% of the 400,000 cases. The labeled display took slightly more space, but 91% of the 400,000 items had room for seven or more lines of holdings on the first screen.

Figure 12.4: Machine-Readable Data File, Brief Cardlike Display

```
Your search: Spikell, Mark A#                            BRIEF
     Finds: 1 record                             Screen 1 of 1
-------------------------------------------------------------------

        Spikell, Mark A.
          Brain ticklers, Apple II, IIe editiokn [machine-readable
        data file] : mathematical problem-solving with the
        microcomputer / Mark A. Spikell & Stephen L. Snover. --
        Prentice-Hall, c1983.
          1 program file on 1 computer disk ; 5 1/4 in. +
        instructions (iv, 6 p.) + 2 books in loose-leaf binder.




-------------------------------------------------------------------

NEXT ACTIONS    Key: ? for help            + to see the next screen
                     L to see a Longer display  - to see the previous screen
                     F to Find other items      Q to Quit

NEXT ACTION? +_
```

Figure 12.5: Machine-Readable Data File, Brief Labeled Display

```
Your search: Brain ticklers, A#                                  BRIEF
   Finds: 1 record                                          Screen 1 of 1
---------------------------------------------------------------------------

         TITLE: Brain ticklers, Apple II, IIe edition [machine-readable data
                file] : mathematical problem-solving with the
                microcomputer / Mark A. Spikell & Stephen L. Snover.
          NAME: Spikell, Mark A.
     PUBLISHED: Prentice-Hall, c1983.
      MATERIAL: 1 program file on 1 computer disk ; 5 1/4 in. + instructions
                (iv, 6 p.) + 2 books in loose-leaf binder.




---------------------------------------------------------------------------
NEXT ACTIONS     Key: ? for help                 + to see the next screen
                      L to see a Longer display  - to see the previous screen
                      F to Find other items      Q to Quit
NEXT ACTION? +_                                                  LBRF1
```

As noted earlier, statement of responsibility is an important part of many bibliographic entries. An informal sampling showed it duplicating the main entry in about 40% of items checked, but providing significant information in another 40%.* Names of illustrators, names of lyricists for music, names of ghostwriters and coauthors all appear in the statement of responsibility. A briefer entry might take up less space, but will not provide basic information for quite a few items.

Medium Display

A medium-level display should show all entries and subjects and provide all the information needed by most patrons, while still showing most items on a single screen.

The most complicated display decisions arise when designing a medium display, which should be the default display for most catalogs. One reasonable goal is that a medium display should satisfy the needs

---

*The remaining 20% had no statement of responsibility or had a statement providing some additional information that was arguably insignificant.

of 90% of patrons and have room to show an item and brief holdings in at least 90% of all possible cases (in other words, a second screen should be required for less than 1 out of every 10 items). An ideal display will satisfy more needs and display more items on one screen while providing clear information in a legible arrangement.

The research project that culminated in the book *Bibliographic Displays in the Online Catalog* studied many different options for medium displays, after determining a minimal definition of "medium." The project also studied displays based on assertions made by Joseph Matthews and Richard Palmer as to elements required to satisfy most users.

The results are mixed. Using the definition for an acceptable medium display used in the research project and explained in the following section, every labeled display required a second screen for more than 10% of the items tested. Two cardlike displays, both without spacing between paragraphs, managed to meet the 90% goal, but labeled displays ranged from 88% to 41%. The display judged to be most readable could show items on a single screen only 41% of the time; in almost two thirds of the cases tested (59%), at least two screens were needed to show an item with minimal holdings.

Figure 12.6 shows information for a sound recording displayed in a traditional cardlike arrangement, using only 60 columns of each line to

Figure 12.6: Sound Recording, Medium Cardlike Display

```
Your search: Ravel, Maurice, 1#                          MEDIUM
     Finds: 25 records         Record 14 of 24        Screen 1 of 2
------------------------------------------------------------------

        Ravel, Maurice, 1875-1937.
          Introduction and allegro, for flute, clarinet, harp, and
        string quarted [sound recording] Angel S 36586. [1969]
          1 disc. 33 1/3 rpm. mikcro. stereo. 12 in.
          1. Septets (Clarinet, flute, harp, 2 violins, viola,
        violoncello) 2. Trios (Piano, bassoon, oboe) 3. Sonatas
        (bassoon and clarinet) 4. Suites (bassoon, clarinet, oboe)
        5. Suites (bassoon, violins (2), viola, violoncello, double
        bass) I. Melos Ensemble. II. Poulenc, Francis, 1899-1963.
        Sonatas, clarinet, bassoon. [sound recording] 1969. III.
        Poulenc, Francis, 1899-1963. Trio, piano, oboe, bassoon.
        [sound recording] 1969. IV. Francaix, Jean, 1912-
        Divertissement, bassoon, strings. [sound recording] 1969. V.
        Francaix, Jean, 1912- Divertissement, oboe, clarinet,

------------------------------------------------------CONTINUED-------
NEXT ACTIONS     Key: ? for help              + to see the next screen
                      L to see a Longer display - to see the previous screen
                      F to Find other items     Q to Quit

NEXT ACTION? +_
```

make the display more readable. Ninety-two percent of items tested leave room for minimal holdings on one screen using this display and only 8% require a second screen.

Figure 12.7 shows the same bibliographic item displayed in a very legible labeled arrangement. This arrangement provides readily understandable information in an open display, but requires a second screen in 59% of the tested cases.

Figure 12.7: Sound Recording, Medium Labeled Display with Spacing

```
Your search: Ravel, Maurice, 1#                              MEDIUM
      Finds: 25 records            Record 14 of 24          Screen 1 of 2
------------------------------------------------------------------------

         TITLE: Introduction and allegro, for flute, clarinet, harp, and
                string quartet [sound recording]
     PUBLISHED: Angel S 36586. [1969]
      MATERIAL: 1 disc. 33 1/3 rp.m. micro. stereo. 12 in.

         NAMES: Ravel, Maurice, 1875-1937.
                Melos Ensemble.

      SUBJECTS: Septets (Clarinet, flute, harp, 2 violins, viola,
                violoncello)
                Trios (Piano, bassoon, oboe)
                Sonatas (bassoon and clarinet)
                Suites (bassoon, clarinet, oboe)

--------------------------------------------------------CONTINUED-------
NEXT ACTIONS     Key: ? for help              + to see the next screen
                      L to see a Longer display  - to see the previous screen
                      F to Find other items   Q to Quit
NEXT ACTION? +_
```

These two figures are almost at the extremes of space usage. *Bibliographic Displays in the Online Catalog* includes a number of other alternatives with extensive information on their performance. Most of the other alternatives require less space than the display in Figure 12.7, but only two of them require less space than the display in Figure 12.6. Libraries should determine the combination of clarity and compactness that will serve their patrons best. There are good reasons not to omit information to make displays more compact; some of these are discussed in the following section.

Elements of a Medium Display

Medium-level displays must include subjects and all names and should include other entries. Medium-level displays should include series statements, edition, physical description and publication information.

Elements included in the medium displays are the complete title field, edition and publication information, physical description, series statements (but not series tracings), subjects and all entries. MARC tags included are 100–130, 245, 250, 260–262, 300–305, 400–490, 600–651 and 700–730. The displays do not include notes, uniform titles (other than as main entries), linking entries, or control numbers.

The elements included in this definition of a medium display were considered carefully, and do not agree with many of the published statements that specify what data elements are needed. Those statements vary widely. The most frequently cited research on actual use of data elements, conducted by Richard Palmer, dates from 1972:

> Over three-fourths of the catalog's patrons used the title, author, and call number (including location). Slightly over half . . . made use of the subject headings. A little over one-third used the date of publication. Just over 20 percent used the contents note. Fifteen percent used the edition statement. About 13 percent used the number of volumes. Ten percent used the place of publication, joint author, and publisher. All other items were used by fewer than 10 percent."[2]

According to the Palmer study, almost 9 out of 100 patrons used bibliography notes; roughly 6 used pagination and author's birth/death dates; 4 used tracings; and 3 out of 100 used the LCCN, series note or indication of illustrations.[3]

Based on the Palmer research, publication information, edition and part of the physical description must appear to satisfy 9 out of 10 patrons. That leaves the rest of the physical description, series statements and added entries as items that could possibly be omitted from medium displays. In each case, the information serves important purposes.

Physical Description

Physical description should appear in all bibliographic displays. The information is needed to identify nonbook materials properly, useful in order to determine what books may be worth scanning and compact enough to require very little space.

A patron looking for a book on a subject may well consider the publication date, but will also be interested in the length of the book. Library users frequently want to know whether a book includes illustrations and can learn to recognize the abbreviated form quite easily.

It is harder to make a case for spine size, but that information usually takes up less than six characters of a display.

Nonbooks present a very different problem. Without the physical description, users may not be able to ascertain what the item is, and whether they will have any use for it. Consider items containing the term *[sound recording]* within the title statement. A medium-sized library may very well have a dozen versions of Beethoven's symphonies, and even two or three by the same orchestra and conductor. Only the material description distinguishes vinyl (long-playing) disc from audiocassette from compact disc from 78 rpm historical recordings.

In a sample of 400,000 records, physical description statements average 24 characters in length—half a line in a citation or cardlike format—and rarely more than one line in a labeled format. Omission of physical description saves little space but eliminates a significant source of information.

Series Statements

Many series statements can be useful or even essential for good patron access at all levels. Presence of irrelevant series statements should not negate the use of relevant series.

Consider the example in Figure 12.8. The series statement is the only element in this display that makes it absolutely clear that the videocassette is not about meteorology in general but is intended for a specific audience. Potential fliers and those interested in air masses will both benefit from the series statement, and fliers might very well use the series to find this and related items. Series statements can also be very useful in fiction, although catalog records tend to lack some of the most useful series statements for fiction.

Series statements will not clutter up most displays. Only about 30% of a 400,000-item sample include series statements, and the average series statement is only 37 characters long.

Added Entries

Patron access systems should not discriminate against joint authors or other added entries and should display access points leading to works.

When a patron access system displays the main entry but not additional entries, it goes even further than cataloging codes in assigning an arbitrary importance to one particular author. No sound argument calls for leaving out other authors, illustrators or editors.

Works entries—uniform titles and added entries containing title subfields—present a different problem. If online catalogs are to fulfill Cutter's criteria, they should not only display such entries but should make them retrieval points. (See Chapter 9.)

While cardlike displays have many problems, they avoid the difficulties of grouping and labeling. Labels present problems for added entries. A system can group all entries together and call them *Entries:*, but the term is not common outside the library field. Entries other than uniform titles can be called *Authors:*, but that causes problems for corporate names and for author-title entries. It also provides a misleading label for names of illustrators and editors.

No single answer will settle the question with finality. One possible answer is to group all "author" fields except those with title subfields in a group labeled *Names:*. Uniform titles and author-title combinations appear in another group labeled *Works:*, even though *Works:* may be library jargon.

Figure 12.8: Visual Material, Medium Labeled Display with Spacing

```
Your search: Meteorology I #                                 MEDIUM
     Finds: 12 items          Item 3 of 12            Screen 1 of 1
----------------------------------------------------------------------

           TITLE: Meteorology I [videorecording]
       PUBLISHED: Vacaville, Calif. : Hayes & Nolly Productions, [1985?]
        MATERIAL: 1 videocassette (VHS) (108 min.) : sd., col.

           NAMES: Hayes & Nolly Productions.

          SERIES: Aviation video instruction.

        SUBJECTS: Meteorology in aeronautics.
                  Fronts (Meteorology)
                  Air masses.



  ----------------------------------------------------------------------
  NEXT ACTIONS     Key: ? for help            + to see the next screen
                       L to see a Longer display  - to see the previous screen
                       F to Find other items  Q to Quit

  NEXT ACTION? +_
```

Arrangement of Information

Subjects and entries should appear before notes. Names should probably appear before subjects. Publication information, edition and physical description should appear in traditional order, as they do in catalog cards and citations.

Those libraries that choose cardlike displays may prefer to use the traditional cardlike sequence. That sequence is appropriate for medium displays without notes. On more complete displays, notes should come after subjects and entries, whether the display uses a tracings paragraph or some clearer arrangement.

Labeled displays require more options. The most important choices may be whether the main entry (other than title) should appear at the beginning of the display and where location and status information should appear.

Figures 12.9 and 12.10 illustrate a labeled display with location and status information placed immediately below a citation. This arrangement allows a single consistent display for all three levels. A brief display consists of the citation and holdings information. A medium display, as illustrated in these figures, adds names, series, subjects and works, appearing below the holdings information. A long display would

Figure 12.9: Map, Medium Citation Display with Labels, Holdings

```
Your search: Saxton, Christoph#                                MEDIUM
        Finds: 1 item                                     Screen 1 of 2
-----------------------------------------------------------------------

        Saxton, Christopher, b. 1492? BRITANNIA INSVLARVM IN OCEANO
        MAXIMA A CAIO. Christophorus Saxton descripsit. [London]
        1583. Amsterdam, Nico Israel, 1974. Map 150 x 184 cm. on
        20 sheets 33 x 49 cm. bound in cover 50 x 34 cm.

LOCATION    COPY   CALL NUMBER                    STATUS
--------    ----   -----------                    ------
Map Room      1    G 5750 1583 .S3 1974           Available
Rare Book     1    G 5750 .S3 1974                Available: Does Not Circ.

        NAMES: Saxton, Christopher, b. 1542?

        SERIES: Imago mundi. Supplement, no. 6.


   ----------------------------------------------------CONTINUED------------
NEXT ACTIONS     Key: ? for help            + to see the next screen
                      L to see a Longer display  - to see the previous screen
                      F to Find other items  Q to Quit
NEXT ACTION? +_
```

Figure 12.10: Map, Second Screen

```
Your search: Saxton, Christoph#                                 MEDIUM
         Finds: 1 item                                    Screen 2 of 2
---------------------------------------------------------------------

         Saxton, Christopher, b. 1492?  BRITANNIA INSVLARUM...[CONTINUED]
      SUBJECTS: England--Maps--To 1800.
                Wales--Maps--To 1800.
                Maps, Early--Facsimiles.

      WORKS: Shelton, Raleigh Ashlin. Saxton's survey of England and
             Wales, with a facsimile of Saxton's wall-map of 1583.
             1974.




---------------------------------------------------------------------
NEXT ACTIONS     Key: ? for help            + to see the next screen
                      L to see a Longer display  - to see the previous screen
                      F to Find other items  Q to Quit

NEXT ACTION? +_
```

add notes and possibly control numbers, appearing after the entries. This arrangement is only one of thousands of possibilities but shows that displays can provide extensive information, serve different levels of need and still retain consistent design throughout a patron access system.

The main entry should appear together with other names in a labeled display, but displays should not put all names above the title. Clarity can be increased by repeating the main entry once at the beginning of the display and once in a group with any other names.

There are good reasons to combine the main entry with other entries in the display, but putting all names above the title can lead to ludicrous displays, particularly in the case of sound recordings. One test of such a display showed some examples where the title did not appear until the second or third screen. Archival records show similar difficulties and could delay the title to the sixth or seventh screen of an item.

When all names appear as a group, it may seem sensible to begin the display with the title. That technique usually seems to work well for books. For sound recordings and scores, the results are decidedly mixed, as a relatively high percentage of items have generic titles such as *Symphony no. 5 in D minor.* Music libraries may find such displays unacceptable.

Long Display

All notes and linking entries should be displayed to patrons on the longest bibliographic displays. Elements that may be omitted include some variant title forms, control numbers, coded elements and other elements of no direct bibliographic significance. Any element that has possible use for even a few patrons should be included.

Notes and Linking Entries

Most notes and linking entries don't appear very often. When they do appear, they are there for a reason and should be available to patrons.

Specialized notes will require room only when they appear, and most notes don't appear very often. The same can be said for linking entries and most other special fields. Serials average about one linking entry per record, though that is an average made by combining many records with no linking entries and some records with several linking entries each. Linking entries help patrons to follow the history of a serial and should certainly be available on long displays.

Consider a few examples of notes, with frequency of occurrence taken from a 600,000-item sample of current (January and February 1986) cataloging on the Research Libraries Information Network (RLIN). Sixty-four percent of records have general notes (USMARC tag 500), but the average general note fits on a single line. Forty-three percent of records have a bibliography or discography note, certainly useful information for many patrons trying to determine whether a book might meet their needs. Only 4% have a formatted contents note, but the average contents note is 215 characters long, requiring four or five lines to display.

Very few other notes occur in even 1% of sampled records:

- 3.5% have brief citations (field 510).
- 1.4% have summary/scope notes.

- 1.7% have reproduction notes.
- 1.3% have issuing body notes.
- 1.8% have local notes.

Including all notes will provide the specialized information important to some patrons but will have little impact on overall display requirements.

Nonbook formats have higher frequencies of certain notes, and the notes are more important in some cases. Of 4450 sound recordings sampled, 65% had notes on participants or performers, 23% had notes on capture sessions and almost 29% had contents notes. The performer notes will serve many patrons and help to serve as a selection tool. Of 1673 visual materials (films) records, 25% had credits, 28.6% had participant/performer notes, 69.6% had summaries and 22% had notes on intended audiences.

Control Numbers and Coded Elements

Most control numbers and coded elements do not appear to serve any patron needs. Some libraries may make exceptions for ISBN, ISSN, publisher number for sound recordings and some other elements, depending on local needs.

Some patron access systems display the values for language, country of publication and the like. Unless a system translates the codes to actual names of languages, countries, etc., the information may not have much value for patrons.

Irrelevant Tracings

No patron access display should simulate catalog cards to the extent of including tracings consisting only of the word "Title" or the word "Series."

Some online catalogs do display those tracings. If they serve any conceivable use for patrons, that use is unknown and highly improbable.

Tagged (MARC) Display

If full MARC displays showing tags, indicators and subfields are available to staff, they should also be available to patrons.

Most patrons will not understand a tagged display and most access systems should not need to show such a display as a standard option. But every library will have the occasional patron with library background who may need very specialized information available only from the MARC record itself. If that display is available for staff work, the computer can already generate it. In that case, there seems no good reason to deny that patron access to the display.

How would a patron get at a MARC display? In a system with normal syntax, any patron knowledgeable enough to use a MARC display would probably know enough to try DISPLAY 1 MARC or DISPLAY 1 TAGGED. A library may wish to include those instructions somewhere in online tutorials and in printed materials.

NOTES

1. Fayen, Emily Gallup. *The Online Catalog: Improving Access to Library Materials.* White Plains, NY: Knowledge Industry Publications, Inc., 1983. p. 29.
2. Palmer, Richard P. *Computerizing the Card Catalog in the University Library.* Littleton, CO: Libraries Unlimited; 1972. p. 81.
3. *Ibid.,* p. 83.

Glossary

AACR 2: *Anglo-American Cataloguing Rules,* second edition.

Boolean logic: A logic that takes several sets of items and prepares one final set by combining the initial sets based on three factors: items that occur in both of the two sets (AND), items that occur in either of two sets (OR), and items that do not occur in one set (NOT). The search FIND WORD SOCIAL AND (HISTORY OR ART) NOT SCIENCE retrieves items that do include the word *social,* that also include either *history* or *art* and that do not include *science*.

Browsing: In an online catalog, using a heading or authority file (possibly including a call number index) with freedom to move backwards or forwards as far as the beginning and end of the file.

Chaining: Issuing a series of commands at once. Commands must be separated by a special *chaining character.* The proposed Standard Command Language uses a semicolon as a chaining character; RLIN uses a slash; this book recommends a backslash.

CLR: Council on Library Resources, Inc.—a funding agency for a variety of projects in the library field. CLR provided funding and leadership for a large study on public use of early online catalogs and for a series of conferences on aspects of patron access systems.

Command: Any sequence of text entered at a keyboard, except for a search string keyed to complete a menu choice.

Conversational system: A patron access system that asks questions in order to prepare a search or carry out other actions.

CRT: Cathode Ray Tube, the most common form of video display terminal (VDT).

Cursor: The point on a display at which keyed characters appear. A cursor usually appears as a blinking square or as a blinking underline.

Database: An organized system of data including indexes or other access methods for that data.

Database engine: The computer or computers, database or databases, and program or programs that provide the underlying support for any library automation system.

Diacritics: Special marks used above and below letters to modify those letters.

Dial-back modem: A modem that accepts a call and some form of authorization, then calls back to the number from which it was called. It is one method of improving security for dial-in use.

Echo: Display what was keyed. A patron access system should echo a command on the display that results from that command. Echoes should make sense, which may not always mean echoing precisely what was keyed.

Explain: Verb recommended in the proposed Standard Command Language to call for online tutorials. For example, EXPLAIN LONG should provide a screen of information about the *long* display.

Explicit truncation: Truncation (which see) explicitly called for by use of a special symbol at the end of (or, sometimes, within) a search.

Feedback: Any information that the system provides based directly on the patron's actions, other than results. Feedback includes echoing and other messages.

Field indexes: Indexes that contain the entire text of a field or subfield, also called *phrase indexes.* In contrast to *word indexes,* field or phrase indexes provide immediate access but require full knowledge of the field's contents.

Function keys: Keys on a terminal or microcomputer that do not enter letters or numbers, but that can be recognized for special functions.

Help: Verb recommended in the proposed Standard Command Language to ask for context-sensitive information, information appropriate to the particular point at which HELP was keyed.

Highlighting: Any way of making information stand out, including capitalization, reverse video, underlining, boldface, different intensity or blinking.

Hybrid system: A system that uses menu choices for all commands, but accepts keyed search statements to complete the commands. Most people would call such a system a *menu-driven system;* this book reserves that term for systems that *never* use keyed text.

Icon: Symbol used in place of a word or phrase.

Implicit Boolean: Interpreting a search as containing Boolean *and* operators even though such operators do not appear. Most command parsers will treat a word search containing multiple words as though an *and* appears between each pair of words.

Implicit truncation: Treating a search as though it ended with a truncation symbol even though no such symbol has been keyed.

Integrated system: A computer system that combines many different functions. An integrated library system would typically combine circulation, acquisitions, catalog maintenance, serials control, patron access and possibly some other functions.

Known item: A specific item that a patron wants to retrieve, using a known title or author and title.

LC: Library of Congress.

LCSH: Library of Congress Subject Headings.

MARC: *Ma*chine *R*eadable *C*ataloging. The term was coined in 1966, and is used for a family of machine-readable formats for bibliographic data around the world. In the United States, MARC is usually a synonym for USMARC or LC MARC. The term covers many other MARC formats, including Britain (UKMARC), Canada (CANMARC) and many others.

Menu: A set of choices, usually numbered. A *pure menu* is one that requires a number, where the system will not accept any other entry.

Modem: *Mo*dulator-*dem*odulator, a device to translate digital information from a computer into sound waves for transmission across telephone lines (modulation) and to reverse the process (demodulation).

NISO: The National Information Standards Organization [Z39], formerly American National Standards Committee Z39. The standards organization concerned with library, publishing and information fields.

NLM: National Library of Medicine.

OCLC: Online Computer Library Center, Inc. America's largest shared cataloging system and one of the largest online systems in the world.

Online catalog: A patron's view, by means of an interactive terminal, of a library's resources. Also *OPAC, Patron Access System.*

Options: Possible commands, displayed on the screen. Numbered options may serve as menus, but options can always be entered directly and completely from the keyboard.

Parsing: Resolving a command into its component parts so that those parts can be acted on.

Patron access: The means by which patrons find out what a library has and how to locate the material they want.

Patron access system: A way of providing patron access through a terminal. Nearly synonymous with *online public access catalog* or *OPAC* and with *online catalog.*

Pixel: Picture element, the smallest part of a display that can be independently defined and turned dark or light. A character is made up of many pixels.

Pointing devices: Ways of moving the cursor to a particular spot on the screen and possibly expanding the cursor to highlight a certain area. A mouse, light pen, cursor keys, trackball and touch-sensitive screen can all serve as pointing devices.

Postings: The number of items held for a given heading or other search term.

Precision: The ability to retrieve only the items wanted or needed. Improved precision means narrower searching, focusing more exactly on the items best suited to a patron's needs.

Presentation: In the area of online systems, how information from the system appears on the screen and how the system requests and accepts information from the user.

Process: For a patron access system, any activity that results in a change in the system's files. Searching is not a process but an underlying support mechanism. Examples of processes include sending a message to the library, placing a hold, ordering a book and charging out an item.

Protection: For a patron access system, the methods used to shield one user from other users or agencies, the user from the system and the system from the user. Examples of protection include automatic separation of patron information from item information when an item is returned, and command logging mechanisms that do not make it possible to identify the patron.

Recall: The power to find everything needed. Recall is improved by broadening search results, through normalized indexes and other means.

Related works: Items that have a subject heading, author, uniform title or series title in common with one another.

Result summary: A display that explains the result of a search. Possible summaries include number of items by field, number of items by physical format and number of items for each term and combination in a Boolean search.

RLG: The Research Libraries Group, Inc. A consortium of universities and libraries that pursue common aims in library and scholarly fields.

RLIN: The Research Libraries Information Network. The computer support for RLG, and a large bibliographic service, with more than 19 million bibliographic records and more than 900 terminals.

Show: Verb recommended in the proposed Standard Command Language to request a display of the state of the current session. That state might include the current search request, any results that have been stored, and files in use.

SideKick: A computer program for the IBM PC and Apple Macintosh that provides a notepad, calculator and some other facilities, available while the user is running some other program. SideKick is relevant to patron access only because it provides an easy mechanism to take a screen full of information—from any source—and incorporate it into a message or file. SideKick is a trademark of Borland International.

Soft keys: *Function keys* that change functions during a program and have functions labeled on the bottom of the display. Soft keys prevent users from learning any pattern for function keys and appear undesirable for patron access.

Term indexes: Indexes that contain sets of words beginning at any point in a field. A term index for *MARC for Library Use* will contain that phrase, *library use, use* and possibly *for library use*.

Terminal: Any combination of an input device and a display device that is connected to a computer or other information system. For most patron access systems, terminals consist of keyboards and video display terminals (VDTs) and may or may not be microcomputers.

Three-P model: A simple model for any library computer system. Aspects of the system are divided into *Presentation, Process* and *Protection*.

Truncation: Shortening the term searched in order to retrieve more items. Right truncation, the most common form, uses a special symbol to mean "and anything that follows." If an asterisk is used as a truncation symbol, *COMPUT** will match *computer, computing, computation* and a number of other words beginning with *comput*.

USMARC: Machine-readable cataloging formats used in the United States. Includes LC MARC, OCLC MARC, RLIN MARC, WLN MARC and others.

VDT: Video Display Terminal.

Window: An area of the screen that presents new information and overlays existing information, obscuring the old information in a way that makes it obvious that the old information can be seen by "closing the window."

Word indexes: Indexes that provide access by any word from a field.

Workstation: Place where work is done, as in *terminal workstation,* the desk or table, chair and other furniture to support use of a terminal. Also used as a synonym for *scholar's workstation,* a powerful microcomputer intended for use by scholars.

Annotated Bibliography

This bibliography includes only those items consulted while preparing this book. An annotated bibliography of recent works on patron access can be found in *Library Hi Tech Bibliography,* cited here.

ALA Handbook of Organization, 1985/1986. Chicago: American Library Association: 1985. 307 p.

Alewaeters, Gerrit [and others]. "VUBIS: A User-Friendly Online System." *Information Technology and Libraries.* 1(3): 206–221; 1982 September.

Anderson, Rosemary [and others]. *Library of Congress Online Public Catalog Users Survey: A Report to the Council on Library Resources.* Washington, DC: Library of Congress; 1982 October 29. 17 p + app. Clear summary of LC's results, how they relate to the overall CLR study and what LC should do about it.

Arret, Linda. "Can Online Catalogs Be Too Easy?" *American Libraries.* 16(2): 118–120; 1985 February. Argues that menu-driven online catalogs limit users and do not allow them to learn. Questions word indexing as a reasonable replacement for access to Library of Congress subject headings.

Atherton, Pauline L. "Catalog Users' Access from the Researcher's Viewpoint." *Closing the Catalog.* Phoenix, AZ: Oryx Press; 1980: 105–122. Discusses "unheeded research findings" regarding access, including suggestions that subject entries should be filed in reverse chronological order and that older items should not have access by subject.

Atkinson, Hugh C. "The Electronic Catalog." *Nature and Future of the Catalog.* Maurice J. Freedman; S. Michael Malinconico, eds. Phoenix, AZ: Oryx Press; 1979: 102–113. Supports fast known-item access as the basic tool and argues that older items need not be fully represented.

Berman, Sanford. "Cataloging for Public Libraries." *Nature and Future of the Catalog.* Maurice J. Freedman; S. Michael Malinconico, eds.

Phoenix, AZ: Oryx Press, 1979: 225–239. Argues that displays for public use should be shorter, should not include collation, ISBD punctuation, etc.

Bibliographic Services and User Needs. Washington, DC: Council on Library Resources; 1984 March. 116 p. Report of a conference (December 14–16, 1983).

Bierman, Kenneth John. *Automated Alternatives to Card Catalogs for Large Libraries.* 1975 June. 43 p. Final report for a CLR Fellowship project. A good early study of attitudes and work done. Includes a modest and fairly accurate projection of when online catalogs might be significant, estimating around 1985.

Books Are for Use. Syracuse, NY: Syracuse University School of Information Studies; 1978 February. 172 p. Report on a project studying enhanced subject access, using phrases from tables of contents and indexes to enrich records.

Borgman, Christine L. *End User Behavior on the Ohio State University Libraries' Online Catalog: A Computer Monitoring Study.* Dublin, OH: OCLC; 1983 August 31. 30 p. OCLC Research Report OCLC/OPR/RR-83/7.

Borgman, Christine L. "Psychological Factors in Online Catalog Use, or Why Users Fail." *Training Users of Online Public Access Catalogs.* Washington, DC: Council on Library Resources; 1983 July: 23–24.

Boss, Richard. "Turnkey Minicomputer Systems as Online Catalogs." *RQ.* 20(1): 40–44; 1980 Fall.

Broadus, Robert N. "Online Catalogs and Their Users." *College and Research Libraries.* 44(6): 458–467; 1983 November. A good review of the CLR study and publications based on it, questions the asserted level of user satisfaction with online catalogs, notes sources of bias in the study method.

Brownrigg, Edwin. "Telecommunications Considerations for Online Catalogs." *Online Catalog Design Issues: A Series of Discussions.* Brian Aveney, ed. Washington, DC: Council on Library Resources; 1984 July; 201–225.

Burrows, Clay. "Online User Prompts and Aids." *Online Catalog Design Issues: A Series of Discussions.* Brian Aveney, ed. Washington, DC: Council on Library Resources; 1984 July; 155–179.

Carpenter, Gai. "LS/2000 and Five Colleges, Inc.: The User's Perspective." *Library Hi Tech.* 2(2): 21–24; 1984.

Christoffersson, John G. "Automation at the University of Georgia Libraries." *Journal of Library Automation.* 12(1): 22–38; 1979 March.

Clinic on Library Applications of Data Processing (17th: 1980: University of Illinois at Urbana-Champaign). *Public Access to Library Automation.* Urbana-Champaign, IL: Graduate School of Library and Information Science; 1981. 128 p.

Closing the Catalog: Proceedings of the 1978 and 1979 Library and Information Technology Association Institutes. D. Kaye Gapen; Bonnie Juergens, eds. Phoenix, AZ: Oryx Press; 1980. 194 p.

Cochrane, Pauline A.; Markey, Karen. "Preparing for the Use of Classification in Online Cataloging Systems and in Online Catalogs." *Information Technology and Libraries.* 4(2): 91–111; 1985 June.

Command Language and Screen Displays for Public Online Systems: Report of a meeting sponsored by the Council on Library Resources, March 29–30, 1984, Dublin, Ohio. Paul Evan Peters, ed. Washington, DC: Council on Library Resources; 1985. 93 p.

Corey, James F. "Search Retrieval Options." *Online Catalog Design Issues: A Series of Discussions.* Brian Aveney, ed. Washington, DC: Council on Library Resources; 1984 July; 23–66. Excellent analysis of uses for various types of indexes, enhanced by the vigorous, lengthy discussion that follows.

Crawford, Walt. *MARC for Library Use: Understanding the USMARC Formats.* White Plains, NY: Knowledge Industry Publications, Inc.; 1984. 222 p.

Crawford, Walt. *Patron Access Project: Phase 1; Report to Phase II: Development Issues.* Stanford, CA: The Research Libraries Group, Inc.; 1985. 152 p. (RLG Document Code 85-52.)

Dowlin, Kenneth E. *The Electronic Library: The Promise and The Process.* New York: Neal-Schuman; 1984. 199 p.

Estabrook, Leigh. "The Human Dimension of the Catalog: Concepts and Constraints in Information Seeking." *Library Resources and Technical Services.* 27(1): 68–75; 1983 January/March.

Farber, Evan. "Historic Concerns in Library Instruction: Teaching the Card Catalog." *Training Users of Online Public Access Catalogs.* Washington, DC: Council on Library Resources; 1983 July: 5–10. Stresses that the catalog is an incomplete research tool and that users must be made aware of its shortcomings.

Fasana, Paul J. "1981 and Beyond: Visions and Decisions." *Journal of Library Automation.* 13(2): 96–107; 1980 June.

Fayen, Emily Gallup. *The Online Catalog: Improving Public Access to Library Materials.* White Plains, NY: Knowledge Industry Publications, Inc.; 1983. 148 p.

Ferguson, Douglas [and others]. "The CLR Public Online Catalog Study: An Overview." *Information Technology and Libraries.* 1(2): 84–97; 1982 June.

Fox, Mark S.; Palay, Andrew J. "Machine-Assisted Browsing for the Naive User." Clinic on Library Applications of Data Processing (17th: 1980: University of Illinois at Urbana-Champaign). *Public Access to Library Automation.* Urbana-Champaign, IL: Graduate School of Library and Information Science; 1981. p. 77–98.

Furlong, Elizabeth J. "Index Access to On-Line Records: An Operational View." *Journal of Library Automation.* 11(3): 223–238; 1978 September. Experience with NOTIS and LUIS, Northwestern's integrated system and its patron access component.

Genaway, David C. *Integrated Online Library Systems: Principles, Planning and Implementation.* White Plains, NY: Knowledge Industry Publications, Inc.; 1984. 151 p.

Golden, Susan U.; Golden, Gary A. "Access to Periodicals: Search Key versus Keyword." *Information Technology and Libraries.* 2(1): 26–31; 1983 March.

Gorman, Michael. "Cataloging and the New Technologies." *Nature and Future of the Catalog.* Maurice J. Freedman; S. Michael Malinconico, eds. Phoenix, AZ: Oryx Press; 1979: 127–152.

Graham, Peter S. "Technology and the Online Catalog." *Library Resources & Technical Services.* 27(1): 18–35; 1983 January/March.

Hammell, Kathryn A.; Goldberg, Kay. "The Evolution of an Online Union Catalog: Impact of User Feedback." *Information Technology and Libraries.* 4(2): 162–168; 1985 June.

Hildreth, Charles R. *Online Public Access Catalogs: The User Interface.* Dublin, OH: OCLC; 1982. 263 p. The first major monographic work on patron access and still an important one.

Hildreth, Charles R. "User Feedback in the Design Process." *Online Catalog Design Issues: A Series of Discussions.* Brian Aveney, ed. Washington, DC: Council on Library Resources; 1984 July: 67–102.

Hines, Spencer C. "OCLC's Remote Terminal Emulation System for LS/2000." *Library Hi Tech.* 3(4): 7–9; 1984 December.

Hudson, Judith. "Cataloging for the Local Online System." *Information Technology and Libraries*. 5(1): 5–27; 1986 March.

Information Technology: Critical Choices for Library Decision-Makers. Allen Kent; Thomas J. Galvin, eds. New York: Marcel Dekker; 1982. 477 p.

Jones, C. Lee. "Subject Access / Subject Authority: Challenge and Opportunity." *Subject Access*. Washington, DC: Council on Library Resources; 1982 December: 6–8.

Kilgour, Frederick G. "Concept of an On-Line Computerized Library Catalog." *Journal of Library Automation*. 3(1): 1–11; 1970 March.

Kilgour, Frederick G. "Design of Online Catalogs." *Nature and Future of the Catalog*. Maurice J. Freedman; S. Michael Malinconico, eds. Phoenix, AZ: Oryx Press; 1979: 34–45.

Larson, Ray R. *Users Look At Online Catalogs; Part 2: Interacting with Online Catalogs*. Berkeley, CA: University of California, Division of Library Automation; 1983 April 29. 60 p. + app.

Lawrence, Gary S. "System Features for Subject Access in the Online Catalog." *Library Resources and Technical Services*. 29(1): 16–33; 1985 January/March.

Lawrence, Gary S. [and others]. *University of California Users Look at Melvyl: Results of a Survey of Users of the University of California Prototype Online Union Catalog*. Berkeley, CA: Division of Library Automation; 1983 June 3. 125 p. + app. Condensed version of survey results, includes good illustrations of search and display sequences in appendixes.

Library Hi Tech Bibliography. C. Edward Wall, ed. Ann Arbor, MI: Pierian Press, 1986. Volume 1, 1986, includes an annotated bibliography on online public access catalogs, pp. 99–106.

Library of Congress. Automated Systems Office. *MARC Formats for Bibliographic Data*. Washington, DC: Library of Congress; 1980. Looseleaf with periodic updates.

Lipow, Anne Grodzins. "Practical Considerations of the Current Capabilities of Subject Access in Online Catalogs." *Library Resources & Technical Services*. 27(1): 81–87; 1983 January/March.

Lubetzky, Seymour. "Ideology of Bibliographic Cataloging: Progress and Retrogression." *Nature and Future of the Catalog*. Maurice J. Freedman; S. Michael Malinconico, eds. Phoenix, AZ: Oryx Press; 1979: 5–19.

Lubetzky, Seymour. "The Traditional Ideals of Cataloging and The

New Revision." *Nature and Future of the Catalog.* Maurice J. Freedman; S. Michael Malinconico, eds. Phoenix, AZ: Oryx Press; 1979: 153–169.

Ludy, Lorene E. "OSU Libraries' Use of Library of Congress Subject Authorities File." *Information Technology and Libraries.* 4(2): 155–160; 1985 June. Good case study of the use of LC subject headings to modify and control an online catalog.

Malinconico, S. Michael. "The Library Catalog in a Computerized Environment." *Nature and Future of the Catalog.* Maurice J. Freedman; S. Michael Malinconico, eds. Phoenix, AZ: Oryx Press; 1979: 46–70. Discussion of the need for authority control in order to maintain collocation, and the usefulness of authority control in a computerized catalog.

Mandel, Carol A. "Enriching the Library Catalog Record for Subject Access." *Library Resources & Technical Services.* 29(1): 5–15; 1985 January/March.

Mandel, Carol A. *Subject Access in the Online Catalog.* 1981 August. 30 p. Report prepared for the Council on Library Resources. A useful summary of research on subject access, with suggested areas for new efforts by CLR and other agencies.

Markey, Karen. "Subject-Searching Experiences and Needs of Online Catalog Users: Implications for Library Classification." *Library Resources & Technical Services.* 29(1): 34–51; 1985 January/March.

Markey, Karen. *Subject Searching in Library Catalogs: Before and After the Introduction of Online Catalogs.* Dublin, OH: OCLC; 1984. 176 p.

Marshall, Joan K. "The Catalog in the World Around It." *Nature and Future of the Catalog.* Maurice J. Freedman; S. Michael Malinconico, eds. Phoenix, AZ: Oryx Press; 1979: 20–33.

Matthews, Joseph R. *Public Access to Online Catalogs: A Planning Guide for Managers.* Weston, CT: Online; 1982. 345 p.

Matthews, Joseph R. *Public Access to Online Catalogs.* Second edition. New York: Neal-Schuman; 1985. 497 p.

Matthews, Joseph R. "Screen Layouts and Displays." *Online Catalog Design Issues: A Series of Discussions.* Brian Aveney, ed. Washington, DC: Council on Library Resources; 1984 July: 103–136.

Matthews, Joseph R. *Suggested Guidelines for Screen Layouts and Design of Online Catalogs.* Paper presented at a conference sponsored by the Council on Library Resources at the Lakeway Conference Center, Austin, TX on March 10–13, 1985. Good summary of display issues, with citations for studies that are asserted to be sufficient to prove Matthews' theses.

McAllister, Caryl; McAllister, A. Stratton. "DOBIS/LIBIS: An Integrated, On-line Library Management System." *Journal of Library Automation.* 12(4): 300–313; 1979 December.

McDonald, David R.; Searing, Susan E. "Bibliographic Instruction and the Development of Online Catalogs." *College & Research Libraries.* 44(1): 5–11; 1983 January. Useful thoughts on the need to consider bibliographic instruction when designing online catalogs.

Miller, R. Bruce. "Radiation, Ergonomics, Ion Depletion, and VDTs: Healthful Use of Visual Display Terminals." *Information Technology and Libraries.* 2(2): 151–158; 1983 June.

Miller, Susan L. "The Ohio State Universities Libraries Online Catalog." *Closing the Catalog.* Phoenix, AZ: Oryx Press; 1980: 75–84. Discusses enhancements needed to make the Ohio LCS system into a workable patron access system: full-record display, upper and lower case display, subject access and some other enhancements.

Monahan, Michael. "Command Languages and Codes." *Online Catalog Design Issues: A Series of Discussions.* Brian Aveney, ed. Washington, DC: Council on Library Resources; 1984 July: 137–153.

Moore, Carole Weiss. "User Reactions to Online Catalogs: An Exploratory Study." *College & Research Libraries.* 42(4): 295–302; 1981 July. A study of actual use of "fledgling" patron access systems.

Nature and Future of the Catalog. Maurice J. Freedman; S. Michael Malinconico, eds. Phoenix, AZ: Oryx Press; 1979, 317 p. Proceedings of ISAD institutes on the catalog in 1975 and 1977.

Noerr, Peter L. "Are Micros Friendly?" *7th International Online Meeting.* Oxford: Learned Information; [1984]: 1–6. Good discussion of what constitutes user-friendliness. Argues that systems must work at levels to suit the user.

Norden, David J.; Lawrence, Gail Herndon. "Public Terminal Use in an Online Catalog: Some Preliminary Results." *College & Research Libraries.* 42(4): 308–316; 1981 July.

Online Catalog Design Issues: A Series of Discussions. Brian Aveney, ed. Washington, DC: Council on Library Resources; 1984 July. 249 p. Excellent presentations on various aspects of online catalog design. The papers represent professional thinking, not simply reaction to surveys and statistics.

Online Catalogs: Requirements, Characteristics, and Costs: Report of a conference sponsored by the Council on Library Resources at the Aspen Institute, Wye Plantation, Queenstown, MD, December 14–16, 1982. Washington, DC: Council on Library Resources; 1983 March. 132 p.

Online Catalog: The Inside Story. William E. Post; Peter G. Watson, eds. Chico, CA: Ryan Research International; 1983. 158 p. Case study of the selection and installation of an early online catalog at California State University-Chico, presenting a variety of professional perspectives. Well done and particularly interesting for the extensive list of requirements for the catalog which were not met by the system selected.

On-Line Public Access to Library Bibliographic Data Bases: Developments, Issues and Priorities. 1980 September. 50p. + app. Final Report to the Council on Library Resources.

Palmer, Richard P. *Computerizing the Card Catalog in the University Library.* Littleton, CO: Libraries Unlimited; 1972. 141 p. Reviews earlier catalog use studies, adds own studies. The work was aimed at testing the sufficiency of very brief records for an early computer catalog and has been heavily quoted and misquoted since publication.

Pease, Sue; Gouke, Mary Noel. "Patterns of Use in an Online Catalog and a Card Catalog." *College & Research Libraries.* 43(4): 279–291; 1982 July.

Price, Bennett J. "Printing and the Online Catalog." *Information Technology and Libraries.* 3(1): 20; 1984 March.

Radke, Barbara S. [and others]. "The User-Friendly Catalog: Patron Access to MELVYL." *Information Technology and Libraries.* 1(4): 358–371; 1982 December. Good brief discussion of MELVYL's patron access design and the reasoning behind it.

Reynolds, Dennis. *Library Automation: Issues and Applications.* New York: Bowker; 1985. 615 p.

Richmond, Phyllis A. "Futuristic Aspects of Subject Access." *Library Resources & Technical Services.* 27(1): 88–93; 1983 January/March.

Salmon, Stephen R. "Characteristics of Online Public Catalogs." *Library Resources & Technical Services.* 27(1): 36–67; 1983 January/March.

Sandler, Mark. "Terminal Ailments Need Not Be Fatal: A Speculative Assessment of the Impact of Online Public Access Catalogs in Academic Settings." *RQ.* 24(4): 460–465; 1985 Summer.

Schroeder, John R.; Herr, Jessie J. "Data Structures and Resource Consumption in an Online Catalog." *Online Catalog Design Issues: A Series of Discussions*. Brian Aveney, ed. Washington, DC: Council on Library Resources; 1984 July: 3–22.

Scilken, Marvin H. "The Catalog as a Public Service Tool." *Nature and Future of the Catalog*. Maurice J. Freedman; S. Michael Malinconico, eds. Phoenix, AZ: Oryx Press; 1979: 89–101.

Seal, Alan. "Experiments with Full and Short Entry Catalogues: A Study of Library Needs." *Library Resources & Technical Services*. 27(2); 1983 April/June.

Senzig, Donna. "Library Catalogs for Library Users." *RQ*. 24(1): 37–42; 1984 Fall.

Shaw, Ward. "Design Principles for Public Access." Clinic on Library Applications of Data Processing (17th: 1980: University of Illinois at Urbana-Champaign). *Public Access to Library Automation*. Urbana-Champaign, IL: Graduate School of Library and Information Science; 1981: 2–7.

Siegel, Elliot R. [and others]. "A Comparative Evaluation of the Technical Performance and User Acceptance of Two Prototype Online Catalog Systems." *Information Technology and Libraries*. 3(1): 35–46; 1984 March.

Stevens, Norman D. "The Catalogs of the Future: A Speculative Essay." *Journal of Library Automation*. 13(2): 88–95; 1980 June.

Subject Access. Washington, DC: Council on Library Resources; 1982 December. 80 p. + app. Report of a meeting (Dublin, Ohio, June 7–9, 1982).

Sullivan, Patricia; Seiden, Peggy. "Educating Online Catalog Users: The Protocol Assessment of Needs." *Library Hi Tech*. 3(2): 11–19; 1985.

Svenonius, Elaine. "Use of Classification in Online Retrieval." *Library Resources & Technical Services*. 27(1): 76–80; 1983 January/March.

Tolle, John E. *Public Access Terminals: Determining Quantity Requirements*. Dublin, OH: OCLC; 1984. 161 p. Clear description of data gathering and statistical instruments, and includes tools for assessing needs, given enough information.

Training Users of Online Public Access Catalogs. Washington, DC: Council on Library Resources; 1983 July. Compiled & edited by Marsha Hamilton McClintock. 122 p. Proceedings of a conference held January 12–14, 1983.

Users Look at Online Catalogs: Results of a National Survey of Users and Non-Users of Online Public Access Catalogs. Berkeley: University of California Division of Library Automation; 1982 November 16. Final report to the Council on Library Resources.

Using Online Catalogs. Joseph R. Matthews; Gary S. Lawrence; Douglas K. Ferguson, eds. New York: Neal-Schuman; 1983. 255 p. A clear summary of the four CLR user study reports.

Williamson, Nancy J. "Subject Access in the On-Line Environment." *Advances in Librarianship.* 13: 49–97; 1984.

Wilson, Patrick. "The Catalog as Access Mechanism: Background and Concepts." *Library Resources & Technical Services.* 27(1): 4–17; 1983 January/March. A contrary view that online catalogs need not have full subject access and should have deliberately limited usefulness.

Index

AACR2 ... 69, 204
Abbreviations ... 127
Access ... 72-74
Added entries ... 229
Adjacency searching ...
   31-32
American Library
   Association ... 160
Amiga ... 116
Anonymity ... 12-13
ANSI ... 203
Anthropomorphism ... 71-72
Apple ... 116
Arcade effect ... 97
Artificial intelligence ...
   188-189
ASCII ... 115
Atari ... 116
Atherton, Pauline ... 65, *see
   also* Cochrane, Pauline
   Atherton
Atkinson, Hugh ... 19
Audible response ... 91-92
Authorities ... 23, 24, 26-27,
   50
   names ... 23
   subjects ... 24
   title ... 24
Authorized form ... 141-142

Backup ... 74-75
Bar codes ... 9
Beeping ... 91-92
*Bibliographic Displays in the
   Online Catalog* ... 193,
   222-223, 225-226
Bibliographies ... 110-111
Blind patrons ... 103
Blinking ... 97, 100
Boldface ... 97
Boolean searching ... *see*
   Search, Boolean
Brevity ... 139-140
Brief records ... 20
Browsing ... 23, 32, 51, 66,
   164-165, 167-170, 172,
   185-188
   search from ... 171
BRS ... 32

Call number ... 199, 202
Capitalization ... 97-98, 128,
   158-159, 170, 197-198,
   210
Card catalog ... 1-2, 4-6, 22,
   26, 39, 41, 57, 66, 175
CD-ROM ... 115
Chaining ... 130-132

Chicago Manual of Style ...
110, 203
Chronology ... 218
Circulation status ... 22-23,
199-201
Citations ... 98
Clarity ... 6, 61-75, 139-140,
182, 192, 217, 222
CLR ... 2, 25, 31, 38, 58, 64,
119, 164, 173-174
Cochrane, Pauline Atherton
... 20-21
Coded elements ... 233
Coherence ... 192, 202-203
Collation ... 69
Color ... 97, 101
Command review ... 66
Commands ... 64-65, 73, 75,
85, 117-136, 177-178
Commodore ... 116
Compactness ... 202-204
Completeness ... 19-21
Computer ... 15-16
Computer capacity ... 35-38
Confidentiality ... 11-12
Consistency ... 55-56, 68-69,
75, 129-130, 138,
150-151, 153, 194, 211
Content ... 16, 18-25
Context ... 39-54, 192
Control ... 72-73, 134-135,
143, 153, 189-190
Control numbers ... 233
Conversational systems ...
119-120
Corey, James F. ... 24, 184
Council on Library
Resources ... *see* CLR
CP/M ... 116
CRT ... 90-91

Customization ... 67-68,
113-114
Cutter, Charles Ammi ...
157, 229

Daisywheel printers ... 109
Database engine ... 15-16,
26-35
DDC ... 25, 167, 174
Derived-key indexes ...
34-35
Dewey ... 25, 167, 174
Diacritics ... 94-96, 159-160
Dialog ... 32
Dialup users ... 97, 115-116
Display ... 74, 90-96, 112,
138, 169-171, 192-234
arrangement of elements
... 230-231
brief ... 222-224
cardlike ... 202-203
citation-style ...
203-204, 217
density ... 216
health and safety ... 103
known-item search ...
179
long ... 232-233
MARC ... 234
medium ... 224-229
multiple-item ... 211,
214-220
numbering ... 219-220
quality ... 92-95, 101
sequence ... 218-219
single-item ... 220-234
single-line ... 215-217
special features ...
97-102

sufficiency ... 221-222
tagged ... 234
Dot-matrix printers ... 108
Dowlin, Kenneth ... 3
Downloading ... 112-113,
172
Dvorak ... 80

Editing ... 132
Electroluminescent displays
... 91
Entry vocabulary ... 25-26
Errors ... 132-134, 154,
177-178
Explanations ... 150-155

Failure ... 131-132, 183-190
Fasana, Paul ... 19
Fayen, Emily ... 5, 19, 31,
221-222
Feedback ... 134, 137-140,
150-156, 187, 194
Ferguson, Douglas ... 64
Files ... 15-16
Flexibility ... 73, 118-125,
129
Fonts ... 97, 102
Forest Press ... 25
Forgiveness ... 131-133,
177-178, 180, 184-189
Function keys ... 42-43,
46-48, 74-75, 81-87,
101, 115

Graphics ... 97, 102
Grouping ... 194

Headings ... 23, 26-27
author-title ... 24
name ... 32, 166

series ... 166
subject ... 166
title ... 24
word indexes to ... 28
Health and safety ... 103
Help ... 83, 85-86, 137,
150-153
context-sensitive ... 154
Highlighting ... 210
Hildreth, Charles ... 31, 65,
84
Holdings ... 22, 199-201,
222-223
Holds ... 8-9
Home computers ... 115
Humor ... 71-72
Hybrid systems ... 118-119

IBM PC ... 84
ILL ... 10
In-process information ...
21-22
Indexes ... 15-16, 26,
158-160
contents, summaries,
notes ... 29
derived-key ... 34-35
full-record ... 28
general notes ... 29
name ... 32
publication statement ...
29
special ... 32-34
term ... 30-31
word ... 27-29
*Information Technology and
Libraries* ... 103
Initial articles ... 159
Ink-jet printers ... 109-110
Input ... 77-90

Instructional materials ...
61-63
Integrated system ... 3
Intensity ... 97-100
Interlibrary borrowing ... 10
ISBD ... 196-197, 203
ISBN ... 33-34, 233
ISSN ... 33, 233

Keyboards ... 77-90
Knowledge Industry
Publications ... 34

Labels ... 84, 138, 203,
205-206, 209-211,
230-231
Lakeway conference ... 57
Language ... 68-72
appropriateness ... 69
Large catalogs ... 35-36
Laser printers ... 109
Lawrence, Gary ... 64, 119
LC class numbers ... 25
LCCN ... 33, 227
LCD ... 91
LCSH ... 24-25, 174
Learning ... 55-57, 61-63, 66
Legibility ... 92-94, 196,
205, 215
Library and Information
Technology Association
... 160
Library Bill of Rights ... 64
*Library Hi Tech
Bibliography* ... 103
Library of Congress ... 16,
24
Library of Congress Subject
Headings ... 33, 227
Light pen ... 9

Linked Systems Project ...
113, 190
Linking entries ... 232
Liquid crystal diode ... 91
LITA ... 160
Location ... 200
Logging ... 12-13
LSP ... 113, 190

Macintosh ... 116
Main entry ... 69, 212
MARC ... 29, 33, 69, 74,
112-113, 162-164, 196,
204, 217
MARC compatibility ... 4,
16-17
*MARC Formats for
Bibliographic Data* ... 16
Markey, Karen ... 162, 184
Matthews, Joseph ... 31, 64,
83, 225
Media ... 18-19
MELVYL ... 59, 137
Menus ... 48, 64-65, 85, 87,
118-126, 140, 177
Messages
direct ... 72
error ... 70-71
from patron to library
... 7-8
system ... 70-71
Metaphor ... 55-57
Miller, R. Bruce ... 103
Model ... 55-57
consistent ... 44
Modes ... 64-65, 120,
125-126
Most likely action ... 141
Most recent action ... 48
MS-DOS ... 116

Names ... 231
National Information
   Standards Organization
   ... 58, 190
National Library of
   Medicine ... 24
New search ... 74-75
Next action ... 49
NISO ... 58, 190
Non-Roman ... 95-96
Nonprint ... 18-19, 213, 233
Normalization ... 32-33, 48,
   128, 131-132, 158-160
Notes ... 232-233
Numbering ... 169, 219-220

OCLC ... 2, 25, 95
Older material ... 19-20
On-order information ...
   21-22
The Online Catalog:
   Improving Public Access
   to Library Materials ...
   31
Online Public Access
   Catalogs ... 31
Open Systems Interconnect
   ... 113
Opening choices ... 120
Opening screen ... 43-46
Options ... 49, 121-126, 141,
   194
Orders ... 9
OSI ... 113

Palmer, Richard ... 225, 227
Parsing ... 126, 133-134,
   177-178, 180-182
Partially-sighted patrons ...
   103
Password ... 11

PC-DOS ... 116
Physical description ... 227
Pick list ... 110-111
Pike's Peak Library System
   ... 3
Pixels ... 92-93
Pointing ... 87-90
Posting ... 168, 170
Power ... 6
Precision ... 157, 162-164,
   172
Presentation ... 6-7, 15-16,
   39-59
Printers ... 106-110
Printing ... 110-111
Process ... 6-10
Profiles ... 67-68
ProKey ... 68
Prompting ... 141-143, 182,
   184, 187
Protection ... 6-7, 10-13
Proximity searching ... 31-32
Public Access to Online
   Catalogs ... 31
Publisher's number ... 33
Punctuation ... 128, 158-159,
   177, 196-197, 203

Queueing ... 36-37
Qwerty ... 79-80

Radio Shack ... 116
Recall ... 157-161, 172
Recalls ... 8-9
Record enhancement ...
   20-21
Redirection ... 50
References ... 168
Related works ... 142,
   160-161, 175

Request and response ... 51
Research Libraries Group ...
    see RLG
Research Libraries
    Information Network ...
    see RLIN
Response time ... 36-38
Restarting ... 44-46, 83
    automatic ... 44-46
Results
    clarity ... 52-54
    display ... 192-234
    multiple-item ... 54
    single-item ... 53
    size ... 52
    source ... 53-54
    storage ... 171-172
Retrieval ... 157-172
Reverse video ... 97-98
Reynolds, Dennis ... 63
RLG ... 5, 193, 196, 202,
    212
RLIN ... 2, 18, 27, 59, 95,
    179, 188, 232

Scanning ... 164-165, 167,
    172
Scholarship ... 19
Screen design ... 194, 196,
    201-202, 204-205, 209
Screen dump ... 110
Screen size ... 93
SDI ... 114
Search ... 48, 83, 173-191,
    see also Results
    abusive ... 13
    adjacency ... 32
    author ... 179
    author-title ... 176-177
    Boolean ... 28, 30-31,
    48, 54, 143-147, 162,

    173-174, 177, 179-186,
    191
    call number ... 167
    classified ... 25
    derived-key ... 34-35
    encouraging ... 65-66
    failure ... 173, 183-190
    flexibility ... 73
    free-text ... 28
    from browsing ... 171
    interpretation ...
    177-178
    ISBN ... 33-34
    ISSN ... 33
    known-item ... 5, 28,
    175-179, 191
    large catalogs ... 35-36
    LCCN ... 33
    limiting ... 114-115,
    162-164
    modification ... 182
    multi-index ... 180-181
    name ... 32, 167, 188
    new ... 74-75
    non-local ... 10, 189-191
    normalization ... 32-33,
    160
    phrase ... 177, 187
    proximity ... 31-32
    results ... 143-149, 170
    review ... 66
    speed ... 175-176
    strategy ... 183-184
    subject ... 20-21, 25, 28,
    65, 166, 173-175, 179,
    218
    term ... 30-31, 187
    title ... 178
    word ... 32, 177
Selective dissemination of
    information ... 114

Self-logging ... 66
Sequence of displayed items
   ... 218-219
Serials ... 232
Series statements ... 228
Session information ...
   155-156
Sessions ... 40-47
Shakespeare ... 115
Sidekick ... 8
Signposts ... 47-54
Soundex ... 188-189
Spacing ... 194, 217
Special characters ... 94-96,
   159-160
Special needs ... 103
Spelling ... 185-186, 188-189
Stacking ... 130-132
Standard Command
   Language ... 43, 47,
   58-60, 69, 86,
126-130, 133, 150, 164, 221
START ... 42-43
Starting point ... 40-44
Statement of responsibility ...
   212
Status information ... 5,
   22-23, 175, 179,
   199-201, 222
Stopping ... 46-47
Stopwords ... 27
Stored results ... 171-172
SuperKey ... 68
Symbols ... 128-129, 131,
   136, 177
Synonyms ... 25-26, 130,
   188-189
Syntax ... 71-72, 75,
   126-136, 177-181

Technical Standards for
   Library Automation ...
   160
Telecommunications ... 11
Terminal stations ... 104
Terminals ... 77-105
Terminology ... 68-69,
   121-122, 126-127, 151,
   179-180, 200-202, 206,
   209-211
TESLA ... 160
Thermal printers ... 108-109
Thesauri ... 25-26, 175, 189
Three-P model ... 7
TOMUS ... 59
Tone ... 70-71, 151
Touch screen ... 88-89
Tracings ... 230
   irrelevant ... 233
Truncation ... 31, 128-129,
   135-136, 139, 177, 184,
   187, 215-216
Tutorials ... 155
Type of material ... 148149
Types of users ... 64

Underlining ... 97
University of California ...
   137
User profiles ... 114
*Users Look at Online
   Catalogs* ... 31
USMARC ... 16-17, 25, 94,
   115, 232, *see also*
   MARC

VDT ... *see* Display
Vernacular ... 95-96

Vietnamese ... 95-96
Voice input ... 90

Weeding ... 20
Western Library Network ...
    95
Windows ... 152
WLN ... 95
Word indexes ... *see* Indexes,
    word

Wording ... 70
WordStar ... 65
Works ... 142, 229
Workstations ... 104, 111-115

Z39.29 ... 110, 203
Z39.58 ... *see* Standard
    Command Language

About the Author

Walt Crawford is the assistant director for Special Services at the Research Libraries Group (RLG). He was manager of the Product Batch Group at RLG from 1980 through August 1986. His previous experience in library automation is from the University of California, Berkeley. Mr. Crawford is currently a member of MARBI and editor of the *LITA Newsletter*. Mr. Crawford also wrote *MARC for Library Use: Understanding the USMARC Formats, Technical Standards: An Introduction for Librarians* and *Bibliographic Displays in the Online Catalog* (all published by Knowledge Industry Publications, Inc.), and *Common Sense Personal Computing* (Pierian Press).